# Non-Western Studies
# in the Liberal Arts College

Library of Congress Catalogue Card No. 64-8091

The research reported herein was performed pursuant
to a contract with the United States Office of Education, Department of Health, Education, and Welfare.

Printed in the United States of America by
The Evangelical Press, Harrisburg, Pennsylvania

# Non-Western Studies
# in the
# Liberal Arts College

*A Report of the*
*Commission on International Understanding*

ASSOCIATION OF AMERICAN COLLEGES

Washington, D. C.

1964

# Members of the Commission on International Understanding

Sister M. Camille, *President*, College of Saint Teresa

Charles S. Casassa, *President*, Loyola University of Los Angeles

James P. Dixon, Jr, *President*, Antioch College

Paul D. Eddy, *President*, Adelphi University

Harold D. Fasnacht, *President*, La Verne College

David D. Henry, *President*, University of Illinois

John A. Logan, Jr, *President*, Hollins College

Herbert E. Longenecker, *President*, Tulane University

J. Ralph Murray, *President*, Elmira College, *Chairman*

Mother Eleanor M. O'Byrne, *President*, Manhattanville College of the Sacred Heart

Robert F. Oxnam, *President*, Drew University

Robert E. L. Strider, II, *President*, Colby College

Donald M. Typer, *President*, Doane College

Paul L. Ward, *President*, Sarah Lawrence College

Herrick B. Young, *President*, Western College for Women

# CONTENTS

# PREFACE

The question whether systematic study of the "non-Western" world should be incorporated into liberal education is one that no college can hope to avoid. Quite apart from arguments of principle, review, if not revision, of the curriculum is being forced on liberal arts colleges by pressures of supply and demand that will become increasingly severe. Sooner or later, expressly or implicitly, every college will have to answer the question.

The primary purpose of this report is to provide information and, hopefully, guidance for those colleges that have not yet reached a decision, by presenting and analyzing experiences that have been accumulated. At the same time some observations may be equally helpful to colleges that are already experimenting in the field and are striving to improve their performance. The record of their endeavors indicates that any college that seeks to give a more nearly universal character to its educational program will encounter some if not all of the problems that have been identified. So far as is known no college has yet found satisfactory solutions for all of them.

At the present stage of development, nobody could devise a detailed prescription that would be equally valid for every college. Moreover, a standard pattern of curricular development is neither practicable nor desirable. "Non-Western" studies are still a new field of exploration, which is far from clearly defined. We recognize that even the term "non-Western" is not satisfactory, possessing obvious limitations, but so far nobody has found a better expression to cover all of the civilizations that have been neglected in American education. For the purposes of this study we have interpreted non-Western as denoting the whole of Africa, Asia, Eastern Europe and Latin America, with all the modern indigenous languages spoken in those regions.

Our inquiry shows that the colleges bold enough to venture into the unknown have been few if not always far between, and their brief experience can furnish only tentative guideposts for other pioneers. Everything that has been done in this field—and anything that is likely to be done in the next few years—is experimental and provisional. Our report suggests some general principles that colleges should bear in mind in formulating policies and plans appropriate to their own circumstances.

This issue has been the central concern of the Commission on International Understanding ever since my predecessor, President Richard G. Gettell of Mount Holyoke, reminded the annual meeting of the Association of American Colleges in January 1961 that we are living and teaching in a world in which "the sun no longer rises and sets in the North Atlantic Ocean."

The commission's ideas about what the colleges might most usefully do in this situation and what the commission could do to help them were stated in our annual report of January 1962. Soon afterward, with the aid of the Association staff, we took the first step in the form of a survey of the non-Western activities, curricular and extracurricular, of the members of the Association. The survey was unavoidably crude and sketchy but it provided a rough idea of the state of non-Western studies in liberal arts colleges in the spring of 1962. Our main practical conclusion was that "further exploration of the obstacles to progress and of the most promising means of overcoming them" was needed. The actual rate of progress is indicated by the fact that the number of colleges reporting any kind of non-Western activity at that time was only just over half as great as the corresponding number that appears, two years later, in this report.

Meanwhile the Edward W. Hazen Foundation, wishing to provide a complement in the field of undergraduate education to the Morrill Committee's report on *The University and World Affairs,* had appointed the Committee on the College and World Affairs, of which the writer subsequently became a member. Realizing that the purposes of the committee were closely akin to our own, we made the complete results of our first survey available to the committee's study director. We were to be more than repaid by the illumination we derived at a later stage of our own inquiries from the committee's report on *The College and World Affairs,* published in February 1964.

Then, while we were still looking for means to support our "further exploration," we received an informal inquiry from the Language Development Branch of the Division of College and University Assistance in the U. S. Office of Education, which also shared our interest in non-Western studies, as to whether we should be willing to undertake a more elaborate survey. The result was a contract under Title VI of the National Defense Education Act of 1958, which made it possible for us to produce this report.

The detailed evidence on which our findings are based is contained in the statistical tables that comprise Appendix I and the case studies of individual colleges and cooperating groups which appear in Appendix II. We should like to record our grateful thanks to the institutions and individuals who graciously gave us permission to publish those items in Appendix II which were not produced expressly for our own study, as well as to the colleges that cheerfully submitted to what may have seemed an endless inquisition involved in the preparation of the *ad hoc* studies. Appendix III contains a brief directory of sources of specialized advice and assistance. We believe that it will contribute to the purposes of this report.

Commissions seldom write reports, but it is with especial appreciation that this commission acknowledges its debt to Mr F. L. Wormald, vice president of the Association of American Colleges, who in the last analysis is responsible for this report. His clarity of mind and facility of expression have produced a report which we believe to be exceptionally significant and helpful. In turn, his debt to others also must be acknowledged: to Mrs Inez Ransom who held the project together from the beginning and saw that everything came out even in the end; to the staff of the Association; to Dr J. Fletcher Wellemeyer who helped formulate the questionnaire and provided the tables which are the basis of the survey; and to Dr Howard A. Reed who, kindly released from the Danforth Foundation to act as director of the study, helped draft the questionnaire, visited a substantial number of colleges and universities between August 1963 and Feb-

9

ruary 1964, collected limitless facts about their programs and prepared drafts of a dozen of the institutional studies included in Appendix II. Lastly, our warmest thanks are due for the help that we received throughout from individual members of the U. S. Office of Education, particularly Dr Donald N. Bigelow and Dr Lyman H. Legters, who made their knowledge and experience available to us and without whose unsparing assistance this report could not have been written.

As chairman of the commission, I should like to add a word of gratitude to my fellow members for their tireless devotion over more than three years to an undertaking which has not been without its difficulties but which, if it fulfills its present promise, may prove to be one of the most important achievements of the Association of American Colleges.

J. RALPH MURRAY
*Chairman, Commission on*
*International Understanding*

Elmira College
Elmira, New York
August 1964

# I

# THE RATIONALE OF
# NON-WESTERN STUDIES

Until quite lately higher education in the United States of America has been almost completely under the sway of an illusion shared by nearly everybody of European descent since the Middle Ages—the illusion that the history of the world is the history of Europe and its cultural offshoots; that Western experience is the sum total of human experience; that Western interpretations of that experience are sufficient, if not exhaustive; and that the resulting value systems embrace everything that matters.

In the present century, and especially since the Second World War, this illusion has been shattered by confrontation with a world of new and renascent nations striving to satisfy the submerged needs of their awakening peoples and to secure a place of dignity and respect in the international community. The need to do what we can, if only for the sake of self-preservation, to steer this restless world into paths of peaceful and orderly development, has forced the American people to look outward. And, looking outward, we have begun to see ourselves more clearly and to recognize our illusion as the product of ignorance, which breeds racial snobbery and intellectual parochialism.

As a result, American institutions of higher education are almost for the first time giving serious attention to civilizations other than our own and the interaction of peoples and cultures. This enlargement of our educational horizons beyond the heritage that we derive from Greek philosophers, Hebrew prophets and post-renaissance scientists is commonly justified on the ground that it will produce American citizens better equipped to understand, to help and to get along with other nations. The argument is sound as far as it goes. If future generations of Americans are to acquire competence for living in the world of tomorrow, their education must transcend its customary limitation to the ways of life and patterns of thought that characterize Western civilization. They must learn to understand, or at least learn what is involved in understanding, other ways of living and thinking. But this is not the essential justification for the study of other civilizations: that justification lies in the intrinsic nature of liberal education.

We understand the purpose of liberal education to be, in the words of a recent report to which we shall make further reference, to help man "to liberate himself from the meanness and meagerness of mere existence."[1] Its ultimate end is the activity of the human spirit at its highest potentiality—Aristotle's definition of happiness. To attain this end requires the development of those capacities that are distinctively human—imagination, judgment, understanding and compassion. A man must come to see himself in relation to his total environment in space and time, and so to locate himself on the map of human experience. This entails both the analysis of similarities and the perception of differences, both an understanding of the cultural tradition that has helped to shape him and a knowledge of competing traditions which provide a standard of comparison. Such self-understanding is incompatible with complacency, parochialism and prejudice. By supplying essential perspectives it fulfills the Roman playwright's maxim that as a man one must not look on anything that is human with indifference.

---

1. *The College and World Affairs,* Education and World Affairs, Inc., New York, 1964, p. 1

In our view, any type of higher education is defective if it is not imbued with this spirit. We do not look upon liberal education as a special brand of education to be furnished exclusively by a particular set of institutions for a particular class of students. Yet the liberal arts college, sandwiched between steadily improving secondary schools and ever more specialized graduate schools, still stands alone in having as its central aim the development of liberally educated men and women. This function transcends differences of space and time, race and creed, country and class, political allegiance and vocational interest.

If our interpretation of the purpose of liberal education is accepted, it follows that any program that purports to provide a liberal education is untrue to its own aim if it neglects the vast mass of human experience represented by civilizations outside the European tradition. This is quite a different matter from making friends of Indians, understanding the aspirations of the Arabs or reaching a *modus vivendi* with the Chinese, important as those aims may be. If the whole populations of Asia and Africa had been wiped out by some monstrous catastrophe two or three centuries ago, and their cultures survived only in literary records and tangible artifacts, it would still be incumbent on liberal education to reflect their part in the totality of human experience. Our good fortune in having them available for study as living cultures rather than archeological remains is purely incidental—though, ironically enough, it may have led us to give them less attention.

These other civilizations have produced a corpus of aesthetic creation, philosophical thought and social organization that challenges comparison with Western civilization. To ignore it is to deprive ourselves of the benefit of a sizeable portion of human achievement. Apart from mere parochialism, there is no reason to believe that the finest products of those cultures are in any way inferior to the best of our own. As literature, for example, the Koran and the Bhagavad-Gita are worthy of study alongside the Bible. Sung painting will stand comparison with the masterpieces of Western art. Indian sculpture is not surpassed by the Greeks for grace and sensitivity. Arabic mathematics and science were unequalled in the Western world until the seventeenth century. China has been the most cohesive and enduring society in human history. Such achievements of the mind and hand of man are part of the heritage of every civilized person. They are not unknown to the Western world, and have in fact influenced it more than is commonly acknowledged, but they are nevertheless ignored to all intents and purposes in formal education.

But the essential reason why the study of other civilizations is required by the very nature of liberal education is that they are rooted in fundamental assumptions which in many cases are totally at variance with our own. Not for nothing were we told as children that China is topsy-turvy land, where everything goes by contraries. It is disconcerting to learn that some of the world's languages reflect patterns of perception so different from ours that they make no distinction between noun and verb. Still more so that Indian philosophy appears to negate our most basic categories of thought—good and evil, material and spiritual, universal and particular—if not the law of contradiction itself. F. S. C. Northrop argues that the typical indigenous cultures of Asia are founded on a radically different attitude from that of Western civilization toward the whole of human experience—the "aesthetic" as opposed to the "theoretic" approach. If liberal education aims at promoting our understanding of reality, it cannot afford to overlook such startling differences of apprehension.

Western civilization, in spite of stupendous achievements in science and technology, has still failed to create a society that offers the individual a reasonably full opportunity for attaining happiness through self-development. It is a commonplace that this failure stems from the fact that our growing understanding of the physical universe has not been paralleled by our understanding of ourselves. Other civilizations may have done no better, but our understanding of human nature might be advanced by bringing their underlying assumptions into confrontation with our own.

We are well aware of the objections that may be brought against the introduction of a new component into undergraduate education. The most obvious is that there is more than enough for the student to learn in four years without the addition of further subject matter to already over-crowded curricula. But this argument would be more convincing if it could be shown that nothing is now included that is not essential and that the attention given to any particular subject is proportional to the educational results. In fact, few liberal arts curricula do not stand in need of more or less drastic pruning. Selectivity is dictated by practical no less than theoretical considerations. The only choice is between selection by design and selection by accident.

Many if not most curricula are less the result of deliberate reflection on the question of what studies and exercises are needed to furnish a truly liberal education than of extraneous factors such as the personal interests of teachers and the ephemeral tastes of students. Teachers naturally teach best what interests them, and students learn best what appeals to their imagination. These attitudes are neither unworthy nor necessarily obstructive, but if they are allowed to dominate curricular development they cannot help frustrating the emergence of a coherent program.

Closely related to these influences is the tendency, noted by some of our most sympathetic critics, for college offerings to become more and more narrowly vocational and, within the scholarly disciplines themselves, more and more highly specialized. Many liberal arts colleges are on the way to becoming professional schools in disguise or mere preparatory departments for the graduate schools. This tendency leads almost inevitably to overstuffed curricula. Increasingly the dominant aim appears to be that of teaching the student everything he needs to know in order to embark on a given occupation or to secure admission to a graduate department. The graduate schools are partly to blame, but less so, we suspect, than the colleges are inclined to plead in their own defense. In any case, this policy is inherently self-defeating since much of the factual knowledge that the college seeks to provide, even if its relevance can be guaranteed, will be outdated as fast as it is acquired. The college's task is to help the student explore the boundaries of knowledge, choose his own field of further study and learn how to go on learning for himself. If it abdicates this responsibility, it destroys its own *raison d'être*.

Even those critics who go to the length of predicting the demise of the liberal arts tradition in America do not, as we understand them, challenge the validity of its aim. They are moved by the impression that, as a general rule, liberal arts colleges are not doing what they claim to do, and by the gloomy corollary that our society, with all its professed concern for "education," does not deeply care whether they do it or not. In so far as society is at fault, the only remedy is for the colleges to return to their forsaken allegiance, with the hope of turning out graduates equipped to enlighten their fellow-citizens. Even though the common man may not comprehend the processes by which the qualities of a liberally educated person are developed, he acts on the tacit assumption that those qualities will remain at the service of society. Let us hope that he will not be disappointed. If our society is not to degenerate into a mass of irresponsible individuals devoted to the pursuit of material comfort, private self-indulgence and anarchic power, and indifferent to the values that have served to ennoble the human race, a fair proportion of its members must, somehow, somewhere, be liberally educated.

If the colleges are to pick up the gage, their most urgent task is to take fresh thought about what makes a liberal education. Critical examination of present practices and future possibilities must not be trammeled by any tenderness for vested interests or blind reverence for fossilized traditions. Nothing should be taken for granted. No subject matter, no method, no procedure should be accepted unless it can be demonstrated to make a significant contribution to the essential purpose of liberal education.

Some colleges—not nearly enough—have already undertaken this task. Their self-studies, and some of the new programs that have grown out of them, show clearly that the solution of the problem centers on the quality of the curriculum. Almost without exception, these colleges have grappled with the hydra of course proliferation. They have recognized that a college can neither be all things to all men nor teach all things to any one man. Any dream of turning out modern polymaths has been illusory for at least three centuries. At the same time, the fruitful but overworked principle of student election should be brought, as many colleges have tried to do, under the restraints imposed by a "core program" or some coherent pattern of prescribed alternatives.

These endeavors have not led in the direction of a universal standard curriculum. There is ample room for legitimate differences of opinion on the blend of subject matter needed to constitute a liberal education. We see no reason to believe that anybody can devise a single prescription equally valid for all students at all times and places. Different babies thrive on different formulas. Educational programs have changed in content, along with changes in the technical, economic and social environment, without necessarily ceasing to be liberal. No doubt they will continue to change. Experimentation and adjustment will always be needed.

It is encouraging to recall how far we have come in a century of thought and argument about the content of liberal education as mental discipline. Some 100 years ago President Woolsey of Yale expressed a widespread suspicion of such new subjects as history and science as encroachments on the traditional study of mathematics and the classical languages. Since then we have admitted many other subjects into the charmed circle of the liberal arts and sciences.

Now we are learning that national and cultural boundaries are artificial and irrelevant limitations on the scope of any academic discipline. The student obtains a better grasp of his own culture if he is enabled to compare it with others, to see it as only one aspect of the unfolding human record. American history makes more sense when explicitly placed in the context of events and ideas occurring in a larger environment. Study of the family is more enlightening if it is not limited to the Western pattern but includes some attention to the Egyptian, Indian or Japanese family. Encouraged or even required to give the non-Western world its rightful place in his quest for understanding, the student will find Chinese history as good a corrective of cramping stereotypes as European history, Buddhist philosophy as good a mental exercise as Hegel or William James, the Russian language as valuable an acquisition as German or Spanish.

In these circumstances, the argument that there is no room for non-Western studies is untenable. Apart from any question of non-Western studies, much needs to be cut out of the curriculum. The only question is what to put in. When we seek answers to that question, non-Western material has no magical properties and no prescriptive priority. It must be judged by exactly the same criterion as more familiar subjects of study: the relative value of its contribution to breadth and depth of understanding. The essential purpose of non-Western studies is not to enlarge the fraction of the world that the student knows about but to redress the present neglect of some of the varieties of human experience that must be taken account of in liberal education.

# II

# ORIGINS AND GROWTH OF NON-WESTERN STUDIES

## The First Three Centuries

Neither in the United States nor in Europe has higher education ever been exclusively national in its outlook, but it has seldom been truly international. Its early history in this country gives no hint of concern with the world outside the pale of European civilization. From colonial times the prime source of intellectual energy was European culture with its roots in classical antiquity. For two centuries after its founding Harvard reflected with fair accuracy the medieval idea of a university, based on the trivium and quadrivium, as modified by sixteenth-century Oxford and Cambridge. The trinity of Greek, Latin and mathematics was firmly established in colonial America, not to be disestablished until after the Revolution.

Then, soon after 1800, a new influence made itself felt. One of the first nineteenth-century colleges proclaimed in an early statement of purpose the need of "civilizing and evangelizing the world by the classical education of indigent young men of piety and talents." Thus it was that the world beyond Europe began to come into focus for American higher education, not under the student's microscope but through the colored spectacles of the missionary.

Most of the new colleges were denominational in both origin and purpose. In the period up to 1860, Yale alone begot 16 Congregational colleges and Princeton 26 Presbyterian colleges. The churches used their educational affiliates to train staff for the mission field, first in what was then the western part of the United States, later in Asia and Africa. Of all the 516 colleges and universities founded before the Civil War, only 104 were still alive in 1929, but while they lasted the central concern of the majority was evangelism.

Although this concern had relatively little effect on the curriculum and almost none on the scholarship of the period, it sowed the seeds of a hybrid growth of moral awareness and intellectual interest which came to fruition in the twentieth century. It is no accident that many of the colleges now embarking on non-Western studies trace their original motives to missionary involvement in various parts of the world. The founder-president of Mills College, Cyrus Mills, and his wife had been in charge of Batticotta College in Ceylon. Western College for Women followed the lead of its godmother, Mount Holyoke, in encouraging its graduates to go into missionary work. John Franklin Goucher, from whom Goucher College gets its name, was one of the founders of the Isabella Thoburn College in India. Moreover, at most of the language and area centers established under the National Defense Education Act of 1958, which are now our largest source of non-Western scholars, some members of the faculty are sure to be children of missionaries.

By the end of the nineteenth century the strands of educational development had become tangled. The partially international tradition that had its ultimate source in the classical world—the mainstream of humane learning—was absorbed by the emerging university, whose German-inspired graduate school introduced the notion of specialized scholarship. Interest in the larger world, on the other hand, remained characteristic of the small denominational college, the seminary and the Bible school. Paradoxically, the more nearly global outlook was associated with a vocational function which, in comparison with the expanding intellectual range of higher education, was relatively parochial. But the narrower, Western outlook was dominant in the maturing system, and therefore the college that sought greater academic respectability tended to emulate the university. Thus the graduate school began to set the pattern for higher education.

Meanwhile, higher education came increasingly to focus its attention on contemporary affairs. While the Western tradition and its classical origins were not forgotten, the land-grant colleges in particular found their *métier* in more or less direct service to the surrounding communities. Attention began to shift from an agreed core of humane learning (which had its chief vocational justification in training for the learned professions) to an almost limitless range of occupational training immediately relevant to a rapidly developing society's need for diverse skills. As a result higher education turned its vision inward to domestic needs, and in so doing it encountered little resistance so long as the world at large impinged but slightly on the consciousness of most Americans.

A concurrent development, fostered by both the growing versatility of the graduate schools and the increasing urgency of practical needs, was the proliferation of course offerings and fields of specialization. The medieval and renaissance conception of liberal learning was submerged in a variety of new departments and professional schools. By the turn of the century the crystallization of new disciplines such as economics and sociology, and the emergence of professional curricula such as business management and engineering, afforded a fresh variety of vantage points from which the human condition might be studied, but they provided no pressing reason to look abroad for material to study.

## Twentieth-Century Reorientation

During the present century the preoccupation of American higher education with domestic affairs has been dramatically reversed—gradually at first, but with growing momentum since the Second World War. The change has been due to the reluctant emergence of the United States as a protagonist on the stage of world affairs, which has at one and the same time admitted a vastly enlarged cast of characters and shrunk the distances that separate them. The result has been a sharp reorientation of our academic outlook.

Five concurrent streams of development may be identified as components of the process of reorientation. Some of them started earlier than others, and all of them followed separate but not entirely independent courses. From time to time they have run together and influenced one another, but each of them is still recognizably represented on the present map of higher education. These streams of development are: (1) extracurricular fascination with the world overseas; (2) course work in international relations or world affairs; (3) general courses introductory to a civilization or a group of civilizations; (4) infusion of non-Western material into regular disciplinary courses; (5) area studies as a formally recognized part of the curriculum.

## Extracurricular Activities

At first sight, extracurricular activities may seem less important than the other streams of development. But their significance lies in their sensitivity as a barometer, for they tend to precede and foreshadow curricular change. Students and teachers generally mirror the prevailing concerns of their society. When the society becomes concerned with the rest of the world, academic people begin to relate their personal activities to this concern. If the curriculum offers an outlet for these interests, well and good. But as a general rule the curriculum reacts belatedly to shifts in public concern and in the academic interests that reflect it. The time lag between extracurricular developments and curricular change might be shorter if it were not easier to charter a plane or organize an art exhibit than to revise the curriculum or revamp an individual course. In any case, extracurricular interest in the world at large, whether expressed in buying airline tickets to faraway places, admiring Oriental or African art, seeking foreign notables as campus speakers or founding international clubs, has never been sustained at so high a level for so long a time.

Nothing exemplifies this interest more strikingly than the dimensions reached since World War II by "educational" travel and the logistical apparatus that has been developed to facilitate it. Academic peregrination, of course, is an old story dating back through the wandering scholars of the Middle Ages to the schools of classical Athens. For the graduate student and the scholar-teacher it is a normal response to intellectual needs: the need of access to additional data for research; the need of enhanced mastery of a foreign language or first-hand acquaintance with a cultural milieu; the need of face-to-face communication with foreign colleagues. But what is unique in our era is the magnitude of the migration, which has grown on a geometric scale for undergraduates as well as graduates and which may combine the best and the most dubious of academic motives.[1]

## Courses in International Relations

A second stream of development, the proliferation of course offerings in international relations or world affairs, was both the earliest and the easiest curricular response to America's twentieth-century confrontation with the shrinking world. That it was the earliest development on a large scale may be attributed to the fact that it was but a short step beyond its academic antecedents and correlates, diplomatic history and U. S. foreign policy. It was easiest because it belonged essentially to one discipline, political science, and courses could be planned and offered by one department without impinging on others and thus raising curricular conflicts.

Even before World War I brought the United States into international politics, several universities had introduced courses dealing with subject matter variously called contemporary politics, world politics and contemporary history. In the curricular conditions of the time all of them could be, and were, described

---

1. See Section I, "Analysis of the Situation," by Stephen A. Freeman in *Undergraduate Study Abroad*, Institute of International Education, New York, 1964

as "trail-blazing." Although unbounded by national frontiers, the subject matter of these courses nevertheless represented, in the perspective of our own age, only slight departures from tradition. They rarely if ever looked beyond the Western world (except to the extent that attention was turned in the opposite direction by the "open door" policy in the Far East) and their conceptual framework derived solely from Western ideas of diplomacy, international law and foreign policy.

A greater widening of horizons occurred between the two world wars, prompted in part by the peace movement and by the war-induced recognition of flaws in the notion that the European great powers should regulate the affairs of the entire globe. The sentimentalism in this academic current—which may be seen as prefiguring a similar ingredient in today's striving for "international understanding"—called forth a counter-tendency to emphasize power politics and the single-minded pursuit of national interests. Thus were born two contending viewpoints within the sub-discipline of international relations.

Especially after World War I that subject, though loosely defined, became a respectable academic specialty. Courses multiplied throughout the country and were commonly accepted into the liberal arts curriculum. It was generally conceded that they fell within the discipline known as political science, in spite of a few devotees who thought that international relations ought to be a separate field of study (as it became at some institutions).

Doubts and confusions, however, were revived and multiplied by the Second World War and its aftermath. Familiar concepts of the relationship between sovereign states were found to have lost much of their pertinence when applied to the new *dramatis personae* of global, as distinct from European, international relations. To make matters worse, the postwar world disclosed the limitations of a purely political or quasi-legal approach. International relations were suddenly (or so it seemed) entangled in a web of economic, social and technical problems, all as upsetting to academic theories of diplomacy as they were to most professional diplomats. It became clear that political science did not exhaust the relevant subject matter. Comparative government courses might add Brazil, India, Japan, Nigeria or the USSR to their spectrum; comparative politics courses might extend their theoretical coverage to the political systems of the entire world—but the characteristic approach of political science was manifestly inadequate to comprehend the intricate network of military strategy, trade relations, technical assistance, cultural exchanges and information services that make up contemporary foreign policy.

In order to cope with its postwar responsibilities, the United States was called on to repair its neglect of broad reaches of human experience—whole countries and regions that were beyond the range of popular knowledge and academic study alike. International relations, as a branch of political science, could not be expected to solve this complex problem. Its province was the superstructure of the international community: it did not penetrate to the roots of fundamentally different social values and modes of thought. It could furnish no substitute for the insights of such basic disciplines as anthropology, geography, history, literature, linguistics, economics, sociology and philosophy, through which alone could genuine understanding be achieved.

From within the professional field, Ambassador George Kennan indicated the limitations of international relations as an academic subject when he emphasized the kind of understanding derived from "the essentials of humanistic study: from history itself, and from all those more subtle and revealing expressions of man's nature that go by the name of art and literature."

The study of world affairs had indeed played a vital part in internationalizing the curriculum. Its inability to furnish a complete solution merely reflected the necessity of enlisting the whole body of liberal studies in the endeavor.

## Introductory Civilization Courses

The third component in the reorientation of academic interest was supplied by introductory, usually interdisciplinary, courses dealing with whole civilizations. They date from the period between the wars and are closely related to the movement, reacting against the more anarchic aspects of the elective system, toward a basic core of "general education." Hence the frequency

25

with which such introductory courses were required of all students. Civilization courses are not peculiarly non-Western, for the approach has been used for Western and later for American civilization at least as often as for non-Western areas. But as the importance of remoter parts of the globe came to be recognized, non-Western and particularly Asian counterparts began to be fashioned on the model of courses in Western civilization and were sometimes offered in a conscious effort to strike a balance.

The best-known examples—probably the Asian courses at Chicago, Columbia and Cornell—utilized instructors from various disciplines to cover the assorted subject matter as well as the geographical area. Usually this technique resulted in the development of special texts to suit the purposes of the course. Subsequently other colleges and universities copied the idea, often using the textbooks compiled for such elaborate offerings as are comprised in the Oriental studies program at Columbia College.

The importance of the civilization course for the evolution of non-Western studies lies in its intent to provide insight into an alien culture not in terms of its relationships with Western civilization but in terms of its own values. This was something new in the American curriculum.

## Infusion

As civilization courses respond to the demand for global understanding by giving complete non-Western cultures a place in the curriculum, a parallel response is to give non-Western material an appropriate place in disciplinary courses. If a balanced curriculum requires an integrated non-Western course to match an integrated course in Western civilization, then a balanced treatment of, say, political science or economics may similarly require attention to systems other than those of North America and Western Europe. Known generally as "infusion," the method presupposes that disciplines and departments are not, or should not be, culture-bound; that the study of government or the family has as much relevance to India or Peru as to England or Belgium, and that examples drawn from the former countries may be as valuable as examples from the latter for comprehension of the underlying principles. The parallel can be developed for numerous disciplines—history, literature, fine arts, music, education, anthropology, philosophy and so on.

It is of course possible to provide a dual approach to non-Western cultures by combining the infusion of disciplinary courses with the offering of an integrated, introductory course, and our case studies show that several colleges have done so.

## Area Studies

The fifth and most significant component in the twentieth-century reorientation of higher education has been the development and acceptance of area studies.

Well before World War II, a few pioneer scholars with a special interest in non-Western areas, such as South Asia or the Middle East, started to experiment with graduate programs combining the ancient and the modern, the humanities and the social sciences, disciplinary training and language learning. Their aim was to make the study of the areas in question as comprehensive as the treatment accorded to Western civilization—at least in theory—by the conventional curriculum. Such programs—notably those offered by the University of Pennsylvania, Yale and Princeton—served as prototypes when war confronted the United States with a sudden need for experts on all parts of the world involved in military operations. The armed forces established their own training programs—located at universities and employing whatever competence was available—and these in turn served as crude models for postwar programs conducted under institutional auspices.

Area studies gained momentum from a reaction against the hardening of the walls between the traditional disciplines. These divisions, which are commonly taken for granted, are in large measure a comparatively recent corollary of the departmental organization of higher education. In only a few decades the several disciplines crystallized in such a way that scholarly study of any society in its totality became all but impossible. Area studies were intended to correct this fragmentation, not by superseding the disciplines but by combining their different perspectives, filling the gaps between them and achieving a unity of treatment which would convey to the student a multidimensional picture of the life and thought of the chosen area. This approach is not necessarily restricted to non-Western studies but, as it was employed at an early stage to meet the pressing need for enlarged knowledge of non-Western areas, it has ever since been closely associated with them.

The area approach was in one sense a return to the time-honored pattern of classical studies, whether they related to the Greco-Roman world or to the traditional Orient. They too attempted to cover the totality of a culture. But, whereas classicists and Orientalists were usually forced to be generalists within their own fields, because they operated alone on most campuses, area studies were deliberately planned to involve a variety of scholars representing disciplines that were otherwise separate. Moreover, although the initial demand was mainly for the man whose field of specialization was the area as such, area study programs came more and more to be directed to the student whose primary specialty lay in a disciplinary field but who wished to give it an added dimension by pursuing it in the context of another civilization.

Area studies culminated in a variety of academic degrees. Sometimes an area certificate was combined with a disciplinary degree; in other cases degree-granting authority remained entirely with the conventional departments (including, however, departments organized on area lines). But it was a common assumption of the early years that an area degree was feasible at all levels—A.B., M.A. and Ph.D.—even though a well-founded caution in face of employment problems sharply restricted the number of students who actually earned the Ph.D. on an area basis.

From the beginning, the area concept was applied at least as often to research as to instruction. One of the major aims was to generate new knowledge which, through the cooperation of a multidisciplinary team of scholars, would be unique in its comprehensiveness. Even when translated into instructional terms, the relatively unfamiliar ground that a non-Western program had to cover required particularly vigorous research activity to provide a foundation for teaching.

The research orientation of area studies may partly explain the relative neglect of the language element in the early instructional programs. At the same time, such programs were trapped in a vicious circle by the desperate shortage, throughout the educational system, of competence in non-European languages. With very little to start from, the staffs of non-Western area programs had to shoulder the double burden of meeting a sizeable share of the national demand for trained linguists and developing within themselves the capability of giving language study its proper place in their own programs. This required years of effort, which bore scanty fruit until it was backed by substantial aid from the Federal Government. But the growing success of the endeavor to bring language into balance with other subjects was marked by the gradual adoption of the term: "Language and Area Studies."

## The Last Two Decades

As the immediate postwar period gave way to the decade of the 1950's, a more or less uniform pattern of development began to appear. Area studies became almost exclusively associated with non-Western civilizations. Undergraduates were admitted in growing numbers to courses initially intended for graduate students, and programs which had originated at the graduate level came to include introductory courses designed expressly for undergraduates. The ensuing success of area studies in attracting students at both levels vindicated the professors, administrators and foundation executives who had supported the area approach to the study of regions beyond the Western world.

Probably the decisive characteristic of what had by 1950 become an educational movement to redress the neglect of non-Western subject matter was the integration of programs. Some universities had previously been content to comb their catalogues for courses relating to a particular geographical area and to climb aboard the non-Western bandwagon by announcing a "program." But it soon became clear that courses so collected into one place in the catalogue were no closer to forming a program than they had been in their scattered state.

By 1951, when Wendell C. Bennett prepared his survey of *Area Studies in American Universities* for the Social Science Research Council, he was able to enunciate the tangible and essential attributes which, in his view, constituted "integration," i.e., the criteria for separating programs from mere agglomerations of courses. His seven characteristics of integrated programs were:

1. Official university recognition and support of the program;
2. Adequate library resources both for teaching and research on the area;
3. Competent instruction in the principal languages of the area;
4. Offerings in at least five pertinent subjects in addition to language instruction;
5. Some specific mechanisms for integrating the area studies;
6. An area research program;
7. Emphasis on the contemporary aspects of the area.

The number of programs that met Bennett's criteria was small. Excluding four programs dealing with Western Europe, he found 25 programs in operation at nineteen institutions. The leading areas were East Asia, Latin America and Russia, with eight, six and five programs respectively. Latin America claimed the largest number of faculty specialists, but the other two had far and away the most students. Other areas lagged behind on all counts. But it was already apparent from Bennett's findings that area concentration had not, as originally feared, become a substitute for other requirements by providing a soft option. On the contrary, the new emphasis on language proficiency and field work was likely to add one or more years to a doctoral program.

The outstanding development of the fifties was the marked increase in the number of programs. The cold war had already launched Russian and East European studies, and this field remained in the lead throughout the decade. East Asia and Latin America continued to show numerical strength, though the latter was feeding on a long and somewhat desultory past and await-ing its boom in the 1960's. But the Middle East and South Asia were growing rapidly, followed by Southeast Asia and, more gradually, by Africa and the Uralic-Altaic field. By 1964 a State Department survey of *Language and Area Study Programs in American Universities,* based on the above criteria for integra-tion, reported 146 graduate programs well distributed over the geographical spectrum, as compared with 55 unevenly distri-buted programs shown in the first edition of the same survey in 1954.

Along with numerical growth, certain other tendencies be-came apparent. The range, intensity and quality of language instruction rose perceptibly, as did the extent of disciplinary representation. By the early 1960's it was commonplace for a graduate program to provide the equivalent of three or four years of instruction in the major uncommon languages: Chinese, Arabic and Japanese. Many departments cooperated to the mutual benefit of the programs and the disciplines.

It had also proved possible to strengthen certain disciplines without sacrificing the integrated character of area programs. As a result, the area degree at the doctoral level was beginning to disappear. Faculty members were able to maintain their disciplinary credentials without abandoning area specialization. Departments involved in area study were coming to accept the desirability of having major world areas covered by their staffs. Nothing did more to promote equilibrium between departmental and non-Western programs, both in recruitment and in teaching assignments.

In short, thanks to the pioneering efforts of many universities, non-Western language and area programs have now won ac-ceptance in higher education. The number of students is still relatively small. But assuming continuation of the necessary sup-port, the country is for the first time assured of a continuing flow of well-trained historians, linguists, political scientists, econ-omists and so forth, conversant with a particular non-Western area as well as with their academic discipline.

## Outside Support

Despite substantial institutional investment, this result could hardly have been achieved in so short a time without generous support from sources outside the universities, especially the great philanthropic foundations.[2] As new and highly specialized ventures, non-Western programs were expensive. Their development might have been seriously delayed by faculty opposition—compounded of distrust of unorthodox innovations and of resentment against any diversion of funds from the traditional disciplines—if the universities had been obliged to rely entirely on their own financial resources. Fortunately they were not.

The Rockefeller Foundation and the Carnegie Corporation of New York played the earliest roles in supporting this development. In the decade beginning in 1951, the Ford Foundation made grants exceeding $65,000,000 for graduate area study programs and related activities. The Foreign Area Fellowship Program, initiated by Carnegie in 1947 and supported on a broader scale by Ford after 1951, has contributed to American society over 1400 people with competence in non-Western areas and cultures.

After the foundations, the chief source of financial aid has been the Federal Government. The critical legislation was the National Defense Education Act of 1958, Title VI of which was directed to the development of language study. It provided for a program of research in language learning, for graduate fellowships in so-called uncommon languages and, above all, for financial support to enable institutions of higher education to strengthen their offerings in modern foreign languages and related area studies within the framework of language and area centers. In the first six years of the act's operation, 55 NDEA Language and Area Centers were designated, and under a matching formula $11,000,000 of federal funds produced a total investment of at least $22,000,000—probably over $25,000,000—at

---

2. The history of the universities' pioneering endeavors and the support they received from the foundations is summarized in Joseph Axelrod and Donald N. Bigelow, *Resources for Language and Area Studies*, American Council on Education, Washington, D. C., 1962, Chapter I, pp. 3-12.

34 institutions. Federal expenditures in the same period for research, fellowships and instruction in language studies amounted altogether to $40,000,000.

In addition, some states (usually with foundation aid) furnished support for non-Western studies at institutions of all levels within their own jurisdiction, through programs administered either by a state university or by an agency of the state government. Outstanding examples are Indiana University and the New York State Department of Education.

These various factors add up to a nationwide network of support for non-Western studies— not as a result of national planning but simply due to widespread recognition of a serious deficiency in the American system of higher education. As we have tried to show, the deficiency goes back to the beginnings of the system and attempts to correct it are comparatively recent. In particular, they have barely begun to affect undergraduate education, especially in liberal arts colleges that are not part of a university. Foundation grants, like the programs they supported, started at the graduate level. Grants to liberal arts colleges have been proportionate to the modest dimensions, as revealed by our survey, of the colleges' ventures into non-Western studies. In 1958, when funds first became available under the National Defense Education Act, it was still necessary to concentrate attention on the graduate schools, which produce the teachers needed at lower educational levels. Only four of the 55 language and area centers assisted by the act were originally intended solely for undergraduates, and only one was established at a liberal arts college—Portland State College.[3]

But two new fellowship programs under NDEA are specifically designed to help the liberal arts college: awards for a limited number of undergraduates to spend a summer in intensive language programs sponsored by language and area centers (200 were awarded in 1964); and a small number of awards for faculty members desirous of doing postdoctoral work at one

---

3. Donald N. Bigelow and Lyman H. Legters, *NDEA Language and Area Centers: A Report on the First Five Years* (U. S. Office of Education, Washington, D. C., 1964) contains the fullest available account of the development of language and area studies and of the 55 NDEA programs.

of the major language and area centers, preparatory to introducing non-Western courses in the colleges where the recipients teach (fourteen were awarded for 1964–65). But the liberal arts college has formidable arrears to overtake.

Verbal encouragement is not lacking. Over the last fifteen years or so, a whole series of books and pamphlets—some the product of lengthy discussion in conferences or careful study by individuals—have dealt with issues related to non-Western studies in the undergraduate college. (The most important of these publications are listed in Appendix III to this report.) Their significance lies less in the exhortations they contain, or even in their recommendations, than in the implied verdict that non-Western studies have passed a climacteric. The enterprise no longer needs to prove its worth or its relevance; it no longer requires a special organizational structure. It is not a mere experiment, not something grafted on to the regular system, but an intrinsic part of higher education. All of the documents form a kind of summing-up of the distance traveled and a challenge to go forward.

# III

# THE PRESENT SITUATION

## Toward a Definition

It follows from our basic assumptions about the nature of liberal education that what we mean by "non-Western" is pragmatically and negatively defined. We are concerned with those sectors of the human venture and those interpretations of human experience that have been left out of account in the customary pattern of American education. An article in the *ACLS Newsletter* of September 1961 stated that "no one has offered a better term than non-Western to denote area studies outside the bounds of the traditional curriculum." While, as we have already noted, area studies are not coterminous with so-called non-Western studies, and while "non-Western" is an unsatisfactory expression, it continues to hold the field in spite of its obvious defects.

"Non-Western" might naturally be taken to denote those areas of the world whose dominant cultures spring from roots other than those of European civilization, as distinct from those areas whose cultural ancestry includes at least a substantial European element. Yet this distinction is not always easy to apply, as is evident from consideration, for instance, of Latin America or the USSR. The cultural origins of many societies—like the genealogy of a good part of the human race—are so mixed up that the boundaries between Western and non-Western may vary with the point of view of the several academic disciplines. Even where the dividing lines seem clear for one discipline, other disciplines may draw them differently.

In practical terms it is indisputable that, notwithstanding a high degree of cultural kinship with Western civilization, Latin America and Eastern Europe (including the Soviet Union) are among the areas traditionally neglected by the liberal arts curriculum. Because of this common factor of neglect, we have accepted non-Western as denoting the whole of Africa, Asia, Eastern Europe and Latin America, with all the indigenous languages spoken in those regions.

The definition of non-Western studies, however, involves a more serious problem than the geographical denotation of the expression "non-Western." What kinds of instruction—what particular courses or programs—may properly be regarded as effectively redressing the neglect of non-Western experience? All is not grist that comes to the mill. On what basis can a distinction be made among the assorted courses that satisfy the geographical definition? How can one determine whether they contribute significantly to understanding of the non-Western world? Courses in non-Western studies are subject to many interpretations, as well by the person answering a questionnaire as by the reader. A course that may plausibly be described as non-Western does not necessarily further the educational aims postulated for non-Western study and may never have been intended to do so. The data yielded by a survey such as ours may therefore be distorted by sheer misunderstanding.

In addition, the prevailing climate of opinion is conducive to distortion and exaggeration, not only in an institution's responses to outside inquirers but in its understanding of its own activities. As often as not, something described as new may be an old course under a new name. Or a dash of "non-Western" spice may have transformed an old course into a new one merely because the teacher took a trip or read a book. On the administrative level, college officials faced with still another questionnaire may have been tempted to lump together a group of ill-assorted courses and present them as the college's non-Western look for the occasion.

Proof of genuine accomplishment is hard to come by. There is little reason to believe that the introduction of non-Western studies is any easier to assess than the growth of general education, the devotees of which became professional magicians over night. They could show at the drop of a hat that general education existed on campus merely by calling History I "Western Civilization" and by substituting an assistant professor for the instructor or graduate student who had formerly run a perfectly respectable "drill session." Now it became a "seminar" which was *taught*. In lieu of salary teachers have often acquired titles. And not without profit have some academicians followed the simple device of Hamilton, Madison and Jay, who called their anti-federal polemics *The Federalist Papers*.

A clue to the relevance of a particular course may be furnished by the date at which it was introduced into the curriculum. Courses in Latin American history, Oriental religions and world literature are certainly non-Western by our geographical definition; they may embody a respectable treatment of non-Western material. But if they date from the 1930's and have survived unchanged down to the present, they are more likely to represent a curricular hangover than a live institutional commitment to non-Western studies. To the extent that they have become fossilized, they serve as a warning that the development of non-Western components in a curriculum can stagnate at any point, particularly at the initial stage of token bows to the non-Western world.

The crucial test is the purpose, in so far as it can be identified, which a course is intended to serve. Some of the courses offered by American colleges as early as the 1880's covered ground that was non-Western by our geographical definition. An obvious example is Comparative Religion, a long-established and popular course in many liberal arts colleges. Somewhat later, Comparative Government began to extend its purview to non-Western systems. But these courses usually had a tendentious character which was at variance with the aim of non-Western studies as we now conceive it. They were designed to furnish support for such theses as that Christianity was superior to the rest of the world's religions, or that Anglo-Saxon patterns of government were superior to all others.

By the 1920's, as noted in Chapter II, courses which, under a variety of labels, dealt with international relations were offered on many American campuses. While less blatantly tendentious than the older courses, they were focused on the effect of external forces on American interests and policies. Their emotional overtones, deriving from both pacifism and isolationism, rendered such courses more a reflection of Western ideas and aspirations than a serious attempt at understanding the life and thought of non-Western societies.

In 1964 we have reached a stage at which courses are being taught all over the country on such subjects as Russian language and literature, the history and politics of the Middle East, Indian religion, Chinese art, and the economics of developing countries. These courses clearly fall within the geographical definition and may be taken to have resulted from a worthy intention to treat non-Western cultures and peoples on their own terms. But unfortunately such courses are often isolated and marginal— reflecting perhaps a professor's pipedream—and have thus far done little to break down the parochialism of higher education. Excepting interdisciplinary courses introductory to an entire civilization, non-Western courses in isolation rarely make a serious contribution to genuine understanding of non-Western societies. And this implies a further criterion: that non-Western subject matter, if it is to make a worthwhile contribution to the central aim of the liberal arts, should be introduced into the curriculum systematically and purposefully and encouraged to grow with it.

The purpose of our survey is to assess the extent to which non-Western studies are currently playing an organic role in the development of the liberal arts curriculum. Three propositions underlie our evaluation of the evidence. Stated axiomatically they are: (1) the study of any civilization contributes to the understanding of human experience; (2) the contemporary world is as important to that understanding as is the ancient world; (3) effective competence in appropriate languages, modern as well as classical, is essential to meaningful study of non-Western civilizations.

## The Evidence of the Universities

Although this survey does not cover undergraduate study at the university, as distinct from the liberal arts college that offers little or no graduate work,[1] the present condition and future prospects of the liberal arts curriculum cannot be fairly assessed without reference to university experience. While in popular belief the liberal arts college may exercise a unique and critical influence on national destiny—like the playing fields of Eton— it is nevertheless part of a larger system of education. Just as it is affected by the performance of the secondary school, so it must be influenced, in the future as in the past, by the example of the university. The way of the liberal arts college is, after all, only one of several alternative roads to the baccalaureate degree. What a student can do at one type of institution is germane to any discussion of what he might do at another.

At the graduate level, as has already been shown, area study programs are often highly developed, with extensive and well-integrated course offerings. To be sure, the superior ability of the graduate school to provide such programs is unquestionable. It has given the university a head start in the non-Western field. The level of scholarly competence and the high degree of specialization available at the university can seldom be matched by the college. But it does not follow that the range of the curriculum offered by the university, and the type of education it makes possible, cannot be adapted to the liberal arts college.

Although originally designed for graduate students and oriented to their needs, most of the non-Western courses offered by universities can be taken by undergraduates. Some of them, particularly in language, are offered for credit only at the undergraduate

---

1. The survey was confined to members of the Association of American Colleges that do not teach beyond the master's degree, plus a handful of institutions that offer a doctorate but, in virtue of their predominant concern with undergraduate teaching, are customarily regarded as liberal arts colleges.

level (although they are also open to graduates). As early as 1959–60, for example, of the 399 students taking Japanese at ten universities, 218 or nearly 55 per cent, were undergraduates.[2] In 1962–63, when more institutions were offering Japanese, a more complete survey showed that 45 colleges and universities had a total of 1600 students registered for that language alone and that 1200, or 75 per cent, of them were undergraduates.[3] Another survey taken at the same time showed that, of all the students taking language and area courses at fifty NDEA centers, 60 per cent were undergraduates.[4] At these centers, which represented about one third of all language and area programs at the graduate level,[5] nearly 10,000 undergraduates were enrolled in at least one area course and many of them took several courses, sometimes including a course in an uncommon language. While it cannot be inferred that the total number of undergraduates registered in language and area programs was three times as great, it is a reasonable guess that they numbered at least 20,000. The important point, however, is that the proportion of undergraduates taking courses in such programs at universities has continued to range from 55 to 75 per cent of all students enrolled in these programs.

These men and women at any rate are convinced that non-Western studies are relevant to their education, and any argument about whether such studies fit into the curriculum becomes purely academic. Is there any cogent reason to believe that these students are receiving less of a liberal education than if they were studying at a liberal arts college with a conventional program—blissfully ignorant of the non-Western world? If they are

2. A survey made in 1959-60 by Dr Joseph Yamagiwa, University of Michigan, included in "Background Data—Prepared by Professor C. O. Hucker, Consultant, for U. S. Office of Education Conference in Stimulation of Undergraduate Programs for Foreign Language Study"

3. *Manpower in the Neglected Languages, Fall 1962; A Report,* by John Harmon, James Simms and Hannelore Tierney, The Modern Language Association of America, New York, N. Y., 1963

4. Unpublished "Summary of Activities at 53 NDEA Language and Area Centers—Fall Semester 1962" in Language Development Branch, U. S. Office of Education, Washington, D. C., 1963

5. *Language and Area Study Programs in American Universities,* Department of State, Washington, D. C., 1962, p. ii, gives 136 graduate programs.

missing the humanizing influence of some poets, some philosophers or some byways of European history, they are surely being compensated by the stimulus of intellectual experiences that the conventional college does not provide.

In the last four or five years, university undergraduates have shown proof on an ever-increasing scale that they can digest such experiences. They have been learning uncommon languages and studying unfamiliar cultures at such a pace that they are beginning to constitute a new breed of graduate student which is already changing admission requirements as well as the content of graduate courses. Students are now so much better equipped than their predecessors that, whereas National Defense Language Fellowships in some non-Western languages have hitherto been awarded to applicants with no previous competence, for 1965–66 at least one year's preparation is a condition of awards in Arabic, Chinese, Hindi, Japanese and Portuguese.

Students like these will be the next generation's leaders in non-Western scholarship; they are this generation's leaders in showing what can be done by and for undergraduates. If they are not the wave of the future, they have at least made more than a ripple on the academic waterfront. They are part of the competition that the graduates of liberal arts colleges will have to face. If, as our survey shows, what the colleges have hitherto achieved in this field is modest at best, the hope of being able to do more and better rests on solid evidence of what has been achieved by the universities.

## The Position of the Colleges

Measured from zero, the progress made by liberal arts colleges in incorporating non-Western studies into the curriculum is fairly impressive. Our survey, taken in the spring semester of the academic year 1963–64, shows that at least 482 colleges were engaged in non-Western activity of one sort or another. Of these, 440 reported formal course work—some of it inconsequential. Thus a majority of liberal arts colleges have clearly tried to do *something* about non-Western studies. A critic who examines individual performances rather than numerical totals might be tempted to add that the result has not always been commensurate with the effort.

Of the 848 institutions that are members of the Association of American Colleges, 122 were excluded from the survey because they could not be classified as liberal arts colleges engaged primarily in undergraduate education. Forty-one more had to be omitted for technical reasons. The remaining 685 provided the basis of our survey. Of these, 152 failed to reply and 51 reported negatively. The 482 which reported some kind of non-Western activity represent seventy per cent of the total surveyed. About one eighth of them are public institutions, the rest private or church-related. Nearly two thirds are coeducational and of the remainder more than twice as many are women's colleges as men's.

The figures that appear in Appendix I must be interpreted with caution and imagination. In our attempt to learn all we could about every kind of activity that might reasonably be related to the development of non-Western studies, we collected a great deal of information that cannot be summarized in statistical tables. Nor can any figures convey an adequate picture of the quality of non-Western studies. Finally, an activity that contributes to study is not the same thing as study itself, and in delineating non-Western studies the distinction is crucial. We have recognized the importance of extracurricular activities as an early symptom of academic interest in the non-Western world and as a stimulus to curricular change. But guest lecturers, art exhibits, international clubs and faculty seminars are no substitute for formal instruction. Nor is student or faculty travel: it may in fact be a distraction from the essential business of a college. So the assessment that follows is based almost entirely on formal courses taken for credit.

Subject to the qualifications noted above, we can report that, of the 440 colleges listing some course work in non-Western studies, nearly three fourths offer five or more non-Western courses including "infusion courses," which were defined for the purposes of the survey as courses with no more than fifty per cent non-Western content. One hundred and fifty colleges, or over a third, offer ten or more courses, a commitment which may be regarded as significant even when no clue is given as to the degree of integration achieved or the goal to which the college aspires. More precisely, 79 colleges offer between ten and fourteen courses; 22 offer 15–19; 22 offer 20–24; and 27 offer 25 or more non-Western courses including infusion courses.

At least the 49 colleges that make up the last two groups—all offering *twenty or more* courses—may be assumed to be firmly committed to non-Western studies. Besides this volume of course work, all but five of them offer one or more of the uncommon languages (including Russian), and half of them state that they have one or more organized non-Western programs in operation.

While the word "program" has a wide range of meanings in academic discourse, it is here taken to mean a series of courses which are explicitly recognized as contributing to a common academic aim and which students may be encouraged to treat as a single sequence of study. The definition used in our survey was "some form of schematic arrangement by which part or all of the non-Western courses . . . are integrated into a coherent whole." Seventy-eight of the 440 colleges offering non-Western courses reported a total of 143 organized programs. Thus more than one sixth of all colleges reporting some formal course work in non-Western studies also claim to have at least one non-Western program.

Analysis of course offerings by world areas shows that three leading areas are almost equally popular with faculty and students. Together they account for more than half of all courses labeled non-Western, including infusion courses. In numbers of courses, first place goes to the USSR and Eastern Europe with 875 courses, followed by East Asia or Asia in general with 656, and Latin America with 625. If infusion courses are excluded the corresponding figures are 735, 655 and 616. Enrolment figures show the same order of preference, except that for all courses, including infusion courses, Latin America is slightly ahead of Asia. The other four world areas—Middle East, Africa, South Asia and Southeast Asia—together account for only about one tenth of all courses if infusion courses are included and less than one seventh if infusion courses are excluded. It should be noted that non-Western courses that are not attributable to any particular area make up nearly 1500 of the total of just over 4000 courses of all types and more than 500 of the nearly 3000 courses other than infusion courses.

A breakdown of these non-Western courses indicates that the leading disciplines or departments are history, political science (international relations and politics) and geography. History is far and away the leading contributor. Certain departments reveal special strength in particular areas: for instance, courses in Latin American or Russian literature are numerous; fine arts are prominent only in Asian areas; religion and philosophy show strength in all Asian areas except the Middle East.

Language courses, which are excluded from the foregoing course statistics, provide independent evidence of the degree to which colleges are committed to non-Western studies. Assuming that no non-Western program will ever be complete unless it includes appropriate language instruction (an assumption that is discussed later in this report), it is significant that, of the 440 colleges reporting some formal course work, 216—very nearly half—offer one or more of the indigenous languages of the non-Western world (other than Spanish). But of these 216, 175 offer Russian alone. Only 41 colleges (including 27 that teach Russian) report any courses in other uncommon languages. Together they cover fourteen of these languages, the most frequent being Portuguese (18 colleges), Chinese (12), Japanese (8) and Arabic (4). While the survey shows that language instruction may be included as part of an organized program of non-Western studies, it indicates equally that language courses may be provided independently of any such program or even of any great concentration of non-Western courses. Finally and most important, the survey suggests that, while instruction in non-Western languages has made a fair and perhaps surprising start in liberal arts colleges, it is still in its infancy.

It cannot be ignored, however, that language learning, in what have always been considered difficult languages, is seriously undertaken in some forty undergraduate colleges. For instance, of the fourteen languages reported, ten are taught at the second-year level, including Chinese, Japanese and Portuguese, each of which is offered at five or more institutions. At the third-year level the number of languages drops to six, but significantly Chinese is still offered at six colleges. Four languages are available at the fourth-year level: Chinese at three colleges, Arabic, Japanese and Modern Hebrew at one each.

Because of the futility of providing only one or two years' teaching of an unfamiliar language, instruction in Chinese illustrates an important conclusion of this survey. Of all the cultural areas covered by substantial work at the undergraduate level, East Asia, with special reference to China and the Chinese language, is pre-eminent. Nowhere else is evidence of the language revolution, to which we shall make further reference, as apparent as in Chinese—traditionally exotic, presumably difficult and hitherto largely inaccessible. For no other cultural area are course offerings in general as complete and meaningful as for the Far East.

Enrolment across the nation in the neglected languages (excluding Russian and Spanish) at the undergraduate level increased from 15,707 in the fall of 1961 to 17,072 in the fall of 1962, according to a recent survey made by the Modern Language Association.[6] Undergraduate enrolment made up approximately 73 per cent of the total. Of roughly 10,000 enrolments reported in our survey for 1963–64, (of which 78 per cent were in Russian), 514 enrolments, or five per cent, were in Chinese, and 460 in Japanese. In short, there were about 1,000 students taking these two languages at the seventeen colleges reported as offering either or both of them.

Cooperation among undergraduate colleges, which has been one of the most striking features of higher education in the past decade, is a factor to be considered in any examination of non-Western studies. Of the 482 institutions reporting non-Western activity, 102 colleges registered their participation in some form of inter-institutional cooperation (excluding arrangements for sending faculty or students to avail themselves individually of another institution's offerings, such as summer language programs or study at language and area centers). Since many colleges engage in several kinds of cooperative activity, there is of course

---

6.   Op. cit.

duplication in the figures showing instances of inter-institutional cooperation.

Joint sponsorship of lectures, exhibits and artistic events takes first place, having been reported by 40 colleges. While only 12 colleges report joint book purchases, 38 share library facilities with one or more other institutions. Students enjoy the option of utilizing the facilities and offerings of other institutions in 34 instances; and there are 24 colleges participating in joint programs of undergraduate study abroad for credit. In the crucial area of faculty participation, 31 colleges report joint faculty seminars, 29 share faculty with other institutions, and 26 collaborate in faculty exchange programs with non-Western areas.

Some extracurricular activities reflecting attention to the non-Western world were reported by all colleges, including the 42 which could report no formal course work. International or similar clubs were the most widespread form of activity, with the Far East leading the field in terms of regional focus, although all world areas received comparable attention. Lecture series, combined with "non-credit seminars," took second place. Visiting exhibits and other artistic events were almost equally popular, followed by resident foreign scholars on campus and travel abroad.

The survey disclosed that 242 colleges have plans in some stage of development for introducing non-Western studies or enlarging their present commitments. Many of them fall within the group already doing something: relatively few represent completely fresh attacks on the problem by institutions new to the non-Western field. It is significant and encouraging that the two types of development most frequently mentioned are library improvement and curricular revision. While each of them is reported by only about a quarter of all the colleges engaged in non-Western activity, it is a good omen for future progress.

For building faculty strength, 113 colleges will attempt to recruit new faculty members with non-Western specialization; 127 intend to invite occasional visiting specialists, and 55 plan to offer visiting specialists resident posts. Several devices for enlarging present faculty competence were mentioned a significant number of times: faculty seminars (60), released time for study on campus (28), summer study leaves (98), a semester or year of study at an American university (41), and a semester or year for study and travel abroad (77).

The survey delineates all of this and much more. It is a helpful guide in estimating the extent to which non-Western studies are already part of the curriculum. In time, perhaps when a subsequent survey is taken, something may be known about the rate of change that is occurring in the liberal arts college. Meanwhile it is clear than non-Western studies have already made an impression that can be measured.

Were the figures yielded by our survey to be compared with *all* courses offered, *all* faculty activity and *total* student population in liberal arts colleges, it would be seen that non-Western studies are as yet playing only a minor part in the life of these colleges. Aside from any such comparison, the difficulty of evaluating the present situation forbids self-complacency. At most, the college effort in non-Western studies can be said to represent a modest beginning.

Yet as a challenge to higher education's long-unquestioned tradition of splendid isolation from the greater part of the world this is a giant step forward. Whether it will add a new dimension to, and whether it will provide a meaningful strategy for, higher education at the undergraduate level depends upon how vigorously and realistically the present effort is maintained. Either from timidity or from over-enthusism, this initial step in non-Western studies could be the last as well as the first.

# IV

# PROBLEMS FOR THE COLLEGES

## The First Hurdle

Whether or not non-Western studies should be undertaken is the kind of question that is always being raised, and resolved, by a college faculty. Any consideration of the claims of non-Western subject matter—whether to add new courses to the curriculum, or to substitute new courses for old, or to incorporate new material into old courses—will engage faculties and administrations in an activity that is altogether characteristic of the academic community. Without this saving grace, liberal education could not endure.

Many faculties have done nothing about non-Western studies. Sometimes this is due to inertia: no reflection has been undertaken, no choice has been made. On the other hand, thoughtful faculties may have soberly considered non-Western studies and decided against them. They may believe that the liberal arts college should remain as it is; that it should be substantially immune to the influence of a changing environment. Whether they are wedded to the classical tradition of Greece and Rome or to the great literature of the West, they have found a satisfactory prescription for performing their task as they conceive it, and non-Western studies appear to them as a distraction if not a blasphemy. A faculty of a different cast of mind, believing that the function of the college is to prepare young Americans for the business of living in American society, may remain unconvinced that academic attention should be given to anything outside the domestic concerns of the U.S.A.

The faculty that wishes to do something may encounter grave obstacles. To be sure, the faculty member who wrote in response to our inquiry: "A non-Western program will not and cannot strengthen the academic posture of a college with a poor academic program to begin with" was overlooking the revitalizing power of a new idea. The spark of interest in non-Western studies may light a fire of enthusiasm that will spread throughout the activities of a faltering institution. But only if non-Western studies are expressly viewed as a factor in the development of an effective total curriculum can they evoke a remedy for basic defects. They will not in themselves make up for or hide fundamental inadequacies. And in most cases it is probable that the teacher quoted above would be proved correct.

Even in stronger institutions the faculty may have reservations about who can do what with what in non-Western studies. Recalling the start of the South Asia Language and Area Center at the University of Chicago, Professor Milton Singer speaks of the doubts felt by some members of the faculty "about the availability of materials that would meet our standards of scholarship, as well as doubts about our own qualifications to deal with the newer areas." Similar reservations have been voiced elsewhere and will be frequently repeated as liberal arts colleges come to grips with the problem. Many faculties may echo Professor Singer's conclusion: "We ourselves had to be more liberally educated to still our intellectual doubts about non-Western studies."[1]

Nevertheless, if our survey has any meaning, it cannot be gainsaid that at least 482 colleges are acting, however haphazardly, as if non-Western studies had a legitimate claim to their attention. One of the main purposes of this report is to encourage

---

1.  In Donald N. Bigelow and Lyman H. Legters (eds), "The Non-Western World in Higher Education," *Annals of the American Academy of Political and Social Science* Vol. 356, November 1964 (forthcoming)

and to help such colleges give systematic and practical consideration to the issues involved.

Once a faculty has decided that understanding of the non-Western varieties of human experience is needed along with the study of their Western counterparts, the question ceases to be whether non-Western studies belong in the curriculum: it becomes *how they can best help to achieve the college's aims.* When the need and the possibility of curricular reform have been recognized, the faculty is called upon to grapple with a whole series of practical problems. Putting aside the problems of student demand and financial wherewithal, not to mention the ticklish question of what if anything should be taken out of the curriculum, questions of content, method and means must be considered and resolved. They are all interrelated but may be isolated for purposes of analysis. In effect they are stages in the planning of a non-Western program.

## Choosing an Area

The first problem is the choice of one or other of the world regions on which to place major emphasis. Since in principle all are equal, there can be no easy determination of priority. It is no longer fashionable, as once it was, to decide for or against a civilization merely by asking what literature it has produced. Nor is it a matter of counting heads—or rivers—or of identifying potential world leadership. Besides, the political scientist could hardly be expected always to see eye to eye with the anthropologist or the literary scholar.

In the absence of theoretical reasons why a particular region should be chosen, the pragmatic approach will normally prevail. Perhaps the two factors that will weigh most heavily are the legitimate claims of the students and the potential ability of the faculty to serve them. A third factor intervenes when, as is often the case, an institution has an historical connection with a particular region. This sometimes proves as decisive as it is helpful in getting started.

In curricular development, existing resources, actual or potential, customarily play the crucial role. The choice of a regional focus is often predetermined. Questions like these may indicate why: What can be taught that is not already offered? Who among the faculty is teaching what? Can it be altered and, if so, how? Who can be properly retrained to add what? Where and how is such training available? What opportunities are there to recruit new teachers? Which of the departments or disciplines are most inclined to cooperate? Finally, who can provide the requisite leadership?

As the answers given to these questions may reveal, it will not always be possible or desirable for a college to focus on a single world region—at least not at first—since a wildly assorted display of experience may be uncovered. It may range from something on life in an African village to a little bit of Russian literature. Still, though the answers may lead in several directions, the question *what area?* makes a good starting point for discussion of a possible program.

Several major areas come up as a matter of course for consideration. Each has its own built-in problems, either because of its history or because of the manner in which American scholarship has approached it. Certain areas are inherently easier than others for some colleges to study, if for no other reason than their ability to use existing manpower. Course work on East European or Latin American countries often presents fewer difficulties in term of available competence than do comparable courses on Africa, Asia or the Middle East. Yet, among the colleges covered by our survey, courses relating to East Asia or Asia in general outnumber courses on Latin America and are second only to courses on the USSR and Eastern Europe. For some colleges the Middle East is the simplest area to tackle, as witness the reported growth between 1950 and 1962 from less than half a dozen to well over 200 undergraduate colleges offering one or more courses on the Middle East.[2] But in our survey the Middle East is well behind the three leading areas.

The other three major areas, South Asia, Southeast Asia and Africa (which includes thirty or more brand new countries), are somewhat more difficult, though not impossible, to intro-

---

2.    *ACLS Newsletter.* XV, 4 (April 1964), p. 1

duce into the undergraduate curriculum as distinct units of study. They have attracted the fewest specialists (and the fewest graduate students) and teaching materials are by far the least adequate. Furthermore, in both Southeast Asia and Africa a great assortment of exotic languages causes all sorts of complications. Even so, in 1963–64 an undergraduate could not only take courses on many aspects of Africa—150 courses were offered at over 20 colleges—but could learn Swahili at Smith College or at Lincoln University in Pennsylvania, as well as at five universities scattered about the country.

According to our survey, out of a total of just over 4000 non-Western courses offered during the academic year 1963–64, 1500 were concerned either with some aspect of Latin America or with the Soviet Union and Eastern Europe. If we exclude infusion courses these two areas account for 1350 out of a total of less than 3000 courses. It is not difficult to see why so large a fraction of the present course work labeled non-Western was focused on these areas. Although scantily treated in the traditional curriculum, they have been more readily comprehensible to both teacher and student than the more remote and alien societies. Of the 216 institutions reporting courses in non-Western languages as we have defined them—excluding Spanish—202 or over 90 per cent offered Russian. (A more specialized and comprehensive survey taken by the Modern Language Association showed a total of just over 500 four-year institutions giving some instruction in Russian in the fall of 1961.) Eighteen colleges in our survey, or 8 per cent, gave courses in Portuguese. (An MLA survey showed 63 four-year institutions teaching Portuguese in the fall of 1962).

The relative accessibility of Spanish, Russian and even Portuguese, and of staff to teach them, enhances the ease with which Latin America and the USSR can be studied. But ease should not be too readily accepted as a decisive criterion: the less accessible languages and areas may also be the most rewarding.

Although language instruction is still the weakest link in the chain of non-Western studies, and is likely to remain so for some time, it is nevertheless the clearest single indication of a college's commitment to the enterprise. It is not hard to see why. The scholarly mind automatically thinks of language when thinking of a cultural region, even though the scholar may be ignorant of the languages he needs for study of the region. Hence in the choice of an area for study, the problem of language is always implicit if not fully articulated.

While for a given college the teaching of an uncommon language may remain an unstated goal when an area is chosen, mistaken ideas about the uncommon languages can contribute to the making of an unwise choice. Modern methods of language instruction are doing much to make all the major languages accessible, but meanwhile the belief that some languages are easier than others not only fosters unworthy and irrelevant motives for choosing a language for study but may inhibit rational choice of a cultural area. In principle, the choice of languages to be studied should be governed by the choice of the total field of study, not *vice versa*. In practice, the choice of an area and the choice of a language or languages will normally be made in tandem. Indeed, before choosing an area, a college might find it illuminating and profitable to review the whole of its modern language instruction.

The essential point is that language teaching should be organically related to the aims of the non-Western program as a whole, and language problems should not be allowed to distort them, much less to dictate the choice of an area. If liberal education is to be emancipated from excessive preoccupation with Western civilization, languages cannot be exempted from the rule that all civilizations are equally worthy of consideration.

Although theoretically the choice of an area for study is the first step, many colleges may feel obliged to give prior thought to some of the problems of method and means that we go on to discuss in this chapter. They may thus be enabled to hit upon an approach congenial to their aims and capabilities. It will not necessarily entail concentration from the start on any one cultural area though in the long run such concentration is desirable. Obviously there is no magic formula for choosing either the area of study or the method of approach. Many choices are possible. Each college must make the best it can. In so doing it will surely reflect its past as well as shape its future.

### Introductory Courses, Infusion Courses and Comparative Studies

Probably no college in the country is so well endowed with books, faculty, time and money that it could undertake programs dealing with all of the main cultural areas. On the other hand, probably no college is too poor to attempt some kind of attention to non-Western experience. The problem is to balance comprehensive coverage against intensity of treatment, breadth of exposure against depth of understanding, available skills against ideal objectives, recognition of what can be done against a vision of what ought to be done. The questions uppermost in the minds of any faculty will be: How much must be added to the curriculum in order to make non-Western studies worth undertaking? Can it be done? If so, how can it best be done?

If it proves impracticable to focus on a single cultural area, intensity of treatment is out of the question. How far can depth of understanding be attained if the whole world is your oyster? If some kind of comprehensive coverage is the alternative, how wide can the net be cast without merely skimming the surface? Comprehensive coverage may provide the largest possible opening for a variety of talents and interests, but barring the coincidence that the whole faculty fought in North Africa or Korea, the resulting program will be pretty much of a hodgepodge. In this situation, non-Western studies would scarcely fulfill their promise of redeeming the liberal arts curriculum from its present fragmentation. Without some sort of coherent plan, the venture had best be left alone.

In the absence of regional specialization, the most promising step is to provide for the study of one or more non-Western civilizations as a whole. Under such a plan the curriculum need not be unreasonably dislocated nor the faculty unseasonably discouraged. An introductory course has the further advantage of fitting neatly into almost any scheme of general education— a fairly common constituent of liberal arts programs. A course on Western civilization might be enlarged to include non-Western subject matter, say on the Middle East or Africa. Or a sequence might be created by adding a new course dealing, for instance, with Asian civilizations. The latter might cover India,

China and Japan, for which reading materials already exist. A course introducing a complete civilization or a group of civilizations is the simplest means of reaching most if not all of the students. It lends itself readily to being made a requirement rather than an elective.

Another possibility is the infusion of non-Western material into conventional courses. As we noted in Chapter II, it is not incompatible with an introductory course and the two approaches are often combined. In theory, infusion may reach a high proportion of the student body, but as the degree of possible infusion varies widely among different disciplines, the actual impact will depend on the college's pattern of requirements, limited options and free electives. History and geography are normally fields more appropriate for separate courses than for infusion, but many general courses in the departments of anthropology, art, economics, literature, philosophy, political science and sociology are particularly susceptible to the incorporation of non-Western material. Infusion is a promising point of departure and it has sufficient validity to justify its adoption by any college that is not yet ready to plunge more deeply into non-Western studies. At the other end of the scale, infusion courses may be useful in providing extended coverage when combined with a program concentrating on a single cultural area. But if infusion is adopted as a complete solution, the limitations of the method will impose themselves on the result. Such instruction cannot hope to provide the same depth of insight and understanding as an area program will furnish for at least part of the student body.

A different approach, with some similarity to infusion, has appeared under the name "comparative studies." This approach may grow naturally out of area studies and it is regarded by some of its proponents as a step beyond and possible replacement for the area approach, mainly in relation to research. It is not yet clear whether comparative studies, which tend to be non-historical and oriented toward the behavioral sciences, can maintain themselves satisfactorily in the university except in conjunction with solid area programs. On the other hand, as a method of instruction in the liberal arts college, illustrated for the purposes of this report by Dartmouth (see Appendix II), the comparative studies approach may be regarded as a variant of the infusion method.

Separate courses on non-Western subjects—for example, the history of Japan as opposed to world history; the economy of India as against the economics of developing countries; Russian literature as against world literature—can achieve a detailed and systematic treatment of the given topic such as no introductory course and no amount of infusion can aspire to. It is much more difficult for the college and the individual faculty member to offer a respectable course on Arab politics than to include a unit on the Arab-Israeli conflict in an international relations course, but the rewards are commensurately greater if the purpose is to come to grips with the Middle East on its own terms.

Yet a college has not moved very far toward an intellectually rigorous confrontation with Japan, Russia or Brazil if its curriculum is merely studded with an assortment of unrelated non-Western courses that available faculty members happen to want to teach. Only when such offerings form a coherent whole can the institution be said to have established a program of non-Western studies. It is no denial of the virtues of other approaches to assert that only such an *integrated program* offers the student an opportunity to achieve solid understanding of another culture. Even when that stage is reached it is by no means final, since the effective exposure of *all* students to non-Western experience may still be far ahead. But meanwhile the college has made a long step toward internationalizing the liberal arts curriculum.

## Language Study

We have emphasized the relevance of language study and its problems to the choice of a cultural area as the focus of a non-Western program. All that needs to be added is renewed emphasis on the critical role of language in non-Western studies and the possibility of successful attack on the problems.

As non-Western studies grow, in depth if not in quantity, language teaching will surely follow, either because it is recognized by the faculty as indispensable to serious study of any culture or in response to the demands of students. While many colleges may find it impracticable for some time to offer any of the indigenous languages of the non-Western areas (excepting perhaps Spanish, Portuguese and Russian), no college can afford to dismiss the possibility once for all. The teaching of Arabic may come to be as much a part of the business of a liberal arts college as the teaching of French or German.

Any discussion of language learning, regardless of the choice of language, calls for recognition of the revolution that has occurred in this field in the last decade. In brief, it is now possible for an undergraduate to learn Arabic at least as thoroughly as his parents learned French, while fulfilling the requirements for an A.B. in the liberal arts. Students at Portland State College have been doing so for the past five years. This is not the place for analysis of modern methods of language learning beyond noting that their kernel is the audio-lingual approach.[3] This approach has won acceptance for the teaching both of exotic languages in universities and of familiar languages in secondary schools. Oddly enough, it has had its smallest impact on the colleges. There is no better example of the wastefulness of college curricula than the prevailing pattern of instruction in foreign languages. Although the old method of grammar book in one hand and dictionary in the other has been completely superseded, most American colleges that boast of a language requirement continue to turn out graduates who cannot speak the language they are supposed to have learned, let alone understand its characteristic subtleties of thought.

As a general rule, faculty members are captives of the same fallacies about language learning as the man in the street. They have no notion of what it actually means to teach Arabic, Chinese or Japanese: they just *know* that it is harder than teaching French or Spanish. Yet Dr Charles A. Ferguson, director of the Center for Applied Linguistics, has stated that "almost any major language can be effectively taught in the same amount of time now given to French or Spanish, depending upon the

---

3. For discussion of the audio-lingual approach see Appendix A of Joseph Axelrod and Donald N. Bigelow, *Resources for Language and Area Studies.*

goals one has in mind, the methods used, and the calibre of instruction that is made available." It is no longer reasonable to think that Spanish is easy and Arabic hopelessly difficult. Arabic can be taught as readily as Spanish, and the adoption of appropriate methods for doing so may incidentally have beneficial effects on the quality of instruction in other modern languages. In fact, besides what some of the universities have been able to achieve in the teaching of uncommon languages to undergraduates, Chinese has been successfully taught at San Francisco State College for five years and Japanese at Earlham for the last two years. Kalamazoo College is experimenting with Chinese, Japanese and Hindi simultaneously.

In any case, academic and national needs cannot wait while graduate students are being belatedly introduced to non-Western languages. The undergraduate colleges ought to play a larger part. In tackling it they must think afresh about the place of languages in liberal education, recognize their vital role in non-Western studies, and grasp the consequences of the revolution in language teaching.

## Faculty Recruitment and Retraining

No college is likely to embark on non-Western studies without first taking stock of faculty capabilities. It is probably a rare campus on which, before any formal discussion, the faculty— or at least its most interested members—has not already expressed itself about area focus, method of presentation and the desirability of language instruction. This expression will have supplied some indications of faculty interest and competence. It is not unlikely that student voices will also have been heard at this stage, affording a rough idea of potential demand. Whether the method under consideration is widespread infusion of non-Western material into existing courses, development of broad introductory courses, or the fashioning of one or more comprehensive programs involving language and several disciplines, there will almost certainly be some talent available. It may take the form of teaching competence capable of more diversified employment or of experience that has been overlooked. Similarly, there may be an untapped source of language skills, such as foreign students, that can be put to use.

But there will surely be a gap between resources and needs. Otherwise there is reason to suspect that the college is cutting its non-Western coat according to its available cloth, a restriction that will neither suit the enterprise nor attract outside support. If the college means business, the gap will sooner or later be evident and means will have to be found to close it.

Visiting professors, American and foreign, can diversify and strengthen a non-Western program and may help to arouse latent interest, but at best they are adjuncts or stopgaps. The only solution lies in the permanent faculty. This means either recruitment of new faculty members, retraining of present members, or a combination of both. Most colleges will be obliged to blend the two procedures as recruitment can rarely be effected on demand and retraining is limited by day-to-day teaching. But whatever the procedure, the goals will be determined by the character of the proposed program.

If the college decides to develop a program focused on a particular cultural area, well-trained language and area specialists will certainly be needed. Retraining of present faculty members can hardly be expected to provide the experience and sophistication that such a program requires. Unless the faculty happens to include one or two genuine specialists in the area—which may of course be one of the reasons for choosing it—recruitment will be unavoidable at the outset. Only thereafter, when the specialists have laid the foundations, will the college be able to build on them by enlarging the competence of other faculty members.

On the other hand, any form of comprehensive coverage may be expected to meet a higher proportion of its teaching needs from existing talent. If for instance, under a policy of infusion, it is proposed to add a unit on Indian politics to a comparative government course, the political scientist already teaching the course could probably acquire the necessary competence in a summer or a semester off campus, or even in the college library. He might well be encouraged by a grant or stipend to devote his whole time to that object. Or if the college plans to offer an introductory course on a single civilization, the multidisciplinary group of faculty members involved may need to make relatively modest efforts to equip themselves for the task.

Neither the recruitment of specialists nor the retraining of present faculty members is free from difficulty. In many disciplinary fields the area specialist is rare and expensive. In face of growing competition, he may be hard to find and harder still to attract to a small college. He would naturally lean toward a larger institution where opportunities for research exist and where he would probably have to do little or no teaching outside his specialty. The best hope of the liberal arts college lies in the growing number of young graduates emerging from language and area centers, some of whom may welcome a change of atmosphere and, responding to the challenge of a developing program, be willing to start their professional careers on a small campus. This, after all, is how great teachers grow on small campuses.

At the same time, in establishing strong non-Western programs, colleges will help to solve their own staffing problems by swelling the pool of graduate students who will be adequately prepared for training as language and area specialists.

For the faculty member, the task of adding a new dimension to his disciplinary training is invariably arduous, the more so if he tries to learn a totally unfamiliar language. But it is by no means impossible. Already a variety of programs offer specific encouragement and assistance. Fellowships are available under Title VI of the National Defense Education Act, as noted in Chapter II, to enable members of the faculties of liberal arts colleges to undertake advanced study of uncommon languages and related subjects. Under the American Institute of Indian Studies, supported by the Department of State with PL 480 funds and by a grant from the Ford Foundation, faculty training fellowships are open to applicants who are non-specialists.

In certain states, notably Indiana and New York, statewide efforts assisted by the Ford Foundation are being made to encourage colleges to use university and college facilities for faculty development. In addition, many colleges are furnishing aid for this purpose to their own faculties.

The cumulative experience of the colleges whose programs are described in Appendix II contains no suggestion of an easy solution for any of these problems. Some colleges have had so little success with recruitment that they have fallen back almost exclusively on retraining. Others have been disappointed with retraining. The nearest approach to a reliable prescription is that a college administration should strive to ensure by the exercise of foresight that the filling of vacancies in the faculty takes account of the non-Western program as well as departmental needs.

## Library Facilities

The problem presented to the college library by non-Western studies does not differ in principle from what is entailed by any major change in the curriculum. The library ought to and tries to keep up with curricular change. But its task is made all but impossible unless the planners of any new program take account of library facilities. Conversely, if the library is not enabled to provide adequate facilities, its deficiencies will cripple the program.

Where non-Western studies constitute an unprecedented challenge to the library is in the magnitude of the gap between the collections it is likely to have and the material needed for any serious non-Western work. In this respect the college library reflects the position of libraries in general. In a recent report, the Commission on the Humanities, sponsored by the American Council of Learned Societies, the Council of Graduate Schools and the United Chapters of Phi Beta Kappa, having observed that "good libraries are needed at all levels in all subjects for teaching and research," goes on to say that "undernourishment tends to force each library to throw all of its inadequate resources into a losing battle to meet the most urgent demands of its own institution."[4]

For non-Western studies the situation is far worse. A yardstick is furnished by Horace Poleman of the Orientalia Division

---

4. Report of the Commission on the Humanities, *ACLS Newsletter*, XV, 5 (May 1964)

of the Library of Congress in speaking of the resources needed for the study of a single region, South Asia, which is not among the regions most amply covered by scholarly material. He maintains that a college library ought "to have at least 3,000 titles before it could meet the normal demands of undergraduate students, while a research library should have at its command not less than 25,000 titles for the humanities, the social sciences, and the natural sciences." [5] Very few university libraries and almost no college libraries reach these standards. Even without the benefit of statistical surveys, inspection of any campus library will suggest how far library facilities fall short of meeting the requirements of non-Western studies. The situation is summed up, in reference to another area, in a report recently published by ACLS: "Almost all liberal arts institutions discover, at the start of instruction on the Middle East, that their area library resources are sparse, even for teaching, to say nothing of faculty research." [6]

In our survey colleges were asked to classify their library holdings as "good," "adequate" or "poor" for the purposes of the non-Western studies at present offered. Of some 500 institutions that claimed some form of activity in the non-Western field, almost exactly half rated their library resources as "adequate" for the present level of activity. Since, as the remainder of the survey shows, that level is seldom high, there is no reason to doubt the accuracy of this particular response. Sixty-eight colleges reported the possession of one or more "important collections of non-Western materials." Ninety colleges reported that they spent ten per cent or more of the operating expenditures of their libraries on non-Western studies; 96 that books relating primarily to non-Western studies make up ten per cent or more of their annual acquisitions; and 55 gave a similar status to non-Western periodicals. If we ignore the problems of definition discussed earlier, the figures are encouraging. At least they

5. In *Resources for South Asian Area Studies in the United States,* ed. by Richard D. Lambert, Philadelphia, 1962
6. "Undergraduate Foreign Area Studies: The Case of the Middle East," *ACLS Newsletter,* XV, 4 (April 1964) p. 3 (See Appendix II to this report)

indicate that librarians, reflecting the current mood of administration and faculty, have become aware of the need for additional resources to meet the requirements of non-Western studies.

When a college undertakes a non-Western program—or preferably when it is planning one—the library staff, with such aid as they can get from interested members of the faculty, ought to make a careful inventory of holdings related to the purposes of the program. This will be an important element in the total inventory of institutional resources which is indispensable for realistic planning. The essential aim is clear: to assemble a collection that will enable faculty members to prepare their courses and assign appropriate readings to students, will furnish students with ready access to the data they need for classwork and the modest research involved in term papers, and will provide faculty members with at least some of the basic tools for their own research. How readily this aim can be translated into a program of acquisitions for the library will depend on the degree of clarity with which the non-Western program itself is defined. Requirements will obviously vary according to the college's choice of a full-blown area program, introductory courses, a policy of infusion or some combination of these various possibilities.

In trying to fill the gaps, the library staff will have the help of bibliographical guides, though many of them are geared to the needs and capabilities of large libraries. University librarians and area specialists will also be able to help and should be consulted. The staff will have to decide whether certain books belong in the regular collection or in a separate section devoted to the non-Western program. Publications in uncommon languages require specialized knowledge for selection, purchase and cataloguing. This problem is serious even for large universities, as requisite language skills and library training rarely go together, but it will be even more acute for the small college.

With growing sophistication in this field, the library staff will be faced with a spiraling problem of search, acquisition, processing and, not least, funds to pay the bill. There is no final solution. But three things are essential to any library: books, space to house them and staff to handle them. All three must be supplied in sufficient quantity and quality if non-Western studies are to flourish.

## Student Interest and the Extracurricular Dimension

Non-Western studies will have no vitality unless they are sustained by a reservoir of interest within both the faculty and the student body. Faculty interest is plainly needed to get a program going; student interest is equally necessary to keep it alive. If either is lacking, non-Western courses will be poorly taught or poorly attended or both.

This is not to say that the absence of visible interest among students is a sufficient reason for faculty and administration to defer curricular decisions. If non-Western studies are agreed by faculty and administration to be a valid component of the college's conception of liberal education, they can no more be ignored for lack of articulate demand than physics or philosophy. If the interest is there, well and good. If not, it must be awakened.

The most obvious and natural way of awakening interest is by encouraging the development of relevant extracurricular activities. As we noted in our historical review, however, extracurricular activities may spring up spontaneously out of the initiative of individual students and faculty members. They will sometimes reflect a demand for exotic entertainment rather than sober academic study. But except where this is patently the case, it is always safer to take them seriously. If genuine interest is denied a curricular outlet it may seep away in frivolities.

We do not mean to imply that extracurricular activities do not have a value of their own, both as an embellishment and as a support for strictly academic programs. In the liberal education of an undergraduate the curriculum cannot furnish the whole of his learning experience. It should not attempt to do so. Summers in Mexico, social intercourse with foreign students, visiting dance troupes are rewarding in themselves and may have educational significance. Certainly no college should hesitate to encourage extracurricular expressions of the kind of interest that adds life and color to the academic program.

Just as certainly, however, a proper relationship between extracurricular activities and the academic program must be clearly established and rigorously preserved. In no circumstances must extracurricular activities be mistaken for academic pursuits or accepted as a substitute.

The risk of pretense and confusion is greatest where study and travel come together, as Stephen Freeman makes clear in *Undergraduate Study Abroad*. Junior-year and summer study overseas has hitherto been confined mainly to Europe and has therefore had little relevance to non-Western studies. But it is growing rapidly in popularity and, according to the same report, "colleges are examining the desirability of study programs in the Near and Far East, in Africa, and in Latin America."[7] Undergraduates may now go for a year in India under a program at the University of Wisconsin supported by PL 480 funds. Our own inquiries show that some liberal arts colleges, and cooperative groups like the Great Lakes Colleges Association, have started such programs. These particular colleges and groups are clearly aware of the special difficulties that language barriers and so-called culture shock create for undergraduate study in non-Western countries. They at least are sensitive to the distinction to be made between travel as an educational experience and overseas study that is an integral part of the curriculum.

## Aims and Resources

At more than one point in the foregoing discussion we have implied that the aims of a non-Western program and the resources to be applied to it stand in a reciprocal relationship. Neither can be determined without reference to the other. The proposed scope of a program, whether formally integrated or merely involving the addition of some course work, will obviously indicate both the optimum and the minimum resources needed. Conversely, the actual scope of the program will be governed

---

7. *Undergraduate Study Abroad,* p. 33

by the college's assessment of available and prospective resources.

A substantial program of non-Western studies is an expensive undertaking. An extreme example is language instruction, which for some years at least may attract relatively low enrolments. But, as we have indicated, both faculty recruitment and strengthening of library facilities may also entail heavy expenditures. Some colleges have made a good start from a slender base, but very few will go far without assistance from outside.

A college's demonstrated willingness to invest its own resources may act as a magnet for outside aid. The ambitious program of Middle East studies at Portland State College was initially undertaken without external assistance, but it immediately showed enough promise to be given federal support under the National Defense Education Act. The designation of the program as an NDEA language and area center was then decisive for its further development. Similarly the modest beginnings of non-Western study at Earlham spread first to Antioch and later helped to inspire the other ten colleges of the Great Lakes Colleges Association, whose International Education Program was, early in 1964, awarded a grant of $500,000 from the Ford Foundation. The omens are favorable for increasing financial support from both private foundations and governmental sources. But such support is likely to be attracted only by tangible proof of commitment, if not visible evidence of accomplishment. It would therefore be a mistake to make so cautious an assessment of the possibilities as to preclude significant achievement.

# V

# RECOMMENDATIONS AND SUGGESTIONS

Clemenceau ridiculed Wilson's Fourteen Points by reminding his listeners that "The good Lord had only ten." We are bold enough to list fourteen recommendations—thirteen addressed to liberal arts colleges that are considering non-Western studies, and a fourteenth directed to the organizations to which the colleges will look for help.

I. *The first step toward effective non-Western studies is a firm commitment on the part of the college.*

We agree with others who have studied the issues involved that the first imperative is *institutional commitment* to a rationally defined academic program,[1] as distinct from naive fascination with the exotic or sentimental yearning for "international understanding." The necessary commitment must be grounded in a consensus of the academic community—students, faculty, administration and trustees—on the aims of liberal education, the

---

1.  *The College and World Affairs*, p. 11; and Howard E. and Florence H. Wilson, *American Higher Education and World Affairs*, American Council on Education, Washington, D. C., 1963, pp. 33–34 and 44–45

goals of the particular college, and the range of studies needed to attain these ends. The inclusion of non-Western studies must spring from reasoned conviction of their relevance to agreed ends, not from slavish imitation of prevalent fashions or competitive emulation of rival institutions.

The process by which such conviction may be reached is neither new nor exclusively bound up with non-Western studies. As we have already suggested, it is simply the process of self-study to which more and more colleges have recently subjected themselves and which every college should undertake from time to time in order to keep its program alive and meaningfully related to the changing environment.

II. *The college should formulate a definite plan of action before seeking outside support for non-Western studies.*

The development of non-Western studies to their present status owes much, as we have noted, to public and private financial support. But outside support did not provide the initiative for this development: it was first attracted by *institutional initiative.* Clearly it is not indispensable for making a start, as witness some of the colleges that have been studied for this present survey. Hanover, Marian, Mills and Western College for Women, for example, all embarked on non-Western studies without any special subvention. If we exclude a modest amount of indirect support through the statewide Project for Extending the Study of Foreign Areas in Indiana Undergraduate Education, the first two have had no such subvention to this day.

Most colleges that intend to introduce a substantial program of non-Western studies will sooner or later need financial assistance, and its availability will govern the rate of development. But, like the colleges themselves, private foundations and governmental agencies have to husband their resources and apply them to projects that offer the best prospect of a satisfactory return on the investment. They cannot afford to spend their money on vague aspirations. Most programs that have received support had *already started* and were engaging the attention of at least a few members of the faculty and a sizeable number of students before aid was forthcoming. In any case, for non-Western studies as for other fields of educational experiment, potential benefactors will expect to be presented with a well-thought-out, practical plan for reaching a defined and attainable goal—together with concrete evidence of the college's intention to commit a suitable proportion of its own resources.

III. *Planning must begin with a realistic inventory and assessment of institutional resources.*

The formulation of a workable plan of action requires a thoroughgoing *inventory of the college's available resources,* both human and material, and a realistic assessment of their potentialities for a non-Western program. Without such an assessment of practical possibilities, planning is little better than dreaming. The smaller the faculty, the more limited the facilities and the lower the income of the college, the more crucial the inventory. Its importance is emphasized by all of the smaller colleges we have studied. Marian and Mills are significant examples. One of the most valuable benefits of an inventory is that it may reveal unsuspected resources, notably faculty knowledge and experience which have hitherto gone unnoticed, or at any rate unused, for lack of appropriate outlets. These assets may make a critical difference to the possibility of undertaking non-Western studies.

Taking an inventory and drafting an effective program is a task for an *interdepartmental committee of the faculty,* in collaboration with the administration. Depending on circumstances, the committee may be a standing committee on the curriculum (as at New Paltz), a committee charged with a comprehensive institutional self-study (as at Hanover), and *ad hoc* committee on non-Western studies or the equivalent (as at Dartmouth, Marian and Portland State) or a special subcommittee of the curriculum committee (as at Mills). What is essential is that the committee, regardless of its formal status, be representative of all the principal departments of the college likely to be involved in any non-Western program. An interdepartmental committee, moreover, reflects the interdisciplinary character of non-Western studies.

IV. *The fullest possible degree of faculty support must be enlisted to insure a sound and enduring program.*

Most programs for strengthening the non-Western component in an institutional curriculum have their genesis in the thinking of one man or of a small group of individuals from the faculty, the administration or both. The awareness and conviction requisite to the initiation of non-Western studies may stem from long-standing personal knowledge of a non-Western area or from more recent interest gained in private or government assignments overseas. Seldom will such experience be possessed by more than a minority of the faculty.

The crucial initiative has sometimes—in such cases as Mills, New Paltz, and California State College at Hayward—come from the president of a college. In other instances—such as Earlham and Portland State—faculty members have spurred their colleges to significant non-Western efforts.

But regardless of source, it is the idea that counts and needs to be nurtured. It must be protected both against the overenthusiasm sometimes aroused by proposals for curricular reform and against destructive sniping by unpersuaded members of the faculty. This makes it *imperative to involve the faculty in all stages of planning* from the inventory onward, so that they will have every opportunity to resolve their doubts and become firmly convinced.

When a new college is to be established, either independently or within a university framework (as at the University of the Pacific), the responsible administrators may find it expedient, or indeed unavoidable, to do their own planning with minimal faculty participation. In all other cases it would be well to heed the advice of experienced administrators that it is unwise "to try to impose . . . ideas on the faculty or to hurry the process of change."[2] Only a convinced faculty will in the long run guarantee the development and continuance of a worthy program.

---

2.   Thomas E. Jones, Edward V. Stanford and Goodrich C. White, *Letters to College Presidents,* Prentice-Hall, Inc., Englewood Cliffs, N. J., 1964, Chapter 12, ("Preparing the Ground for a New Curriculum"), p. 74

V. *New faculty appointments should be made with a view to strengthening non-Western competence as well as filling departmental vacancies.*

Few colleges that come fresh to the undertaking will be able to get very far without the addition of at least one or two new faculty members. What particular additions are needed will largely depend on the content of the program adopted, and unless the college is exceptionally well-heeled, some desirable appointments will have to await the availability of financial assistance.

If we are right about the essential role of languages, some *language teachers* will be needed. Teachers of non-Western languages are scarce. American students seldom want to become language teachers and they have continually resisted preparing for this occupation: they prefer to become linguists or men of letters. You can lead a man to a language program but you can't make him teach. The language fellowship awards under NDEA, for example, have produced far more area specialists than language teachers. This state of affairs will continue to hamper the development of undergraduate programs, but it is by no means hopeless. Some language teachers are available and more will appear, and some area specialists will be able to contribute to language teaching.

The main demand, however, will be for *area specialists*—not in the old sense of persons whose specialty consisted entirely in a general knowledge of the principal features of a cultural region, but in the sense of persons who combine a broad, general knowledge of the area with a high level of scholarly competence in their own disciplines and, normally, have considerable field experience in the area and competence in its languages.[3]

The graduate programs of universities, and especially the language and area centers supported by the National Defense Education Act, have begun to provide a flow of suitably qualified men and women. Many of them, as we have already suggested, will be ready to respond to the challenge of developing

---

3.  Cf. Donald N. Bigelow, "The Center Concept and the Changing Curriculum," *Higher Education*, July 1962

non-Western studies at a liberal arts college, in spite of the probable dearth on a small campus of colleagues and books in their special fields. Sometimes they will be able to help in teaching one of the appropriate languages. In any case, they are trained to fill a dual role—teaching courses within the particular sphere of their own departmental discipline and non-Western courses of a more general character.

VI. *Every opportunity should be utilized to fortify and extend the non-Western competence of present faculty members.*

At most colleges, the opening phases of a non-Western program must be built around the faculty resources already present. For this purpose the institutional inventory is obviously of capital importance. The paramount need of most faculties will be to enlarge their scholarly competence in non-Western fields. Their members must be given every opportunity and encouragement to satisfy this need. Private study on campus, attendance at summer courses, full-year study at graduate schools, participation in the activities of scholarly organizations, study and teaching abroad, either on sabbatical leave or on special leave for service under educational exchange programs, should all be utilized, as appropriate, for this purpose.

Whether through released time or through direct financial support, *faculty members must be assisted to broaden their academic foundations.* A realistic budget for a sound and enduring program must make adequate provision for these purposes. Limited help is available from the U. S. Office of Education, with its special postdoctoral awards under Title VI of NDEA, from the Fulbright-Hays program, and from some of the major foundations, but further help is needed.

VII. *The interdisciplinary faculty seminar is a valuable means of maintaining interest in a program while enlarging faculty capabilities.*

The experience of a sizeable fraction of the colleges whose programs we report on in detail (e.g., Marian, Mills, Western

College for Women, the colleges of the Atlanta University System, the Gettysburg group and the Winston-Salem group) suggests that the most valuable single device for creating and holding faculty interest, increasing scholarly competence and maintaining a sense of common purpose is the *interdisciplinary faculty seminar*. Designed to increase faculty members' acquaintance with the historical, social and cultural background of a particular non-Western area, it may also encourage them in further study and research. In addition, the seminar provides opportunities for informal interdisciplinary discussion of the content and procedures of the college's non-Western program.

In most but not all of the colleges studied, the seminars made use of outside specialists as directors or participants. Weekly or monthly meetings were held, usually throughout the academic year. Released time for preparatory study was sometimes but not always allowed. Attendance was voluntary, but broad and active participation was encouraged, especially from the departments most directly concerned with the non-Western program. In fact, at most of the colleges that organized seminars an impressively high proportion of the whole faculty took part in at least one such series of meetings.

For many liberal arts colleges the interdisciplinary seminar will remain an important means of developing and sustaining an effective non-Western program, but it can become superficial and at best is essentially a spur to individual effort. Evidence exists that seminars did not always strike a spark, that released time was sometimes all but wasted. Yet ideally the device may provide a concrete realization of the power of non-Western studies to break through departmental barriers and help to unify and strengthen the liberal arts curriculum.

VIII. *College resources should be supplemented by visiting scholars from abroad and from other U. S. institutions and by judicious use of foreign students.*

Scholars brought to the campus as visiting professors or occasional lecturers on non-Western subjects may be citizens of one of the countries studied in the college program. Such persons can often convey a feeling for their ancestral culture rarely matched by an American scholar, no matter how profound his intellectual grasp of the culture. Suitably qualified men and women (including some Americans of non-Western descent) are more readily available than most colleges realize. Some of the organizations named in Appendix III have been of notable assistance in locating them.

Clearly a foreign scholar will make the greatest impact on a college if he comes to it for a semester or longer, under such arrangements as the Fulbright-Hays program, rather than for a brief visit. If, as at New Paltz, Portland State and Winston-Salem, for instance, well-qualified scholars who are natives of the region which the college has chosen to focus on can be found for regular appointment to the faculty, so much the better. But even brief visits from sensitive indigenous interpreters of non-Western societies help to sustain the interest of faculty and students.

No less valuable assistance has come from U. S. scholars who specialize in non-Western areas. Their contributions may range from brief visits, during which they provide advice and occasional lectures or take part in a faculty seminar, to a semester or an academic year of formal teaching. Teachers who have participated in university language and area programs and have taught undergraduates can be especially helpful. Also, it is frequently possible to invite, for shorter or longer periods, professors who have recently spent time in the target area, whether for research or on a government assignment.

The benefit of having on campus living and breathing exemplars of a non-Western society is a strong argument for admitting a reasonable number of foreign students. Not every college will find it expedient to have as high a proportion of foreign students as Western College for Women (some ten per cent of the whole student body in 1963-64), but any college with a non-Western program stands to gain from the presence of at least a few students from the relevant area. They too can be valuable interpreters of their culture, through classroom discussions, organized extracurricular activities and the casual contacts of daily life. But foreign students should be neither exploited nor enthroned.

Just as the chief business of the college is to educate Americans, so it must be borne in mind that foreign students come to the United States in pursuit of their own educational aims rather than to serve any local interest.

IX. *Non-Western programs must include the development of adequate library holdings and staff.*

After faculty, if not before, the most essential resource of a college is teaching material. For the humanities and the social sciences, which embrace all courses normally embodied in a non-Western program, this means, above all, books and periodicals. Our inquiry shows that *library facilities* reveal as serious deficiencies as do faculties for the purposes of non-Western studies. With few exceptions, even among the colleges that have already made a start on a non-Western program, libraries are woefully inadequate for student reading, let alone further study on the part of the faculty. The cost of filling the gaps will be high and a generous allowance for books and periodicals will have to be made in the budget. At the same time, economy dictates careful discrimination in the choice of items. This may well be beyond the capacity of the average college librarian with no special training in non-Western fields. Outside advice will almost always be needed. In addition, either through re-training or recruitment, the library staff itself will have to undergo the same process of development as is needed by the faculty, if it is to play its proper role in serving the non-Western program.

X. *Provision ought to be made for the teaching of relevant languages.*

Opinions differ on the place of indigenous languages in non-Western studies, but we believe that the teaching of at least one major regional language is all but indispensable to an effective program. The Committee on the College and World Affairs cites the argument that "for the undergraduate a good translation may be a better vehicle for understanding than a poor knowledge of the language." This is quite true in so far as understanding derives from the acquisition of information. As a matter of speed and convenience, the student will usually study a good part of his non-Western material in translation—if good translations exist. But for grasping the thought patterns of an alien society nothing takes the place of a working knowledge of its language. Certainly no foreign scholar would be accepted as a serious student of American culture if he did not know a word of English.

Most of the colleges we have studied have developed substantial non-Western programs that do not include language instruction (except in Spanish, which is almost universal, and Russian, which is fairly widespread). Mills, for example, reports that it "acts on the assumption that high-quality substantive instruction relating to non-Western cultures can be offered without teaching non-Western languages at the undergraduate level." (See Appendix II.) Yet the same report states that the college "is willing to grant credit to students who learn such languages elsewhere" and that members of the faculty and the administration are "open to the possibility of introducing certain major non-Western languages into the curriculum at a later stage if funds and personnel to do so can be found."

The inference is inescapable that the omission of non-Western languages derives less from conviction that they are not necessary than from concern over the practical difficulties involved in introducing them. The difficulties are real enough but they are by no means insuperable. Good teaching is necessary and well-qualified teachers are scarce, but thanks to the graduate language and area programs the supply is gradually increasing. Moreover, language learning in general has been made easier and more effective by new teaching methods and mechanical aids which have been developed in the last few years and which continue to be refined.

XI. *Cooperative arrangements of all sorts should be used to assist in the development of adequate programs and especially to ease the burden of language teaching.*

In non-Western studies as in many other fields, much that is beyond the reach of an individual college can be achieved through inter-institutional cooperation. In the broadest sense of the term, cooperation ranges from nationwide programs open to any college student, through collaboration among colleges that are members of a regional organization, to a variety of joint enterprises involving two or more neighboring colleges. For any given college it is important to be aware of the full range of possibilities and to utilize those that are pertinent to the college's own plans.

An outstanding example of programs serving the whole country is the Cooperative Undergraduate Program for Critical Languages organized by Princeton University to enable students from other colleges to study uncommon languages for a full academic year, in tandem with summer study in one of the NDEA intensive language programs. It may be expected that the example of Princeton will be followed by universities in other parts of the country that are able to offer instruction in uncommon languages to undergraduates.

Regional collaboration is typified by the Indiana project, enabling the state university to help private colleges in the state solve particular problems involved in the introduction of non-Western studies, and by the Great Lakes Colleges Association, which helps any of its twelve member colleges that are interested in developing non-Western studies by organizing joint arrangements for faculty development and for overseas study and research. Recent endeavors by the New York State Department of Education to foster non-Western studies in both public and private colleges in the State are among the most comprehensive of regional experiments thus far undertaken.

Cooperative arrangements among neighboring colleges (not only for the purposes of non-Western study) are a growing phenomenon on the academic scene. In the field of our present concern, participation in such arrangements was reported by over 100 of the colleges responding to our survey. Examples are furnished by the cooperative groups that appear in Appendix II. Cooperation may entail a variety of aims, curricular and extracurricular, but essentially it is a *pooling of resources to enable each of the partners to enlarge the scope of its non-Western activities more economically and sometimes more effec-*

*tively than it could do alone.* Cooperation may enable the participating colleges to avoid duplication of library facilities, of specialized courses (notably in uncommon languages) and consequently of scarce teaching skills. It provides students with a wider range of opportunities and faculty members with increased mobility, which may enable them to teach a higher proportion of courses in their own specialties and sometimes even to find time for private study.

Yet cooperative arrangements are no panacea. Some have worked well, others have not. As in any partnership, much depends on the congeniality of the partners. Any divergence of basic aims may well prove fatal. If one college wants to establish a full-scale program on a particular area, replete with language offerings and library holdings, and another prefers to move around from one cultural area to another in successive years, cooperation between them will be difficult. At best, one school would be disappointed: at worst, the whole edifice might collapse, with the investment wasted and the impulse to innovation dissipated.

The simplest form of cooperation consists in the exchange of information and experience, either between an undergraduate college and a university that is better versed in the problems of non-Western study or between colleges that are grappling with similar problems. Among the colleges we have studied, the Atlanta University group and Florida Presbyterian College have taken pains to investigate the experience of comparable institutions, but as a general rule there has been too little mutual consultation. One of the purposes of this report is to help correct this omission, but it cannot take the place of direct communication.

Perhaps the most concrete benefit of cooperative action now visible occurs in the teaching of uncommon languages. All of the various types of cooperative arrangements provide means of sharing the cost, in manpower and money, of language instruction. Above all, the existence of summer programs for intensive language study at many of the major universities should encourage undergraduate colleges to undertake the teaching of non-

Western languages, in the knowledge that even modest efforts on the home campus can be augmented and reinforced.

XII. *A variety of means may be employed to incorporate non-Western studies into the liberal arts curriculum, but for optimum understanding an integrated program is the most promising.*

Any non-Western component embodied in the curriculum must be both internally coherent and integrated with the rest of the institutional program. Most colleges may have to be content with a modest start, but in any case the undertaking must be capable of organic growth within the framework of the college's present and prospective resources. Piecemeal introduction of individual courses on non-Western subjects has historically served a useful purpose in awakening interest in the larger possibilities of non-Western study, but this *ad hoc* procedure has been outdated by the march of events. It would be a waste of time and effort and would tend to obstruct rather than foster the development of satisfactory programs if all colleges undertaking non-Western studies had to grope their way through the same series of mistakes. A higher degree of sophistication is now possible, especially in the earlier stages of launching a program. Not only must non-Western courses be illuminating in themselves but they must make a recognizable contribution to the over-all aims of the institution.

Appropriate courses may take several forms: the interdisciplinary introduction to a non-Western civilization, the regular departmental course infused with non-Western subject matter wherever it is pertinent, and the course—in any of several disciplines—devoted entirely to a non-Western subject. Any of these types may be used as they fit in with institutional aims and available competence, and there is no reason to avoid mixing them in any reasonable relation to each other. *The essential principle is that they should in total constitute a coordinated program,* rooted in the individual disciplines but integrating their contributions by organizing them around a non-Western culture or society.

Such a non-Western program would offer the possibility of concentration with a major or minor. If an introductory survey course were included, this might be required and therefore reach all students, in contrast to the smaller number that might be expected to elect the entire program or any of its parts. To be sure, the survey course does not achieve adequate depth, the integrated program fails to reach all students, and therefore even a combination of the two does not afford an ideal solution. Yet a combined approach remains, at this point in time, the most promising means of providing for all students the opportunity of achieving a general understanding of the non-Western contribution to the human venture and for some the option of beginning more specialized study of a particular culture.

XIII. *In order to provide for systematic modification and adjustment, machinery should be established for continuous review and appraisal.*

Programs of the kind we have suggested represent for most colleges an ideal that will take several years to realize. Our recommendations are intended as guidelines for the administration and faculty in working out, in consonance with their own vision of liberal education and their prospective resources, a program that can be put into effect through a gradual process of planned development. However good the initial planning, progressive experience will reveal a need for changes and adjustments. No curriculum is final, perfect and unalterable. Non-Western studies in particular are a long way from that condition. So it behooves every college that undertakes a non-Western program to charge the curriculum committee, or some other appropriate body, with express responsibility for *coordinating the development of the program, evaluating its performance* and *verifying its assumptions.*

XIV. *Governmental agencies and private foundations need to step up their assistance to non-Western studies at the college level now and in the years just ahead.*

Our final recommendation is addressed to the various agencies representing American society which have seen non-Western studies as vital to higher education. As the Committee on the College and World Affairs pointed out, non-Western studies offer the major benefactors of higher education a great opportunity to serve both a national need and the cause of liberal education. What the philanthropic foundations and the Federal Government have already done in this field encourages us to believe that they will continue their invaluable contribution to the rate of progress and the quality of programs. But their assistance has been overwhelmingly concentrated at the graduate level (where it was natural and proper for it to start) and has barely begun to touch undergraduate education.

At this stage, the encouragement of non-Western studies in undergraduate colleges will not only serve to sustain and enliven the liberal arts but will also furnish help where it is likely to yield the highest returns. The quality of graduate education depends upon the quality of the undergraduate experience. This is the business of the liberal arts college.

Our report has shown that the majority of colleges are at least aware of the challenge presented by non-Western study. A sizeable minority have already responded to this challenge. Others seem anxious to do so. But, if progress is to continue, help is needed—for students, for faculty and for libraries—and it is needed *now* when the critical step has been taken and the will to go forward is strong.

# APPENDIX I

# STATISTICAL TABLES

# TABLE 1

## Number of Colleges Surveyed,
## By Highest Level of Offering, Institutional Control, and Sex of Student Body

### A. HIGHEST LEVEL OF OFFERING

| Level of Offering | Total | | Reporting Non-Western Studies | | Reporting No Non-Western Studies | | Not Reporting | |
|---|---|---|---|---|---|---|---|---|
| | Number of Colleges | Per Cent | Number of Colleges | Per Cent | Number of Colleges | Per Cent | Number of Colleges | Per Cent |
| Total | 685 | 100.0 | 482 | 70.4 | 51 | 7.4 | 152 | 22.2 |
| Bachelor | 447 | 100.0 | 302 | 67.6 | 38 | 8.5 | 107 | 23.9 |
| Master | 216 | 100.0 | 165 | 76.4 | 13 | 6.0 | 38 | 17.6 |
| Doctor | 22 | 100.0 | 15 | 68.2 | .. | .. | 7 | 31.8 |

### B. INSTITUTIONAL CONTROL

| Type of Control | Total | | Reporting Non-Western Studies | | Reporting No Non-Western Studies | | Not Reporting | |
|---|---|---|---|---|---|---|---|---|
| | Number of Colleges | Per Cent | Number of Colleges | Per Cent | Number of Colleges | Per Cent | Number of Colleges | Per Cent |
| Total | 685 | 100.0 | 482 | 70.4 | 51 | 7.4 | 152 | 22.2 |
| Publicly controlled | 79 | 100.0 | 61 | 77.2 | 1 | 1.3 | 17 | 21.5 |
| Independent | 166 | 100.0 | 124 | 74.7 | 10 | 6.0 | 32 | 19.3 |
| Church-related | 440 | 100.0 | 297 | 67.5 | 40 | 4.1 | 103 | 23.4 |

### C. SEX OF STUDENT BODY

| Sex | Total | | Reporting Non-Western Studies | | Reporting No Non-Western Studies | | Not Reporting | |
|---|---|---|---|---|---|---|---|---|
| | Number of Colleges | Per Cent | Number of Colleges | Per Cent | Number of Colleges | Per Cent | Number of Colleges | Per Cent |
| Total | 685 | 100.0 | 482 | 70.4 | 51 | 7.4 | 152 | 22.2 |
| Men | 73 | 100.0 | 51 | 69.9 | 6 | 8.2 | 16 | 21.9 |
| Women | 154 | 100.0 | 116 | 75.3 | 14 | 9.1 | 24 | 15.6 |
| Coeducational | 458 | 100.0 | 315 | 68.8 | 31 | 6.8 | 112 | 24.4 |

## TABLE 2

Frequency of Non-Western Course Offerings in Liberal Arts Colleges in 1963-64, Distinguishing between Courses with Over Fifty Percent Non-Western Content and Infusion Courses with Fifty Percent or Less Non-Western Content (Language Courses Excluded)

| Number of Courses Offered Per College | Number of Colleges If Infusion Courses are Included | If Infusion Courses are Excluded |
|---|---|---|
| 1 | 18 | 43 |
| 2 | 34 | 63 |
| 3 | 35 | 74 |
| 4 | 36 | 50 |
| 5–9 | 167 | 125 |
| 10–14 | 79 | 36 |
| 15–19 | 22 | 21 |
| 20–24 | 22 | 12 |
| 25 and over | 27 | 11 |
| Total | 440 | 435 |

NOTE: The difference between the totals represents five colleges which reported infusion courses only.

## TABLE 3

Distribution of Non-Western Courses (Other than Language Courses) and Enrolments by World Region, Distinguishing between Courses with Over Fifty Percent Non-Western Content and Infusion Courses

| World Region | Number of Courses Including Infusion Courses | Excluding Infusion Courses | Number of Enrolments Including Infusion Courses | Excluding Infusion Courses |
|---|---|---|---|---|
| USSR and East Europe | 875 | 735 | 21,784 | 17,840 |
| Asia (general) or East Asia | 656 | 655 | 16,181 | 15,460 |
| Latin America | 625 | 616 | 17,229 | 15,442 |
| Middle East | 200 | 194 | 5,459 | 5,324 |
| Africa | 149 | 146 | 3,168 | 3,107 |
| South Asia | 52 | 50 | 892 | 860 |
| Southeast Asia | 17 | 17 | 383 | 383 |
| Worldwide | 1,471 | 530 | 66,707 | 18,758 |
| Total | 4,045 | 2,943 | 131,803 | 77,174 |

# TABLE 4

## Non-Western Language Offerings (Excluding Spanish) by Numbers of Colleges, Courses and Enrolments

### A. ALL COURSES FIRST, SECOND, THIRD AND FOURTH YEARS

| Language | Colleges Offering Courses | Courses Offered | Enrolments |
|---|---|---|---|
| Russian | 202 | 552 | 7,996 |
| Portuguese | 18 | 27 | 332 |
| Chinese | 12 | 62 | 514 |
| Japanese | 8 | 41 | 460 |
| Arabic | 4 | 10 | 166 |
| Polish | 2 | 4 | 134 |
| Persian | 2 | 3 | 16 |
| Hindi-Urdu | 2 | 2 | 6 |
| Swahili | 2 | 2 | 33 |
| Modern Hebrew | 1 | 6 | 527 |
| Czech | 1 | 2 | 22 |
| Modern Greek | 1 | 1 | 2 |
| Turkish | 1 | 2 | 12 |
| Sanskrit | 1 | 3 | 1 |
| Tagalog | 1 | 1 | 6 |
| Total | | | 10,227 |

### B. SECOND-YEAR COURSES

| Language | Colleges Offering Courses | Courses Offered | Enrolments |
|---|---|---|---|
| Russian | 146 | 177 | 2,642 |
| Portuguese | 5 | 5 | 68 |
| Chinese | 6 | 16 | 96 |
| Japanese | 5 | 10 | 120 |
| Arabic | 2 | 3 | 48 |
| Polish | 2 | 2 | 9 |
| Persian | 1 | 1 | 3 |
| Modern Hebrew | 1 | 2 | 81 |
| Czech | 1 | 1 | 10 |
| Modern Greek | 1 | 1 | 2 |
| Turkish | 1 | 1 | 9 |

# TABLE 4

## (Continued)

### C. THIRD-YEAR COURSES

| Language | Colleges Offering Courses | Courses Offered | Enrolments |
|---|---|---|---|
| Russian | 58 | 83 | 501 |
| Portuguese | 1 | 2 | 17 |
| Chinese | 6 | 20 | 179 |
| Japanese | 2 | 11 | 59 |
| Arabic | 1 | 1 | 21 |
| Polish | 1 | 1 | 7 |
| Modern Hebrew | 1 | 1 | 7 |

### D. FOURTH-YEAR COURSES

| Language | Colleges Offering Courses | Courses Offered | Enrolments |
|---|---|---|---|
| Russian | 16 | 16 | 66 |
| Chinese | 3 | 4 | 21 |
| Japanese | 1 | 3 | 17 |
| Arabic | 1 | 1 | 12 |
| Modern Hebrew | 1 | 1 | 11 |

# TABLE 5

## Status of College Libraries
## in Relation to Non-Western Studies

### A. NON-WESTERN SHARE OF OPERATING EXPENDITURES

| Expenditures for Non-Western Studies as Percentage of Total Operating Expenditures | Number of Colleges |
|---|---|
| One per cent or less | 50 |
| 2–4 per cent | 111 |
| 5–9 per cent | 98 |
| 10 or more per cent | 90 |

### B. NON-WESTERN SHARE OF ACQUISITIONS

| Acquisitions of Non-Western Materials as Percentage of Total Acquisitions | Number of Colleges |
|---|---|
| *(1) Books* | |
| One per cent or less | 43 |
| 2–4 per cent | 104 |
| 5–9 per cent | 124 |
| 10 or more per cent | 96 |
| *(2) Periodicals* | |
| One per cent or less | 83 |
| 2–4 per cent | 125 |
| 5–9 per cent | 73 |
| 10 or more per cent | 55 |

### C. INSTITUTIONAL EVALUATION OF NON-WESTERN HOLDINGS

| Evaluation | Number of Colleges |
|---|---|
| "Good" | 32 |
| "Adequate" | 250 |
| "Poor" | 119 |

## TABLE 6

### Number of Colleges with Cooperative Programs Relating to Non-Western Studies

| Type of Cooperation | Number of Colleges |
| --- | --- |
| All Types Taken Together | 102 |
| Joint Faculty Seminar | 31 |
| Faculty Exchange | 26 |
| Other Sharing of Faculty | 29 |
| Joint Sponsorship of Lectures, Artists, Exhibits, etc. | 40 |
| Cooperation in Programs of undergraduate Study Abroad for Credit | 24 |
| Other Sharing of Students | 34 |
| Sharing of Library Facilities | 38 |
| Joint Book Purchases | 12 |
| Joint Visual-Aid and Teaching-Aid Purchases | 7 |

## TABLE 7

### Extracurricular Programs by Type of Program and World Region

| Type of Program | Total Number of Programs | Africa | Asia (general) or East Asia | Latin America | Middle East | South Asia | Southeast Asia | USSR and East Europe | Worldwide |
| --- | --- | --- | --- | --- | --- | --- | --- | --- | --- |
| Non-Credit Seminars | 45 | 12 | 14 | 14 | 4 | 5 | 4 | 9 | 13 |
| Lecture Series | 122 | 42 | 42 | 34 | 21 | 17 | 10 | 32 | 59 |
| Dance or Drama | 44 | 10 | 19 | 10 | 2 | 7 | 4 | 6 | 9 |
| Art or Other Exhibits | 97 | 28 | 55 | 23 | 11 | 14 | 6 | 10 | 34 |
| Travel Abroad | 69 | 16 | 16 | 32 | 13 | 5 | 4 | 12 | 21 |
| Off-Campus Study or Other Work in U.S.A. | 32 | 13 | 11 | 15 | 5 | 1 | 1 | 1 | 7 |
| Visiting Foreign Scholars | 74 | 28 | 37 | 28 | 14 | 19 | 9 | 5 | 9 |
| International Club | 196 | 63 | 71 | 55 | 41 | 25 | 30 | 33 | 149 |
| Other | 40 | 11 | 12 | 14 | 7 | 4 | 3 | 10 | 15 |
| Total | 719 | 223 | 277 | 225 | 118 | 97 | 71 | 118 | 316 |

# TABLE 8

## Number of Colleges Reporting Plans for Expansion or Introduction of Non-Western Studies

| Type of Plans | Number of Colleges |
|---|---|
| All Types Taken Together | 242 |
| Faculty Seminar to Extend Competence of Present Faculty | 60 |
| Released Time for Faculty Study on Campus | 28 |
| Resident Visiting Specialists | 55 |
| Occasional Visiting Specialists | 127 |
| Specialists Shared with Another Institution | 65 |
| Summer Study Leaves for Faculty | 98 |
| Semester or Year Leave to Study at Major United States University | 41 |
| Semester or Year Leave for Study and Travel Abroad | 77 |
| Hiring New Faculty Specializing at Least in Part in Non-Western Studies | 113 |
| Curriculum Revision | 132 |
| Programs for Students in the United States | 25 |
| Programs for Students Abroad | 46 |
| Foreign Students | 80 |
| Affiliation with Foreign Institution | 31 |
| Library Improvement Program | 133 |
| Other | 14 |

## APPENDIX II

# REPORTS ON
# INDIVIDUAL PROGRAMS

*Area Programs*
1 Earlham College
2 Florida Presbyterian College
3 Portland State College
4 The State University College at New Paltz, New York
5 Williams College

*Infusion-Type Programs*
6 Hanover College
7 Marian College
8 Mills College
9 Western College for Women

*Combination Programs*
10 California State College at Hayward
11 Occidental College

*Cooperative Programs*
12 Atlanta University Center
13 The Gettysburg Group
14 Great Lakes Colleges Association
15 The St Paul Group
16 The Winston-Salem Group

*Other Types of Program*
17 Dartmouth College
18 University of the Pacific

*Report of a Conference*
19 Undergraduate Foreign Area Studies:
    The Case of the Middle East

# 1

# EARLHAM COLLEGE

Earlham College's comprehensive effort to develop non-Western studies has focused on improving the competence of existing faculty, particularly in regard to East Asia, and on infusing materials on the non-Western world into a wide variety of courses in a number of disciplines. The endeavor grew out of the concerns of several faculty members who believed that Earlham needed to expand its already considerable emphasis on world areas as an integral part of liberal education. Faculty discussions of this concern extended over several years and led to the planning of specific innovations after 1958. After careful study and discussion, the college committed itself to enlarge the non-Western aspects of the academic program. Major factors in implementing this policy included the appointment of two new non-Western specialists to the faculty and a commitment to strengthen library holdings relating to the non-Western world.

## Historical Background

As a Quaker college Earlham has for many years been concerned with international affairs. These interests were reinforced

---

Earlham College, Richmond, Indiana. President Landrum R. Bolling. (Society of Friends; coeducational; quarter system; liberal arts and teacher training to master's degree; 1061 students)

by William C. Dennis, a former diplomat and international lawyer, who was president from 1929 to 1946, and his successors. In 1930 President Dennis inaugurated an annual Foreign Affairs Institute to focus on a topic of contemporary significance in world affairs. President Thomas E. Jones (1946–58) who had taught in a Japanese university, introduced a community dynamics program, with summer work and study opportunities for students and faculty in the Caribbean and Mexico, encouraged foreign students to attend Earlham, and invited many speakers from non-Western areas to the campus.

The international emphasis was strengthened by President Landrum R. Bolling, who had been a foreign correspondent and had taught international politics before he succeeded President Jones in 1958. As a professor of political science he had given leadership to the development of Earlham's foreign study program. From the early weeks of his administration he pushed hard within the faculty and with outside agencies and foundations for an ambitious expansion of Earlham's international involvements, particularly in the non-Western areas. He brought to the faculty two new history professors, Lewis M. Hoskins, who had had extensive relief-work experience in postwar China under the American Friends Service Committee, and Jackson H. Bailey, who had spent five years in Japan and who did his Ph.D. work in East Asian studies at Harvard.

## Initial Planning

One of the first steps taken at Earlham was to prepare an institutional inventory of faculty, courses and library resources relating to non-Western areas. This survey revealed some elements of hope but also much that needed to be done. In 1957–58, the year before Earlham embarked on its cooperative program in non-Western studies with Antioch College, it had about sixty full-time teachers. About a third of them taught some 25 courses with substantial international or foreign content. Only ten of the courses dealt to some extent with the non-Western world and only five or six of the teachers had had significant non-Western experience. None was a specialist on a non-Western area. Aside from president-elect Bolling, who had had extensive experience in Eastern Europe, the Middle East and Africa, this group consisted of a professor teaching Russian history, a linguist introducing Russian language instruction, a professor of education, two chemists, and an economist with experience in the State Department and a background of scholarly interest in the problems of international trade and of economic development.

In a paper read at a conference on non-Western studies at Indiana University in September 1959, Professor Joseph D. Coppock described Earlham's plans as follows:

> . . . the most important things we might do in pursuit of these aims must be in connection with the curriculum, although we recognize the value of the extracurricular. . . . our curriculum should offer more and better courses dealing with Eastern Europe, Asia and Africa. Most, but not all, of these courses will fall in the departments of political science, economics and history. We see no need for new organizational arrangements. . . .

> We have given most thought to an effective means of providing a new lower-class course dealing with the non-Western world which many students would be strongly encouraged to take. The main choices, in our view, are among (1) Contemporary World Problems, (2) A Survey of the Non-Western World, and (3) the study of a single major foreign area. Our present thinking runs toward the third alternative. . . . A survey of the non-Western world is beyond our teaching competence in a college of 850, and I think beyond the competence of all but the large universities. We do not want to be superficial. We are thus led to the third alternative, a single major foreign area.

He then outlined the cooperative plan for Earlham and Antioch Colleges to offer a basic course on the Far East, mainly China and Japan.

> Both Earlham and Antioch would have accepted another area, say Russia, India, the Near East, or Africa South of the Sahara, but an examination of our faculty resources, present and prospective, led us to choose the Far East. Each college expects to appoint a person with a specialty in Far Eastern history, economics, politics, or culture. The two faculty members will create the basic course together. Each will give one advanced course. We feel that some depth in one foreign area, including American relations with that area, would go far to

provide the educational effect on students which is so sadly lacking at present.

In terms of faculty members with special competence on a non-Western area, Antioch and Earlham concluded that

> . . . the new faculty members concentrating on the Far East must have special arrangements and facilities if they are going to maintain high standards of performance. They must be able to travel to the area occasionally, they must be able to attend conferences on the Far East in this country, they must have easy access to materials for their own intellectual and professional development. They must have somebody to converse with! (This last is another reason for the cooperative program.)

Earlham stressed three crucial points: That the program must be "institutionalized" so that it does not depend on only one or two people; that any non-Western course intended to reach many students must be one of a few courses which will satisfy the distribution requirement in the social sciences; and that the success of the program depends on expansion of the library collection.

## Non-Western Area Specialists and Extending Faculty Competence

President Bolling has stated that Earlham's "objective is to increase the non-Western elements in our curriculum." He finds that this "involves essentially three things: a few new non-Western courses; the infusion of several existing courses with non-Western materials; and the inclusion of a non-Western distribution requirement for graduation. . ." He points out that

> The means of providing these increased and improved non-Western curricular offerings consist primarily of developing or acquiring faculty members competent to teach them, and of providing books and other library materials needed by teachers and students for such courses. Satisfactory courses—revised or new—can be offered only as the faculty members are reconditioned or newly hired. Therefore, Earlham places first priority on the obtaining of better qualified faculty members—by retraining and by hiring new ones on a permanent or temporary (visiting) basis.

From the start, Earlham has considered it essential for its non-Western program to be directed by a member of the faculty with excellent disciplinary training who is also a specialist on a non-Western area and knows its major languages. Members of the administration and faculty have repeatedly stressed this point. They appreciate the dual competence of Professors Bailey and Hoskins and their unusual academic and administrative skills. Professor Bailey's direction of the cooperative program in Far Eastern studies, his teaching at both Antioch and Earlham, his careful planning and supervision of the faculty and student field projects in Japan, his work on building library resources and his ability to continue research on nineteenth-century Japanese political history have been acknowledged on both campuses. His leadership in this field has been further recognized by his appointment as part-time coordinator of the non-Western studies program of the Great Lakes Colleges Association.

The college has helped to provide the special facilities which it was recognized would be essential for such a specialist in a small liberal arts college. It has provided for three-sevenths released time to administer the program. It encouraged Professor Bailey to teach a course on Far Eastern History each winter term at Antioch. It has built up the library, developed a new, enlarged language laboratory and assisted in the procurement of other teaching aids. The college has facilitated Professor Bailey's making three or four trips to Japan to prepare for the faculty and student field projects and allowed him extra time for his own research abroad and to attend professional and Asian study conferences in the United States. Professor Hoskins has had comparable opportunities to develop his competence on Africa and to plan for the extension of the foreign study program to Latin America and the Middle East as well as Japan.

While other members of the faculty have not had such extensive opportunities to develop specialization on a non-Western area in depth, several of them have added new dimensions to their competence by means of study and field experience. After five years of endeavor to train and develop the skills of existing faculty, Earlham could tally these results by 1964. It had two specially qualified historians, one on Africa and Latin America, and the other on the Far East. Sixteen members of the faculty representing eleven departments had studied and had first-hand experience of some part of the non-Western world. Two faculty members had developed their knowledge of Russia. One each had spent at least a summer in Africa, India and Mexico. Eight had spent a summer in Japan and had traveled in other parts of the Far East. Two of them had lived in Japan with their families for at least an academic year. Another was living in Beirut and half way through a two-year research project on international economic instability in the Middle East. Nine others had prepared research plans for further study in or about the non-Western world. Nearly half of the faculty had participated in one or more of the annual seminars on the Far East, India, the Middle East and Africa, and the entire college had felt the impact of the program.

The cumulative effect of the seminars and study opportunities on the faculty has been substantial. The chance for first-hand field experience seems to have been a critically important factor in building on earlier study and in consolidating interest and competence for those who have had a chance to continue study in a non-Western area. It has also provided incentive to seminar participants and others still hoping for such an opportunity. The fact that three members of the Earlham Educational Policy Committee and four department heads studied in the non-Western world underscores the strong interest of key faculty members in the non-Western study program.

Earlham plans to continue giving top priority to opportunities for present faculty members to get further training on non-Western areas, primarily by means of grants for formal study. These will go initially to teachers of art, drama, education, history, literature, music, political science, religion and sociology. The next most urgent issue is the preparation of courses with non-Western content. Twelve teachers from eight departments (art, chemistry, economics, English, geology, history, philosophy and religion) are ready to undertake such course revision. Earlham's third priority is for research on the non-Western world. Funds are available for one teacher (or full-time equivalent) per year to engage in such research. Faculty members in economics, geology, history and political science have submitted requests to undertake research projects on the non-Western world. The college hopes to attract to the faculty competent scholars from a variety of cultural and national backgrounds either as full-time, regular members of the staff or as visiting lecturers shared with neighboring institutions for shorter periods. It has brought to its campus for a two-year period an able young Japanese economics professor on leave from Doshisha University in Kyoto. Trained at Amherst and Harvard, he has proved unusually effective in communicating with American undergraduates and in strengthening the interests of his Earlham colleagues in Japanese life and culture.

## Curriculum

Faculty members from Earlham who drew up a statement for the Great Lakes Colleges Association's workshop on non-Western studies held at Oberlin College in November 1962 described their aims and criteria in these terms:

Earlham is committed in the development of its liberal arts program to include substantial attention to the non-Western world. This commitment is based upon two beliefs. First is the belief that a liberal arts education must include knowledge of the great achievements—including, of course, great ideas—of all the world, not just the Western world, and that knowledge of other traditions will deepen the student's understanding of the world generally. Second, our responsibility to equip young people to deal effectively with the world in which they live requires that attention be given to international relationships in a world context. In addition, we feel a responsibility to provide for those students who may have vocational interests in non-Western studies, an introduction and a beginning which will help them as they pursue advanced study.

Earlham maintains interest in a number of areas of the non-Western world (East Asia, South Asia, the Soviet Union, Africa and Latin America). We feel clear, however, that our academic resources should be committed to coverage in depth of East Asia only. We are therefore interested in coordinating our efforts with those of the other colleges in the Association in the fields of library, language, course work and faculty appointments. We hope to proceed with cautious dispatch in these matters, judging each step by the following criteria:

1. How much better would our liberal arts program be by doing this?
2. Assuming that a given change would mean improvement, can we afford it?

The non-Western studies program had produced substantial curricular changes by 1963–64. Earlham was then offering over thirty courses relating to non-Western civilizations in a dozen departments, plus two new courses in the Russian language and three in Japanese. Sixteen of the courses dealt primarily with the non-Western world. The rest had substantial infusion of non-Western content. Several of these courses were taught by the two language and area specialists. Each of the other courses was taught by a scholar who had engaged in serious study of one or more non-Western areas and had usually spent at least a summer in research and travel in the region about which he was teaching.

By 1964 it was reported by the faculty and a Ford Foundation consultant that well over half the students at Earlham took at least one course with considerable non-Western content. Courses dealing with the non-Western world were by then accepted as fulfilling distribution requirements in English, foreign languages, the social sciences, fine arts, philosophy and religion. Three of the nine most popular and well-attended courses which met distribution requirements gave special attention to the non-Western world.

## Language

One of the basic aims at Earlham is that each student achieve an understanding of the language and culture of at least one non-English-speaking people. Competence in a foreign language equivalent to that reached by the end of the third course is required for graduation. Four levels of instruction, plus opportunities for independent study, are offered in both Russian and Japanese. Russian was introduced in 1957 and Japanese in 1963. Either of these languages fulfills the graduation requirement in foreign languages.

In recent years Earlham has experimented with new techniques in the teaching of Russian, Spanish and Japanese. This has grown out of its pioneer work in self-instruction methods whereby "instructors in several departments (e.g., biology, foreign languages, mathematics and religion) have developed supplemental materials which have enabled them to make more effective use of their time and energy." The leader of this project has been Professor M. Keith Myers, a trained linguist, who has developed new techniques and materials for Russian language instruction. He has also worked closely with Dr M. Daniel Smith, director of self-instruction, who spent two years in Professor B. F. Skinner's research group at Harvard, with Professor Bailey and Miss Misako Hagino. They hope to develop materials and techniques which they believe are effectively adapted to sound instruction in Japanese in a small college with minimal staff. Within a year or two they hope to assess these experiments and, if they prove worth while, to share their findings with other colleges.

## Study Abroad

Earlham inaugurated its foreign study program in 1956. This consists of from three to six months (usually a summer and a term) of study, travel and work in another country for a group of some twenty students under the supervision of an Earlham professor. Instruction in the language, history, arts and social conditions is given by professors native to the country. Whenever possible, students live with local families, take concentrated language training and are exposed to rural and urban communities and various social classes. They also carry on independent study related to their fields of concentration at Earlham. From two to six course credits may be earned. The college tries to keep costs comparable to those for an equivalent period on campus, but must provide some supplementary scholarship aid. The program has been directed by Professor Lewis Hoskins since 1959.

By the end of 1964–65 foreign study groups will have been to Austria, Colombia, Denmark, England, Finland, France, Germany, Italy, Japan, Mexico, Norway, Spain, Switzerland and the USSR. The current plan calls for sending Earlham groups each year to France, England and Japan, and in alternate years to Germany, Austria and a Spanish-speaking country.

Earlham makes use of the foreign study centers established or to be established cooperatively under the auspices of the Great Lakes Colleges Association. The first centers are located in Beirut, Mexico, Tokyo and Bogotá. By 1962, some eighty Earlham students annually took part in foreign study, primarily in Western Europe (Austria, England, France, Germany and Italy). It is expected that 150 will take part each year by 1966. From 1958 to 1964, 89 Earlham students studied for credit in the non-Western world (Eastern Europe, Russia, East Asia and Latin America).

Earlham is also starting a winter-term, off-campus study program at the Hoover Institution for the Study of War, Peace and Revolution, on the Stanford campus. This will be primarily for history majors doing independent study projects on the Soviet Union and China or other topics related to recent wars and revolutions.

## Library

In 1963 Earlham opened its new Lilly Library with a capacity of 200,000 volumes. The library includes a large audio-visual area with the latest language laboratory equipment in forty booths, a separate self-instruction laboratory, projection, slide, listening and photo-processing rooms used in Japanese and Russian language courses and for independent study, and a tranquil Japanese alcove. The library had 113,000 volumes in 1963 and was spending about $27,000 annually for books and $5000 for periodicals. These figures compare with total holdings of some 80,000 volumes and less than $10,000 annually for books and periodicals in 1957–58.

Mr Philip Shore, associate librarian, has participated in the faculty seminars on East Asia and spent a summer in Japan getting acquainted with librarians, booksellers, publishers and others in order to improve his ability to deal with Far Eastern materials and to serve the non-Western studies program more effectively. He reported that by the end of 1963, for purposes of instruction, library holdings were "good" for Asia in general and East Asia; "adequate" on Africa, South and Southwest Asia and for Slavic and East European studies; but "poor" on North Africa, the Middle East and Latin America. For student research he rated the holdings as "good" on Asia, "adequate" on Sub-Saharan Africa, but "poor" for all other non-Western areas. For faculty research he rated the library "adequate" on East Asia but otherwise "poor."

Earlham's most urgent library need for its non-Western studies is for series of journals, then for bibliographical materials and thirdly for out-of-print books. During the next two years, with the assistance of a foundation grant, the library plans to spend about $6500 annually for some 1200 volumes with an emphasis on East Asia. Mr Shore hoped to complete purchasing all items on the Far East listed in the American Universities Field Staff bibliography and to obtain all of the works in categories A and B of this bibliography for all other world areas. He calculated that in 1963 fifteen per cent of the books and three to four per cent of the periodicals received related primarily to non-Western studies.

Earlham has consistently stressed the importance of building strong library resources as essential to serious study of the non-Western world. Its representatives took the lead in the Great Lakes Colleges Association in calling for training in non-Western bibliography for reference librarians and cataloguers. Under a recent foundation grant to the association, one of a series of faculty workshops on non-Western studies will be devoted to librarians. Plans are being made for a common catalogue of non-Western works, some joint purchases of expensive books, and interchange of books within GLCA.

## Students and Extracurricular Activities

A variety of lectures, art exhibits and musical and dramatic performances have supplemented the formal non-Western studies program at Earlham since 1959. Many students are members of the international club. A special Foreign Student Committee raises funds to aid foreign students by means of talent shows, movies and other projects. The committee also maintains close personal contacts with foreign students when they arrive and throughout their stay. The Student Political Affairs Committee sponsors a model United Nations and other conferences or talks on world issues.

In addition to the annual Foreign Affairs Institute, the entire college participates in convocations each Tuesday and Thursday morning. During the last six years the programming has given an unusual amount of attention to non-Western topics, and this has had important results in developing general campus interest in the non-Western world. Among the convocation speakers who have dealt particularly with the non-Western world have been Ambassador Reischauer, Professors de Bary of Columbia and Scalapino of the University of California, Lebanese cabinet minister Charles Malik and Indian President Sarvepalli Radhakrishnan.

Earlham attracts relatively few students from abroad—about fifteen a year—and only five to seven of these come from non-Western countries. In 1963–64 there were seven, all on Earlham scholarships. These students make a definite contribution to non-Western studies, as some are used as native informants in language classes, occasionally as resource persons in class, and often in debates, on radio and television panels or as regular participants in foreign language tables at meal times.

## Cooperation

Although Earlham's efforts in non-Western fields have grown out of the institution's own aims and resources, they have also gained from the several cooperative arrangements in which the college has participated. At the same time, Earlham must be credited with a strong catalytic influence on the other cooperating colleges.

The primary cooperative arrangement was with neighboring Antioch in a program begun in 1959 with assistance from the Ford Foundation. Antioch with its similar international outlook was a natural partner, especially because of its well-developed system of work and study abroad and a strong contingent of faculty members with non-Western experience.

Originally conceived more broadly, this collaboration gradually focused on East Asia for the sake of greater depth in preference to wider coverage. It involved the several dimensions of joint faculty seminars, exchange of faculty and students, and collaborative arrangements for overseas study and library development. As the joint program drew to a close in 1964–65, the two colleges planned to continue their curricular ties with respect to Far Eastern course work and their avoidance of undue duplication in library acquisitions.

Earlham has also been one of the moving spirits in the Great Lakes Colleges Association, especially in connection with non-Western studies; has contributed notably to the state-wide effort in Indiana in behalf of strengthening non-Western elements in college curricula; and has been a member of the Regional Council for International Education. Professor Hoskins has been a leader of the last-named group, and Professor Bailey has been named coordinator of the GLCA international studies program.

## Conclusion

As a result of the non-Western program at Earlham and the cooperative enterprises with which it has been associated, Earlham's students, those of many other mid-Western colleges, and their teachers now have access to opportunities for study of the non-Western world—on their own or on nearby campuses, as well as abroad—which simply did not exist a few years ago. Throughout, Earlham has kept to its original standard of good teaching, of developing non-Western studies under the direction of qualified scholars, and of giving them the library resources, field experiences and other incentives necessary to extend their knowledge and share it with other teachers and students.

# 2

# FLORIDA PRESBYTERIAN COLLEGE

Florida Presbyterian College was chartered in 1958 and began instruction in the fall of 1960. Located on a new campus in St Petersburg, it received its initial financial support from the United Presbyterian Church in the U.S.A. and from the Presbyterian Church, U.S., and its board of trustees is appointed by the synods of Florida of these two denominations. Within the college community this identification with the church is recognized as a positive asset in liberal arts education rather than as a restriction. This is especially true with reference to an approach to polycultural studies. Since the Christian tradition is not the product of a single cultural heritage and since the Christian concern is by its very nature extended across cultural lines, a college which is identified with the church finds a natural involvement in those issues which transcend national and ethnic boundaries.

The fact that the college came into being in the latter half of the twentieth century seemed to call for a program which

Florida Presbyterian College, St Petersburg, Florida. President William H. Kadel. (Presbyterian; coeducational; semester system; liberal arts to bachelor's degree; 560 students)

This report was prepared in March 1964 by Professor E. Ashby Johnson, director of the core program of the college, for the Council of Protestant Colleges and Universities.

recognizes the special needs and circumstances of the era. There is no call to set aside the basic standards of the liberal arts tradition but there is good reason for design of a curriculum which is adapted to changing conditions in secondary education, educational aids and broad currents of cultural concern.

**Florida Presbyterian College** is coeducational. It opened with a freshman class of 154, and in its fourth year of operation had 560 students. It has made the deliberate choice for slow growth in numbers for the sake of maintaining the admission standards which assure that the students who are enrolled are able to profit from the academic program.

## The Core Program

In an effort to deal with the problem of fragmentation of the academic life, with the need for a common intellectual experience for all students and with the inter-relatedness of all inquiry, the academic program of the college has been built around a four-year course for all students, involving staff from all areas of the faculty. One of the opportunities presented to a new college was the possibility of building a core curriculum around which the division courses could be built, rather than constructing a course to supplement departmental offerings. The core curriculum makes up about thirty per cent of the student's academic program.

*Objectives and Structure of the Core Program.* The formal statement of the objective of the core program is to "develop competence in the formation and articulation of informed, independent and responsible judgments of value." Quite obviously the formation and articulation of such judgments call for certain skills (reading, analysis, dialectic, writing), for accurate knowledge over a wide range of concern and for some insight into the interrelationship of these fields of knowledge. The acquiring of skills and of information, however, are not ends in themselves but means toward the formation of mature judgments and decisions.

During the freshman and sophomore years the materials of the program are drawn primarily from the literature, history, art, natural science, social science and philosophy of the European and American traditions. The staff is drawn from all three divisions of the faculty. Three lectures or other presentations are given each week to the class as a whole. Three hours are spent each week in small groups in the analysis and discussion of the documents which make up the materials of the program. Each discussion leader supervises the writing program of the students in his group. At the end of the second year there is a comprehensive examination which determines the credit for the two years' work.

The third-year program focuses upon institutions and works which do not belong to the Western tradition and is designed to apply to the analysis of other cultures the skills acquired during the first two years. The fourth-year program is built around a series of lectures presented by visiting scholars and is designed to familiarize the seniors with some of the pressing issues of the contemporary scene.

*Western Civilization and Its Christian Heritage.* The freshman and sophomore years of the core program are assumed to make up about two fifths of the student's academic load during those years. The first semester focuses upon various means of approaching our contemporary culture: literature, philosophy, art, psychology, science. Major emphasis is placed upon the skills necessary for the analysis of works and institutions. The second semester gives major attention to the Hellenic and Judeo-Christian sources of the Western world. Materials of the third semester are taken from medieval, reformation and renaissance sources. The fourth semester is an examination of efforts to discern or devise structure or order for the modern world.

*Asian Studies.* The core program in the junior year is the primary means by which the college undertakes to familiarize all its students with the cultural forms, institutional structures and historical movements which lie outside our major traditions but which are becoming increasingly significant for our civilization. Much of the educational procedure of the first two years carries over into this program. There are two lecture sessions a week for the entire class. As in the freshman and sophomore years, many of these sessions are given over to movies, dramatizations or panel discussions which can enrich the program. The class is divided into smaller sections for an additional discussion period each week. Each student selects one specific field of individual research, preferably associated with his major field.

*Christian Faith and Great Issues.* The fourth year of the core program is a lecture, reading and discussion course focusing upon twelve issues selected by a joint faculty-student committee. Persons of national and international prominence in economic, political and scientific life are brought to the campus for lectures and informal discussion with the senior class. Preparatory lectures and discussions from members of the college faculty are coordinated with the program of visiting lecturers. Each senior submits a personal journal on the issues considered during the year and prepares an analysis of two periodicals which he has followed during the course.

*The January Term.* The college year is so ordered that a month is cleared of regular classes and devoted to directed research. One semester closes with the Christmas holidays. The second semester begins early in February. During the fall members of the faculty post descriptions of special projects which they intend to offer for directed study in January. Students may select their January programs from this list or may, with faculty approval, follow research programs of their own design.

In the interest of intercultural involvement, one or more projects each year is offered outside the United States. Student groups have undertaken several projects in Latin America and in Europe. Initial steps have been taken for a program in the Near East in January 1965 and for possible programs in the Far East in future years.

*Independent Study.* Academic policies of the college provide for and encourage student's meeting a significant part of their academic requirements, particularly during the junior and senior years, in programs of independent study. This makes it possible for students who have become interested in intercultural studies to pursue their concerns in specific areas for which there are no catalogue courses.

## Experience and Experiment in Polycultural Programs

Several inherent characteristics of Florida Presbyterian College made it almost inevitable that there would be a serious effort to incorporate in its program some emphasis upon cultures other than the Western European and American traditions. The formation of its curriculum at a time of increasing awareness of the interaction of cultures dictated that attention be given to this area. Social responsibility indicated the justification for helping to prepare young people for leadership by giving them some insight into the thought forms of other peoples. Identification with the church indicated the propriety of sharing a Christian vision which transcends ethnic patterns.

In setting the approach to intercultural studies the faculty undertook to consider not only the characteristics of this particular college but also the experience of other institutions in the study of Asian and other non-Western materials.

Several general conclusions seemed justified. Although provision should be made for a degree of undergraduate specialization, the intercultural studies should be a part of the program of all students rather than an elective discipline. This pointed to incorporation in the core program. Although it is necessary to have one or more specialized scholars on the staff, extended faculty involvement is desirable. One all-college course should be provided, but this program needs the reinforcement of other studies throughout the four years. The faculty recognized that there is conflicting evidence regarding the best approach to intercultural studies: the relative worth of primary focus upon a humanist or a social science approach, the relative importance of the native and the foreign scholar, the relative value of intensive and extensive studies.

Comparison and contrast of works and institutions from different cultures run through all four years of the core program. The many subcultures within any tradition furnish material for analysis and evaluation. The program at Florida Presbyterian

College is not based on the assumption that "the West" and "the East" are two poles but rather upon the assumption that there are materials in a multitude of traditions from which insight may be drawn. Within the so-called Western tradition there is the necessity for selection and exclusion. Similarly it is necessary to limit the scope of studies outside that tradition. The decision for this college was to select a single segment of the non-Western world, focus upon its works and institutions, and seek to give only secondary attention to other ethnic or cultural groups.

## Asian Studies at Florida Presbyterian College

The junior course in Asian studies is set up like the other three years of the core program—participated in by all members of the class, involving common reading and lectures, drawing materials from several academic disciplines. The nature of the course calls for a structure which differs at some points. In the first, second and fourth years an interdisciplinary staff has responsibility for the design and materials of the program. In the junior course a single professor has responsibility for the plan and execution of the program. Greater use is made of student-led discussions.

There are two lectures or other presentations each week and one discussion session. The reading program is drawn from translations of source materials, periodicals and standard secondary works. In addition to common course readings there is provided a selected list of titles for students to use in following particular lines of interest.

Chinese works and institutions have been chosen as a basis of course organization at this college. Several considerations are involved in this decision. The plan to begin a program in the Chinese language makes this a logical choice. Further, it affords a ready reference to Korea, Japan, India and Southeast Asia, as they are culturally and politically related to China. Finally, the dominance of China on the political scene makes this an extremely significant topic for contemporary emphasis.

In the first year of the Asian studies program (1962–63), the structure of the program was determined largely by the decision to attempt to reach an understanding of another culture through an examination of the literary, artistic, philosophical works of the culture. Students were encouraged to enrich this program by personal study of the history, institutions and social structures of the culture, and they were provided with bibliographies to guide them. Further, each student was called upon to initiate a project relating his Asian studies to his academic major (political science, natural science, psychology).

In the second year of operation (1963–64), the program was redesigned to provide for a systematic study of the history, geography and institutions of China and of regions closely associated with its culture. As during the first year, rather extensive use was made of films, performances and guest lecturers. Students were provided with bibliographies of source material and were encouraged to make reports on this reading. During the first semester emphasis was placed upon the cultural and political heritage of China. During the second semester attention was shifted to the modern social and political situation in the Far East.

We would be deceiving ourselves if we did not acknowledge that there have been significant advantages and disadvantages to both of the approaches which we have followed. We would also be quite shortsighted if we did not heed the almost universal response of the students: "How can we combine the merits of the two programs?" To heed the question, however, is not to find a ready answer to it. A brief consideration of this question is presented in the section, *Evaluation and Conclusions*. Even when a year of the core program is devoted to an Asian studies course, any single approach is far from adequate. Some preparation in terms of knowledge and skill on the part of students is needed. A false picture is presented if intercultural concerns are limited to a particular year and a particular course.

## Institutes on the Non-European World

To support our international and intercultural studies we hold an annual institute on some aspect of the relationship between the United States and a non-European nation. The leadership for these institutes is drawn from universities, embassies and news media. The program involves students in all four years of their college work.

The program is carried on in cooperation with Rollins College, Florida Southern College and Stetson University, under a grant from the Danforth Foundation. A joint committee from the four institutions designs the program. In 1963 the theme of the institute was the crises in Southeast Asia. In 1964 attention was directed to the struggle for Asian leadership between Communist China and India.

## Bibliography and Materials

Over the past four years a continuing effort has been made to locate and secure the books, periodicals, art works and exhibits necessary for stimulating study and serious research in a polycultural program. In the summer of 1963 Otis Shao of the department of political science prepared a selected bibliography of the Far East (China and Japan) as a basis for systematic acquisition by our library of works, papers, journals and documents for undergraduate teaching. The bibliography is divided according to the major academic divisions of the college: humanities, social science, natural science. Our library now contains about a third of the titles listed in this 2000-item bibliography, with additional works on India, the Middle East and Korea.

## Language Studies

The original plan for the college called for the addition of Chinese language to the curriculum in 1965. Interest in the field has prompted consideration of a plan to begin this program in 1964.

The general college requirement for graduation calls for a third-year level of competence, conversation and reading, in at least one language other than English. It has been the experience here, as at other colleges, that this emphasis upon language competence has stimulated extensive participation in programs of foreign study in French-, German- and Spanish-speaking countries. (Language requirements may also be met in Greek, Latin or Russian.)

We anticipate that the addition of Chinese to the language options will make possible an addition of staff for Asian studies as well as providing a base for students who may choose to enter graduate programs of intercultural character.

## Faculty Institutes and Training

One of the most rewarding aspects of the first two years of the core program has been the extensive faculty participation which has been possible. Both in program design and in teaching, staff members have been drawn from all academic areas. This makes possible not only a continuing conversation across divisional lines but also a coordination of core program and divisional programs. We are concerned that the Asian program should have some corresponding involvement throughout the faculty. If this is to be of sound quality, some type of faculty study program is necessary. To this end we propose:

*A summer institute of two months led by two of our own Asian specialists and one visiting scholar.* It would be designed as retraining for six of our own faculty members and six from other Florida colleges.

*Faculty seminars during the following year.* We plan toward four seminars of three days each, involving the participants in the summer program but also additional visiting specialists.

*Summer institutes in the Orient.* These would serve to give a depth of insight into other cultures which cannot come from study at a distance.

If financial support for this program can be provided, we anticipate being able each year to add to our faculty six persons who are able to relate their particular disciplines to intercultural concerns, make a contribution to the Asian studies program and guide students in research and independent study related to polycultural programs.

## Cultural Programs

In planning the film series, artist series and general lecture series of the college each year, care is taken to include art forms which are polycultural in character.

## Coordination with Other Aspects of the Core Program and with Divisional Programs

A number of works selected for the first two years of the core program are chosen with view to making possible more ready insight into the cultures of the Middle East and Far East. The Christian Faith and Great Issues Program of the senior year reemploys the materials of the third-year program in approach to the contemporary problems which are under consideration.

Limited but significant efforts have been made in divisional programs, particularly in the departments of literature, philosophy and religion to tie the work of the third year to course offerings within the departments.

## Evaluation and Conclusions

Even before the graduating of its first class the college has experienced significant rewards from placing emphasis upon polycultural studies. Serious consideration of the works and institutions which lie outside the mainstream of Western civilization has served to sharpen the social and aesthetic discrimination of a large number of students. Although no systematic effort has been made to measure the effect, it seems clear that attitudes and values as well as information and understanding have been affected. One indication of this is the large number of students who are applying for Fulbright study, Peace Corps service and other programs involving residence outside the United States.

It is quite clear that there are educational losses and gains involved when primary focus is given either to the humanities or to the social science approach to polycultural studies. When the program at Florida Presbyterian College emphasized "reaching an understanding from the inside," i.e., by way of the drama, art and other creative works, there was a greater sense of discovery and involvement on the part of students but an acknowledged lack of systematic knowledge of the institutions which produced these works. When the program was built around a lecture and reading program which emphasized descriptive and secondary materials, there was a significant gain in historical and geographical knowledge but some loss in student excitement and involvement. In neither year was the emphasis an exclusive one. Revisions and redesign of the course for future years, however, will be made with a view to even further synthesis of social science and humanities.

Quite obviously, when a program is presented as a program for all the students of the college, it is desirable that the program reflect the thinking and methods of several individuals and disciplines. We anticipate that two projected programs will make this wider involvement of faculty in Asian studies a possibility. The addition of Chinese language to the curriculum will probably mean that there will be three professors giving part of their time to the design of the junior year of the core program. The faculty retraining program should furnish us with a steadily increasing number of faculty members who are prepared to participate in the program and to relate it to departmental courses.

# 3

# PORTLAND STATE COLLEGE

Portland State College has developed since 1959 a unique undergraduate program in Middle East Studies. This program includes three years of required Arabic or other Middle Eastern language, and courses in six disciplines culminating in two senior seminars on Political and Economic Trends, and Cultural and Social Change in the Middle East. Students who wish to work toward the Certificate in Middle East Studies major in the usual disciplines but must complete three years (33 hours) in Middle East language (Arabic, Hebrew, Persian and Turkish are offered) and 43 hours in subject-matter area courses with at least one course each in anthropology, economics, English, geography, history and political science. There is no separate major in Middle East Studies, so that candidates for the certificate fulfill all the requirements for their major in their selected discipline, then in effect earn what comes close to a second major in Middle East Studies.

Students at Portland State may also take courses in several departments dealing with the Far East, the Slavic world, Eastern Europe, Africa and Latin America, and may study Portuguese

---

Portland State College, Portland, Oregon. President Branford P. Millar. (State; coeducational; quarter system; liberal arts and teacher training to master's degree; 5,787 students)

and Russian. But the Middle East Studies program is Portland State's distinctive element in non-Western studies.

In 1963-64, 80 undergraduates were enrolled in the program leading to the certificate of the Middle East Studies Center. There were 130 other students taking one or more of the courses offered under the auspices of the Center. While this represents a small proportion of the 5,787 students enrolled at Portland State, it is one of the largest undergraduate groups studying the Middle East in any U. S. college. Those taking Arabic were the largest number of undergraduates doing so in any college.

The college was also engaged in training a group of Peace Corps volunteers for service in Iran and another group for Turkey. Staff affiliated with the Middle East Center were responsible for all the language, area and culture instruction for these special programs.

The typical undergraduate program outlined below indicates that it is practicable for any competent student to combine study in general liberal arts education and a disciplinary major with a substantial concentration in Middle East language and area courses, yet still have room in his schedule for a reasonable number of electives. This combination provides a substantial link between liberal arts education and Middle East studies which is without parallel in U. S. undergraduate education.

The Middle East Studies program has reached its present status as a result of many interrelated factors. First, the program was devised and came into being with strong administration and faculty support. It has had consistently able leadership and a focus provided by a director, an assistant, central offices for staff and a commonroom. The program has been interdivisional and interdepartmental from the start. While it began with the exclusive support of the college budget, it was designed to elicit NDEA matching funds, which were granted in February 1960 during its first year of operation. From the beginning it has drawn on existing tenure faculty in several departments for the core of its disciplinary instruction and has benefited from the appointment of specialized new staff in several departments willing to appoint teachers in their respective disciplines with competence in the Middle East, several of them natives of the area.

All courses relating to Middle East Studies are offered in the respective departments by their own staff members and are open to any qualified undergraduate. This is the case even with the four levels of Arabic, and two each of Hebrew, Persian and Turkish, which are integral parts of the foreign language department offerings and are so listed in the catalogue. These languages are accepted as fulfilling the graduation requirement for competence in a foreign language.

The program has attracted able students and a good deal of favorable notice in the college, within the metropolitan area and nationally. This has helped to consolidate its already friendly relationships with various other units in the college. The success of some of its students in winning national fellowship awards has been a stimulus to staff and students and reflects credit on this new institution which only became a four-year college in 1955.

## Historical Background

Portland State College's interest in the Middle East stems from that of Professor F. J. Cox, a historian who was a Fulbright research professor at Cairo University in 1950-52. In 1958-59, a year after his appointment at Portland State, Dr Cox introduced a course on the history of the Middle East. Within a year the college had established its Center of Middle East Studies. The center's creation was stimulated by the prospect of aid under the National Defense Education Act. In November 1958 a group of faculty members, including the dean and the assistant dean of the faculty, the chairmen of the divisions of education and the humanities and the heads of the foreign languages and geography departments, represented the college at a conference for Northwest language teachers and institutions interested in establishing programs under the NDEA. As an outgrowth of this conference, the dean of the faculty, with the approval of the divisional chairmen concerned, appointed an *ad hoc* interdisciplinary faculty committee headed by Professor Cox to study the future role of non-Western studies, with special attention to language and area focus. During the spring of 1959 this committee met and recommended that Middle Eastern language and area courses be established as a program in the college.

The committee early decided to concentrate on one major world area and to build on existing faculty strength as practicable. Aside from Russian, no non-Western languages were then taught and few courses on non-Western areas were offered. A course on Far Eastern history had been offered for several years, and there was Professor Cox's new course on the Middle East. The Middle East and the Far East were considered to be the most important regions for undergraduate study because both had an unusually long and varied cultural tradition and at least one major language. The Middle East was finally chosen because there were a few faculty members who had considerable experience and competence in the area. The recommendation involved a request to approve the start of instruction in Arabic and the introduction of a new course on Islamic civilization as first steps in implementing the new program.

The faculty and administration approved, and the college requested matching support from the NDEA for the new Middle East area and language program in the late spring of 1959. No funds were granted for 1959, in part because NDEA grants were then being given only to graduate centers. But the college was encouraged to revise and re-submit its request. This second proposal was accepted in February 1960 when NDEA made a matching grant of just over $25,000 to an exclusively undergraduate language and area program for the first time.

These steps were not taken without serious question by some faculty members. However, Dr Cox reports that the dean of the faculty gave "persistent encouragement," President Millar added his full support, and various departmental and divisional officers were enthusiastic. Professor Franchere, chairman of the division of the humanities, was particularly interested in the sound development of language training.

The faculty committee's recommendation included a five-year plan with these nine goals:

1. The teaching of the major languages of the Middle East, including Arabic, modern Hebrew, Persian and Turkish at the undergraduate level;

2. The understanding of Middle East society through the vehicle of language training in order to give the undergraduate student an appreciation of a non-Western culture;

3. The encouragement of a liberal arts education for the undergraduate plus the acquisition of a knowledge of a non-Western area in depth and breadth through language and area training without sacrificing the former for the latter;

4. The education and awakening of an interest in Middle Eastern affairs in the Oregon community through workshops, seminars, lectures and institutes;

5. The inauguration of faculty and student research papers on Middle East problems and projects;

6. The attainment of scholarships for undergraduate specialized training;

7. The establishment of a training program on a non-credit basis for interested personnel in government, industry and public affairs;

8. The development of a library of materials dealing exclusively with the Middle East, including manuscript, monographic and reference works, films and other audio-visual materials in English and Middle Eastern languages;

9. The creation of a center as a location for staff, students, and library materials.

## Administration

The Middle East Studies Center is an administrative unit, run by a director and an assistant, with no other staff. Professor Frederick J. Cox, the director, is a regular teaching member of the department of history and served until recently as its executive officer. His assistant is an experienced secretary. The center is not a department, offers no courses of its own for undergraduates, and does not offer a major. It is a functional center for the integration of a multi-disciplinary approach to language and area training, and a geographical focus for the offices of staff from various departments to participate in teaching the courses on the Middle East, for seminar rooms, classrooms, select library holdings and a commonroom for students and staff. Professor Cox reports to the dean and the president through his department and division heads as a member of the history faculty, and through the heads of the divisions of the social sciences and humanities in his capacity as director of the center.

During 1963-64 there were eleven faculty members attached to the center. They represented seven departments: anthropology, economics, English (linguistics), foreign languages, geography, history and political science. Their primary duties were to their respective departments rather than to the center. Dr Cox explained that "these disciplines were chosen chiefly because the executive officer in each was willing to hire staff with Middle East competence or because he already had faculty members able and well-qualified to take part in the program. No department was obliged to employ faculty or to participate in the center program."

The Middle East Studies program has been a beneficiary of the fact that Portland State College is a new, rapidly growing urban college. It is the only state-supported institution of higher learning in the metropolitan area where 40 per cent of the state's population reside. This type of institution is often more flexible, ready to try new approaches to learning, and less bound by tradition, established policies or administrative structure than older colleges might be. President Millar, Dean Swarthout and divisional chairmen Franchere (humanities) and Hoffman (social sciences) have stressed experimentation and the teaching emphasis of the college. They have also done much to encourage personal contacts between students and teachers. The new student center and library building, and provision for regular meetings with faculty advisers, have fostered the interchange of ideas and openness to innovations such as the Middle East Center.

It should be emphasized that the center has had to compete from the start for very limited funds in the budget of an institution hard pressed to meet many burgeoning demands and dependent upon a state in which tax support for higher education has not been generous. The college is nevertheless strongly committed to the support of the center, which has its own budget, allocated mainly through the chairmen of the humanities and social science divisions in consultation with the director.

## The Middle East Studies Center: Growth and Program

The Middle East Studies program began in September 1959 with 34 students taking four initial courses. These were: beginning Arabic, Geography and Resources of the Middle East, History of the Ancient Middle East, and History of the Modern Middle East. There were less than 100 volumes in Middle East languages in the library. The center had three teachers, Professors Brooke (geography) and Cox (history) and newly-appointed Assistant Professor Farah (history). Only twenty of these students registered for the second quarter in January 1960, but seven new students joined the program. A special section in Arabic was set up for them to catch up by the fall of 1960 so that they could then begin second-year Arabic.

New language and subject-matter courses have been added to this modest beginning, together with more staff and students. For example, in 1960-61 there were eight teachers, two Arabic and eight area courses, 52 students enrolled for the certificate in Middle East Studies and 109 other students taking one or more of the area and language courses offered under center auspices. By the 1963-64 academic year the program had grown to eleven instructors offering ten language courses (four years of Arabic, and two years each of Hebrew, Persian and Turkish) plus nine disciplinary courses dealing with the modern history and society of the Islamic Middle East. As noted above, eighty undergraduates were enrolled for the certificate program and some 130 others were taking one or more courses on the Middle East. The center had assembled some 6,000 specialized volumes relating to the Middle East and was receiving hundreds of new accessions annually under the Library of Congress and Public Law 480 exchange publications program with Egypt.

The Robert Bogue collection of some 250 Egyptian lamps and funerary urns was donated to the center in 1962. These lamps represent Egyptian, Greek, Roman, Christian, Hebrew and Arab art and will form the nucleus of a small museum of Middle Eastern artifacts. In 1964 the local community leaders of Middle Eastern descent donated a large Persian rug and other works of art to the center, in which they take a keen interest.

From the start, it was decided to develop a Middle East Studies program based on a broad and fairly specialized range of substantive courses offered in several disciplines coupled with substantial language instruction. The committee considered an alternative approach through a general survey course to introduce Islamic and Middle Eastern civilization, as well as revision of the standard Western Civilization course to include more attention to the Middle East, but decided against either approach. The main reason was that they thought that both of these solutions tended to remain superficial and left out language instruction, which the committee considered essential to a sound program.

## Faculty Reactions

In the early stages, certain faculty members were opposed to having the college spend funds on an experimental, specialized non-Western language and area program without prototype at the undergraduate level. They also had serious doubts as to how such a program might be integrated into a liberal arts education without sacrificing the normal curriculum to what they regarded as the doubtful benefits of premature specialization on the Middle East. Their fears were allayed in part by the administration's appeal to let the center serve as an experiment to ascertain whether or not such studies could find a viable place in undergraduate liberal arts education. The early grant of matching funds from NDEA also helped to persuade the faculty that the test was worth the effort.

Part of the success of the program in gaining faculty support stems from its continued stress on multi-disciplinary course offerings with at least one course from each of the seven cooperating departments required for all students enrolled for the Certificate in Middle East Studies. This, plus the required language courses and the fact that the instructors and courses offered by the center remain under the administration and control of the various departments, helped Middle East Studies to fit into the established patterns and avoid the stigma of over-specialization. The fact that no student majors in Middle East Studies but simply elects to concentrate on the area *in addition* to his regular general education and major departmental requirements for the bachelor's degree has also helped to win over members of the initial opposition. Finally, the success of the Middle East Studies program in attracting many able students from a wide range of departments, such as mathematics, foreign languages (German and Russian), business administration and economics, as well as majors in history and political science, has had a healthy, interdisciplinary influence on classroom and informal discussions in the center, whose effect has not been lost on other members of the faculty.

The continual encouragement of key members of the administration and faculty has been a vital element in the development of the center, according to Dr Cox. His colleagues point out that the center owes much to his own keen interest, tact, strong standing in history (he still teaches the basic Western Civilization course), and desire to find a balance between sound liberal arts education in conventional disciplines and concentration on Middle East Studies. Professor Cox collaborates closely with the executive officers of departments and with the divisional heads concerned in regard to all faculty appointments, course revisions, and the development of new courses relating to the center. Staff salaries, fringe benefits, promotions and kindred matters are determined by the departments in consultation with the director of the center. Center funds are used to assist with appropriate faculty salaries, particularly for new appointments, on a pro-rata basis temporarily.

### Center Staff

The first two faculty members to teach courses offered by the center were tenure professors in geography and history who were native-born U. S. citizens. Each had extended his competence to the Middle East by means of two-year tours of research in the area and by individual study. Neither was an "area specialist" in spite of his competence in the region, and neither had more than slight control of any of the major Middle East languages. Nevertheless, they adopted the view that sustained study of at least one major Middle East language was essential for their under-graduate program. Consequently, the first new appointment in 1959 was given to an Arabic-speaking Middle Easterner with a Ph.D. in history from a major U. S. university, who taught the introductory Arabic course as well as the Ancient History of the Middle East.

Most subsequent appointments of new staff to teach in Middle East Studies were made to qualified candidates native to the Middle East, with graduate training primarily in the U. S. In 1963-64 five of the eleven instructors affiliated with the center were Middle Easterners and another was a Latin American graduate of the University of St Joseph in Beirut. Four of these men taught Middle Eastern languages, while the fifth taught the geography of the area. In previous years native Middle Easterners had taught center courses on the history, political science and economics of the area.

Portland State has been satisfied with the teaching and re-search of these native Middle Easterners but has had the chronic difficulty of being unable to retain some of these highly qualified teachers with specialized competence. Consequently, it has lost the services of five former staff members to other institutions. These losses are serious, but the college has been able to find competent replacements without serious loss of momentum to the program. The fact that they have been able to find faculty members with dual competence suggests that qualified teachers with both disciplinary and area training willing to teach at the undergraduate level are more readily available than some ad-ministrators think. Professor Cox points out that various agencies, particularly the American Association for Middle East Studies, have assisted the center in recruiting prospective staff members. Organizations such as the Middle East Institute, Modern Lan-guage Association, American Council of Learned Societies and American Universities Field Staff have provided assistance, advice and encouragement in planning for the Middle East Studies pro-gram, particularly in regard to visits by specialists, the provision of course syllabi used elsewhere and of bibliographic aids.

## Non-Western Language Instruction as Part of a Liberal Arts Education

The Middle East Studies program at Portland State is unique in its requirement that candidates for its certificate begin Arabic during their freshman year and satisfactorily complete at least three years of Arabic. There are very few colleges, even among those affiliated with graduate institutions, which offer Arabic to undergraduates. In the handful of colleges where instruction in Arabic is available, it is rarely taken except as an upperclass elective. Few institutions permit undergraduates who take Arabic or some other "non-Western" language (aside from Portuguese and Russian, which are classified for the purposes of this survey with non-Western languages), to offer this language in fulfillment of the foreign language requirement for the bachelor's degree. Portland State accepts competence in Arabic, Hebrew, Persian or Turkish for the foreign language requirement.

The following sketch of a *typical undergraduate course of study for a student* at Portland State College *who enrolls for the certificate in Middle East Studies* may help put the center's language instruction into its proper context. A freshman would take the general requirements in composition, elementary science or mathematics, physical education and first-year Arabic plus one course in his major, if this has been identified, or an elective. During sophomore year the student would continue with required science or mathematics and physical education and get introduced to cultural anthropology, economics and geography. He would take the survey of Islamic civilization, second-year Arabic and a course in his major field. In junior year he would continue Arabic, take upper division courses on the economics, geography and history of the Middle East and two courses in his major discipline. A senior would take two more courses in his major, required courses in Middle Eastern anthropology and political science and a seminar on cultural and political change in the area.

This four-year program allows the student to earn a major in disciplines such as geography, history, mathematics, philosophy, political science or in general studies (the humanities and social sciences) and to have an additional 24 hours of electives which can be taken in the major field, or devoted to further language study or any other liberal arts subject. The student enrolled for the Middle East Studies certificate is assigned two advisers, one in his major department and another from the center. This provides coordination of his entire study program and assures that all necessary requirements for graduation and the certificate are met.

A minimum number of 186 unit hours is required for graduation under the quarter system at Portland State. Consequently, the typical student in the Middle East Studies program takes about 33 hours in general education and college requirements, some 55 hours in his major field, 24 hours of electives, 43 hours of disciplinary courses relating to the Middle East and at least 33 hours in Arabic language. This breakdown indicates that the required substantive courses for the Certificate in Middle East Studies approach those necessary for a departmental major and exceed them if language requirements are included. However, as any student would have to fulfill some other foreign language requirement if he or she were not taking Arabic, the language hours count primarily as a general graduation requirement rather than as an additional load imposed only on candidates for the certificate.

The language offerings of the center are intended primarily to give the student an appreciation of the culture of the area based on the capacity to use Arabic (or in some cases Hebrew, Persian or Turkish) intelligently for simple conversation and reading. Language instruction is not intended to produce translators nor, with the accompanying area courses, to turn out an "area specialist," but rather to give students a broad and fairly substantial knowledge and understanding of the Middle East as representative of a major world culture and region which he can study to include a dimension of cultural pluralism in his undergraduate liberal arts training.

The center is committed to the ideal that it is practicable to make a comprehensive study of Middle East civilization, with language instruction central to the program, an integral part of undergraduate liberal education. While the director and staff recognize that their enterprise is still experimental, they hope that the center's progress to date and the opportunity to continue developing their program for a few more years may prove that their goal can be attained.

Dr Cox has described the center's language instruction as follows:

> Believing that the spoken and written word is the vehicle through which a society transmits its culture, our objective is to introduce the selected Middle East language to English speakers as a living tongue. Despite the wide gap between the spoken and written forms, every attempt is made to achieve a smooth transition between the two elements as we take the student from sounds to letters and from cultivated speech patterns to literary forms. At the conclusion of four years of language training, the student is expected to have mastered the use of a spoken dialect; to have acquired a facility in script writing but without imitating the printed form; to have learned the rules of classical grammar; to have acquired some appreciation of literature through the study of great writers in all periods of Middle East history.

The center lists the following basic materials required for language instruction in descending order of priority:

1. basic language texts currently used in college classes in the U. S. A., i.e. readers, grammars and elementary books on prose and poetry;

2. supporting tapes and recordings to help students review grammar and conversation;

3. current dictionaries in Western and Middle Eastern languages;

4. the elementary-to-high-school text books used in the country where the language is spoken in order to provide materials for study and discussion at all levels (The center has found that such materials are invaluable in teaching non-Western languages to English speakers as they provide transitional materials to help the student grasp the ideas presented by prominent native writers. It is very difficult for third year students to understand Arabic literature without some prior experience with intermediate writings which the elementary and secondary texts provide.);

5. musical records in vogue which illustrate simple and well-pronounced phrases and thoughts, mainly to provide the student with an appreciation of native musical forms and to serve as a review for language usage.

The Portland center has faced *three main issues* which must be dealt with *in an integrated approach to area and language instruction.* The first is to find an appropriate balance between area and language courses. The next is how to choose and then implement the best ways to teach a non-Western language such as Arabic to U. S. undergraduates. The third question revolves around the issue of whether language instruction for liberal arts students should be intensive or not.

The center's experience on these issues is not definitive. They have found that in practice their tentative solutions to these problems have worked out quite well. They prefer to have students devote about 60 per cent of their program to substantive disciplinary courses on the Middle East and 40 per cent to language. This represents a slight reduction of time devoted to language, since the first year's proportions were about 54-46. Although only three years of Middle Eastern language instruction is required for the certificate, most of the students take a fourth year of Arabic, or else three years of Arabic and a year of either Hebrew, Persian or Turkish. In such cases, language courses take up roughly half of the units in the Middle East Studies program.

*Portland State is committed to the audio-lingual approach to teaching Arabic* and other Middle Eastern languages. Its objective is to introduce Arabic as a living language with a rich and beautiful literature. From the start Arabic is spoken at close to normal conversational speed in class. The guided-imitation system is used to deal with basic structural patterns of learning. Students are expected to practice in the 85-booth language laboratory. Colloquial speech is first introduced. Grammar comes later, in conjunction with writing, presented in handscript materials specially prepared by the staff. By the end of the first year a student will control a vocabulary of about 600 words and have acquired the skill to use them correctly in conversation and in simple, handscript writing exercises.

Students of Arabic at Portland learn two dialects, that of Cairo and Eastern Arabic, so that they may be accustomed to hearing two variants of the language which together can help them to understand the colloquial and be understood in most of the cultivated Arab Middle East. In the second year printed materials are used for reading and sentence structure, and translation skills are developed. During the third year students read and translate from modern Arabic newspapers and authors and enlarge their vocabulary and grammatical knowledge. They are expected to converse on simple topics. Fourth year Arabic stresses literary readings in prose and poetry drawn from the wide range of traditional and contemporary writers. The capacity to speak as well as read is stressed at every level.

Professor Cox and his associates declare that *the problem of intensive verses non-intensive language instruction for undergraduates is crucial* because of the time limitations imposed on such language teaching by other student responsibilities. Like many other colleges, Portland State's schedule provides for a maximum of five hours of class time per course per week. Consequently, in order not to distort student schedules, the center's first two years of Arabic classes meet for five hours weekly. Four hours in class and a fifth with the instructor in the language laboratory is the usual pattern. Students carry on their own drill in the language laboratory at other hours. Classes in third and fourth year Arabic meet normally three times weekly, but each student is expected to spend several more hours in the laboratory. The staff of the center agree that more rapid progress could be made in learning Arabic if undergraduates could have from eight to ten hours weekly with the instructor. They have found, however, that the combination of frequent instruction spread over a span of time, coupled with regular encouragement to students to practice on their own in and out of the laboratory, produces satisfactory results.

In 1963 the Peace Corps prescribed that five of the ten hours of daily instruction for trainees headed for Turkey be devoted to language. Experience with this group indicated that *no more than two hours of instruction at one session could be absorbed efficiently*. Experimentation with different schedules showed that "for optimum learning, the five hours of study each day should be presented at five different intervals" (of one hour each) "for maximum results." Teachers in the University of Chicago 1963 intensive summer program in Hindi, which was taken by both Peace Corps trainees and other students, came to somewhat similar conclusions. For the time being, the center believes that its language courses and methods have proved effective and manageable within the liberal arts curriculum.

The record of certificate winners thus far confirms the effectiveness of their preparation. For example, in 1962-63 three won scholarships to spend their junior year studying Arabic at the Middle East Study Center, Shimlan, Lebanon, run by the British Government. These awards were made by the new National Undergraduate Program for Overseas Study of Arabic (NUPOSA) administered by Princeton University under a grant from the Carnegie Corporation. Another three Portland students again won these scholarships for 1963-64 and also won awards to study Arabic intensively at the inter-university summer program at Georgetown University in 1963. Two others have received Fulbright grants to study at the Cairo University Center for Arabic Studies and another a fellowship at the American University of Beirut. Three others are at Princeton Graduate College, one with an NDFL award, and another has a similar fellowship to continue with graduate studies in Persian at UCLA. Between 1961 and 1963, eighteen Middle East Studies Center students were awarded a total of $55,000 in scholarships, almost exclusively from outside sources. The program has only one modest scholarship at its disposal. Some of its students win general state awards and a few earn some of their expenses as library assistants.

The center encourages undergraduates to carry on their language learning elsewhere during the summer. They find that this helps both the students and the center. For students learn more, encounter differing ways of teaching and get independent checks on the relative strengths and weaknesses of their previous instruction plus a chance to compare their progress with that of students from other colleges. The comments and increased proficiency of these students, especially those who have spent their junior year in Lebanon, have proved beneficial to the other students and their instructors at Portland.

## Faculty Research

Research by staff members of the Middle East Studies Center has been subordinated to teaching, particularly during the initial years. Yet six of them published three volumes and nine professional articles during the first three years of the program. Thus far, the center's limited budget has not provided for overseas travel or research funds, although it does assist staff to attend some professional meetings in this country. The center hopes to be able to obtain funds to assist in research projects by faculty and students, and to enable its staff to carry out periodic field research in the Middle East.

## Conclusion

The Middle East Studies Center is demonstrating that its program broadens and deepens the liberal arts curriculum in addition to providing a concentration on a non-Western culture. The new courses on the Middle East represent a net increase in the number of courses offered by various departments. As all the center's courses are open to any student, the choice of electives is enlarged. Students taking even a single area or language course on the Middle East learn about a different civilization rather than simply more about their traditional Western heritage.

Center staff have introduced fresh interdisciplinary competence into their respective departments. Some of them are discovering that concepts and methods developed in the study of an area such as the Middle East can be applied effectively to other aspects of learning or to the analysis of other civilizations. Several members of the faculty at Portland State mentioned these factors as beneficial side-effects of the center's activities. Students get enthusiastic over such cross-cultural learning and bring new insights into all their recitations and written work. However, except for the course in Western Civilization, the influence of the center's teaching and program is not yet apparent in the main introductory courses required of most liberal arts undergraduates nor in upperclass courses relating to other non-Western societies.

Dean Swarthout and Dr Cox emphasize that the Middle East area and language program could not have been sustained without the continuing support of NDEA funds. Even with eighty students taking the certificate program, the college would be hard pressed to finance the center entirely out of its regular budget. They would like more resources in order to introduce new courses in philosophy and sociology. The program also needs strengthening in religion, for an understanding of Islam is central to Middle East studies. The center hopes to obtain substantial scholarship funds and money to build stronger library resources, in addition to funds to assist research projects.

The college is proud of the center's progress. The administration wants to continue to develop and experiment with the Middle East Studies program. They think that during the next five years they can evaluate it and reach some conclusions "as to the effectiveness of developing at the undergraduate level an understanding of a non-Western society through the medium of language training . . ." The program has gained considerable faculty and community acceptance. Its best students have won national recognition. The center's sponsors believe that this initial success justifies their hopes that an undergraduate program for the study of a major non-Western culture, built on area and language competence, can be fruitfully integrated into general liberal arts education.

# 4

# THE STATE UNIVERSITY COLLEGE
# AT NEW PALTZ, NEW YORK

The State University College at New Paltz, New York, has been a pioneer in requiring non-Western studies as part of the general education of all candidates for the bachelor's degree. New Paltz has also introduced many non-Western courses at the junior-senior level and majors on Africa and Asia. President William J. Haggerty has provided vigorous leadership for an institution-wide effort to develop a faculty and curriculum which would assure that no student could graduate unless he had taken at least four courses dealing with non-Western cultures. This has been achieved without special financial aid. New Paltz has assembled some 25 specialists on one or more non-Western areas. Twenty members of the faculty in 1963-64 had been born and raised in a non-Western area and had had advanced academic training in the West.

## Historical Background

New Paltz is a former state teachers college which was one of several such institutions incorporated into the State University

The State University College at New Paltz, New York. President William J. Haggerty. (State; coeducational; quarter system; liberal arts and teacher training to master's degree; 3,453 students)

of New York when it was organized in 1948. President Haggerty was inaugurated in 1944, six years after New Paltz became a four-year college. He has helped to introduce many changes in the curriculum, with a growing emphasis on solid disciplinary content. The entire program is now based on general education in the liberal arts, including required introductory courses on non-Western areas, followed by academic majors. The first minor in liberal arts was introduced in 1948. Two of the elective courses in this minor were History of the Far East, and Asia in Modern Times. These were taught by teachers without special qualifications or first-hand experience in the Orient.

Non-Western studies at New Paltz really began with the introduction of the revised curriculum in 1957, partly as a result of President Haggerty's service during 1952-53 as chief educational adviser to the Government of India for the U. S. technical assistance program. Dr Haggerty returned determined to provide a better education for world understanding than the Western-oriented curriculum at New Paltz. A few influential members of the faculty, such as the chairman of the division of education who had served the World Health Organization in Taiwan and professors who had severally taught in India, Iran, Japan, Lebanon and Thailand, were ready to support efforts to "globalize the curriculum."

Two preliminary steps were taken in 1955 and 1956 to promote world understanding among the faculty and students of the college and in the surrounding area. The first consisted of a series of television programs which began in 1955 and continued for several years. The initial series was called "Know Your Neighbors" and focused on understanding other peoples. The second series dealt with India and the third with Asia.

Secondly, at commencement time in 1956, Humayun Kabir, Minister of Scientific and Cultural Affairs in the Government of India, dedicated a World Study Center in the college library. At the center there are displays and collections of books, periodicals, pamphlets, films, pictures, artifacts, slides and maps dealing with all parts of the world but especially with Africa and Asia. By 1963 the center had over 6,000 items and received some 300 periodicals annually. It is widely used by students, teachers and others in the

Mid-Hudson region. The center has published a few booklets and study guides on non-Western countries such as Afghanistan and Thailand.

The Curriculum Committee made a study in 1956-57, concluding with recommendations for broadening the pattern of teacher education in two ways. The first was to provide a two-year required general education program for the freshman and sophomore years. The second was to develop an academic major of 24 semester-credit hours in the liberal arts (increased to 54 quarter units in 1963) which every student would take in addition to his professional training. This new curriculum provided fewer electives and more required courses stressing important concepts and interrelationships in various disciplines, with at least 15 credit hours in science and mathematics for each student, and tried wherever possible to present all subjects in a world-wide frame of reference. *Every student was required to take a course in Asian Civilization and one on Africa and the Near East.* A faculty with special skills and interests was essential to such a curriculum.

## Administration and Faculty

President Haggerty and his senior associates have consistently tried to strengthen the faculty. Their success may be gauged by the fact that between 1951 and 1956 four members of the faculty won Fund for the Advancement of Education faculty fellowships for their outstanding teaching ability in liberal education. While Professor Willard N. Hogan had received a grant to work on revision of the UN Charter at the Brookings Institution in 1952, and three members of the staff had received Fulbright appointments to India (2) and Japan (1) during these years, New Paltz did not have any specialists on the non-Western world before the new curriculum was recommended.

The college has strengthened its faculty resources in relation to the non-Western world by two chief means. First, it has recruited teachers with special competence in non-Western areas. Second, it has encouraged existing faculty members to seek Fulbright awards and other opportunities to study or serve in non-Western countries.

Recruitment of scholars with area specialization has been facilitated since the administration introduced a new criterion for faculty appointment after 1957. It provided that as between two or more candidates of equal merit preference was to be given to the one who had the most significant international experience relevant to the college's needs.

This policy has led to the appointment of twenty members of the faculty who are natives of a non-Western area dealt with in the curriculum. Normally these teachers are responsible for instruction in regular courses in their disciplines and also teach a course or two relating to the non-Western world. These faculty members include eleven in social sciences, seven in the humanities, and one each in art and education. Fourteen of the twenty earned at least their first degree in a non-Western country before taking advanced degrees in this country. Four others completed all of their higher education in the U. S. A. The two remaining foreign-born faculty members earned their advanced degrees in European universities. All of these teachers have had considerable graduate study or teaching experience in the U. S. A. in addition to their non-Western training.

The dean and his colleagues at New Paltz learned that it is important for every teacher in an American college to have a thorough understanding of the Western tradition and the American cultural heritage even if he is instructing students in courses dealing exclusively with a non-Western society. This explains why particular care is taken in reviewing candidates for the faculty from non-Western countries, and why most of those appointed combine advanced training and research at American universities with education in their own lands. The administration has found that, if problems of acculturation and adjustment for teachers from non-Western countries are surmounted by careful planning and good will, these teachers can add important dimensions to the intellectual and social life of the college.

In recent years nine members of the faculty have won Fulbright awards to lecture or engage in research in India, Indonesia, Iran, Japan, Pakistan and Thailand. These awards have gone to members of the divisions of the arts, education, humanities, and the social sciences, including the chairmen of the last two divisions. President Haggerty took part in educational missions to India in 1961 and 1963. Dean Pyle participated in a special study group on India during 1962-63. A member of the music faculty took part in a Fulbright summer seminar in India in 1962. Other arrangements have taken staff members as visiting professors, researchers or consultants to such places as the American University of Beirut, teacher training colleges in Indonesia, and the University College of Rhodesia.

By these various means at least 36 members of the administration and faculty have acquired substantial experience in one or more non-Western areas. As a college with an expanding enrolment, New Paltz has had to enlarge its faculty considerably in recent years. This has facilitated its employment of specially qualified instructors for required and elective courses on the non-Western world. The growing competence of the faculty in non-Western areas has been reflected in the curriculum at many points.

## Curriculum

The Curriculum Committee is responsible as part of its broader functions for the development of international and non-Western studies. The dean of the college serves on the committee along with representatives of the divisions of the arts, humanities, sciences and social sciences. The chairmen of the divisions of the humanities and the social sciences, and the director of liberal studies, to whom they report, have general administrative responsibility for non-Western area studies and for the majors in international relations (introduced in 1957) and in African or Asian studies (inaugurated in 1962).

The introduction in 1957 of a major in international relations and of the two required general education courses on Asian civilizations and on Africa and the Near East was the start of a continuing growth of non-Western studies. The regular addition of new teachers with special qualifications to teach about non-Western areas, and the gradual extension of competence to such areas by other members of the faculty combined to provide the human resources and interest out of which these curricular changes have developed.

By the academic year 1963-64, twenty-nine additional courses relating to the non-Western world had become part of the curriculum. Fourteen of these were disciplinary courses dealing primarily with one or more non-Western cultures. Five represented two years of instruction in Chinese and three in Russian language, offered for the first time in 1961 and 1962 respectively. The remaining ten were courses of the infusion type dealing in part with non-Western areas. Two of this last group of offerings, Art and Culture, and World Literature (including Kalidasa's *Shakuntala* and Murasaki's *The Tales of Genji*, were also required. This makes a total of four mandatory courses in general education relating to the non-Western world, an exceptional set of requirements for a liberal arts college.

Teachers at New Paltz have wrestled with the issues involved in choosing the most effective approach to general education courses on non-Western areas. By 1962 those teaching the semester course on Africa and the Near East had arrived at a consensus that their needs would be met best by a multi-disciplinary approach. Dr Ahmad Haffar, assistant professor of Near Eastern studies, has described certain aspects of the New Paltz approach as follows:

> The New Paltz program includes a one-semester (changed to one quarter in 1963) general education course on Africa and the Near East which all students must take within their first two years at the college. . . . Each member of the program staff alternately addresses a weekly general meeting of approximately 300 students. Sections of 25 or fewer students then meet two one-hour periods each week throughout the semester with one staff member, during which time the broad topic of the general lecture is explored and discussed on a seminar basis. The student is exposed, therefore, to the views of the specialist, who may or may not be his group leader, and to his own instructor from whom he can continue to learn without interruption.
>
> The Africa-Near East staff numbers four (now eight) people and includes an anthropologist, an economic geographer, a sociologist and a political scientist. . . .
>
> Certain administrative considerations relevant to a multi-discipline program must be pointed up to safeguard the basic goals of the program.

Because topics are introduced in a major lecture to a large audience, attendance of all staff is necessary in order to familiarize them with the specialist's views, to create an atmosphere of unity, and to facilitate further development of the general topic in discussion groups. Frequent meetings of the staff are necessary in order to pull together the major points which are to be raised with the students during discussion periods.

It may well be that the Africa-Near East program, now combined in a one-semester course, could profitably be divided, with each area comprising an offering of one semester. There is no doubt that the combination of Africa south of the Sahara with the Near East and North Africa in a single semester is staggering. To make the most of the time now available, a problem approach is being tried on an experimental basis, allowing comparative analysis of considerations common to the areas. Until September 1961, there had been a rather clear-cut division on the basis of time, with ten weeks devoted to sub-Saharan Africa and five weeks to the Near East and North Africa. The current attempt to consider common problems has been somewhat successful, because, despite variations, general characteristics of the areas have been found to be more similar than dissimilar. The problem approach has also alleviated considerably the pains associated with the transition from one area to the other.

There are other concerns which stem from the multi-discipline approach: (1) financing a staff of such diversified disciplinary backgrounds, (2) availability of personnel, (3) the danger of substituting breadth at the expense of depth, and (4) rivalry among disciplines within the program.

Increasingly, the specialists who are sought are those who combine training in one of the recognized disciplines with their speciality in a given non-Western area. This is true at New Paltz, where faculty members play a double role: teaching non-Western courses in addition to courses within their own discipline. The matter of financing is somewhat less acute in this instance, and the arrangement seems to be very satisfactory for the staff involved.

Recruiting is a major concern. There is little doubt that the discrepancy between available, well-trained specialists and the demand for them is considerable—but it is not irreducible. Even today, when the need is so apparent, contact with the right institutions often brings unexpected surprises. Until recently, non-Western studies have been almost exclusively offered in a few of the leading colleges, and the relatively small number of non-Western scholars have directed their attention to those institutions. Public colleges, with increased government and state aid, have become keen competitors, however, and often lure top personnel to their campuses with challenging responsibilities in new programs, satisfying salaries, advancement opportunities and relatively secure futures.

The third consideration is the problem of shallowness of offerings under the multi-discipline approach. While this may be generally true, it must be kept in mind that the non-Western courses required at New Paltz, for example, are introductory courses and presume to be nothing more. Advanced electives are open to students who want to pursue their interests further. In the advanced courses the scope is considerably narrowed and deeper inquiry is made possible. The problem of shallowness nevertheless remains a constant concern. It has been suggested that honor sections be introduced to the General Education program in which students will be permitted to go as far and as fast as their ability and interest will permit.

Inter-discipline rivalry seems to be common to virtually all universities and all programs. The multi-discipline approach to non-Western studies may sharpen rivalry and bring it into clearer focus when compared to other methods of presentation, but unless the content gets out of hand, both students and faculty can be stimulated by it.[1]

The adoption of the quarter system in 1963 forced the revision of all courses. The introductory courses on Africa and the Near East and on Asian Civilization, which Dr Haffar found "staggering" to handle in a semester, have been further condensed. This has sharpened the need for a problem approach. The revised version of Introduction to Africa and the Near East first offered in 1963 was taught by seven instructors in an eleven-week quarter. Dr. Haffer was coordinator of this staff consisting of himself, three Africans and three Americans. There were two main lectures and two discussion meetings in small sections weekly. The course began with three weeks on the Near East. The first week dealt with present conditions, and physical and human characteristics; the second with the traditional value system and the impact of the West; the third with the Near East present in relation to the future, as seen in the dynamics of Westernization, and the character of Near Eastern nationalism.

---

1. *Middle East Studies*, Fall 1962, pp. 13-14

Africa was studied under comparable headings in eight weeks. Present conditions were viewed in the light of (a) African emergence on the world scene; (b) impacts of the United Nations on today's Africa; (c) physical characteristics; (d) human characteristics. "Africa's Present in the Light of Its Past" reviewed (a) traditional value systems; (b) pre-European Africa; (c) Africa and Europe; (d) the impact of the West; (e) African renaissance. "Africa's Present in Relation to the Future" was examined from the point of view of (a) economic problems; (b) political problems; (c) social problems; (d) contemporary colonialism and racism in Africa; (e) new "concepts" and "themes" in Africa; and (f) Africa in relation to the non-African world.

Students were required to buy and read the following texts:

Kimble, G. H. T., *Tropical Africa*, Vols. I and II (1962)
Hitti, P. K., *Islam and the West*, (1962)
Kingsbury, R. C. and Pounds, N. J. G., eds., *An Atlas of Middle Eastern Affairs* (1963)
Antonius, G., *The Arab Awakening* (Selections)

They were also assigned readings from eighteen other books placed on reserve. Independent study and research papers were optional.

The companion course on Introduction to Asian Civilization followed a similar pattern, with a slightly more topical approach to the cultures of India, China and Japan and special consideration of the role of communism in Asia and its impact on the rest of the world. Three films were used as integral parts of the course. This course was taught by six instructors, consisting of a Chinese coordinator, an Indian, a Korean, and three Americans with first-hand experience in Asia. One of the staff was a former Korean ambassador to the United Nations and special envoy to newly independent African nations, with a Ph.D. from Princeton and previous teaching experience there and at Chatham, Lehigh and Yale.

The texts used in the autumn of 1963 were:

Spear, P., *India, Pakistan and the West* (1958)
Goodrich, L. C., *A Short History of the Chinese People* (1959)

Creel, H. G., *Chinese Thought from Confucius to Mao Tse Tung* (1960)
Reischauer, E. O., *Japan, Past and Present* (1952)
Storry, R., *A History of Modern Japan* (1960)

In addition to the required general education courses relating to the non-Western world, any candidate for the B.A. may elect to *major in African or Asian Studies* at New Paltz. Either of these majors calls for 52 quarter-credits out of the total of 180 credits needed for graduation. Required courses account for 28 credits, and electives for 24. The standard requirements in general education, two years of satisfactory, college-level foreign language competence (which may be established by examination), and additional electives in liberal arts, make up the rest of the program. African studies majors must take seven of the following eight courses, each carrying four credit units:

| | |
|---|---|
| Cultures of the Middle East | History of West Africa *or* |
| Economic Problems of Africa | History of East Africa |
| Geography of Africa | Systems of Government in Sub- |
| Religions of the World | Saharan Africa |
| | Africa in Transition |

Asian studies majors take the following seven required courses:

| | |
|---|---|
| Geography of Asia | History of Japanese Civilization |
| Religions of the World | Government and Politics of East Asia |
| History of Chinese Civilization | History of World Social Thought |
| Social History of India | |

Neither of these majors requires any African or Asian language. But instruction in Chinese was introduced in 1961 and Russian in 1962. During 1963-64 eleven students were taking elementary and five intermediate Chinese. The audio-lingual method of instruction was used, with four hours a week in class and at least one hour a week in the language laboratory. Each course consisted of three eleven-week (one-quarter) sequences, making up a full academic year. Ten students were taking elementary, six intermediate Russian, taught according to a similar pattern, with five class hours instead of four a week. An advanced course in

Russian Literature was also offered but was not elected by any students. It is scheduled to meet four hours weekly and provides for one hour of practice in the language laboratory.

Members of the faculty at New Paltz could teach Arabic, Hindi or some African languages instead of other courses. But thus far there has been almost no demand for such instruction, and the focus has been on acquiring personnel with special competence to teach the required general education courses and more advanced courses dealing with non-Western areas. The administration prefers to consolidate its present non-Western area and language offerings before adding instruction in other critical languages.

The electives relating to the majors in African and Asian studies consist of the following courses, each of which carries four units of credit unless otherwise indicated.

Cultural Anthropology
Art of China and Japan
Art of Africa and Pre-
    Columbian America
Art of India and Persia
Ancient Art
Basic Economics I and II
    (8 units)
Money, Banking and Public
    Finance I and II (6 units)
Economic Policy I and II
    (6 units)
History of Economic Thought
    (8 units)
Asian Literature

Introductory Chinese
    (12 units)
Intermediate Chinese (8 units)
Economic Geography
Earth and Man
Land and People of Japan
Comparative Government
History of Political Thought
Near East Politics and Institutions
Modern Political Thought
General Sociology
Social Statistics
Modern and Contemporary
    Social Theory
Methods of Social Research

## Library

The State University College at New Paltz is fortunate in having had an experienced librarian with first-hand knowledge of Asian publications and libraries. Librarian Robert P. Lang spent the year 1960-61 in Pakistan on a Fulbright appointment. Consequently he was able to arrange exchanges of periodicals and gifts of books for the library from Asian institutions which he visited. His experience helped him to acquire the relatively rare special skills necessary to deal efficiently with the complexities of Islamic publications, authors' names and other problems inherent in the integration of Oriental materials into a Western college library.

The library contains upwards of 100,000 volumes and is growing at the net rate of 5,000-6,000 books per year. The current budget for accessions is $37,000, of which $8500 is for the 700 periodicals received annually. Roughly ten per cent of the books and 35 per cent of the periodicals (many of the latter being gifts from this country and abroad) relate primarily to the non-Western studies program. The staff rated the library as "good" for student instruction and research on Africa (general), Asia (general), East, South and Southeast Asia, but only "adequate" on the Middle East and "poor" on Latin America and Slavic and East European studies. In terms of minimal faculty research for courses, it was rated only "adequate" in the categories evaluated above as good for instruction, and "poor" on the Middle East, Latin America and for Slavic studies. The three most urgent library needs are materials on Latin America, Eastern Europe and the Middle East.

## Foreign Students, Visitors and Extracurricular Activities

New Paltz welcomed its first foreign students in 1948. Two were from Latin America and two from Europe. Since then a growing number of foreign students from sixty nations have come to the college to add their contributions to its aims to education for world understanding. In 1961-62 there were 35 students from nineteen foreign countries. Fifteen came from Africa and others from India, the Philippines, Greece, Mexico, Peru, Argentina, Korea, Taiwan and Indonesia. In 1963-64 there were thirty students from non-Western areas.

Foreign students have been used occasionally as native informants in language courses and are often called on to serve as resource persons in classes. They also speak in debates, at forums or on radio and TV panels. Some are responsible for the staffing of the World Study Center in the library and take pride in this work. The administration believes that the greatest contribution which foreign students make is through their extracurricular activities, in special programs relating to their native lands and simply by living with American students.

In 1963-64, for the first time, two undergraduates were studying in Japan for credit. New Paltz hopes to expand opportunities for American students to study in non-Western areas but finds that most of its students cannot afford the cost in time or money. The Central Institute of Education at the University of Delhi, India, and the College at New Paltz began an affiliation in 1959 looking toward an exchange of publications, of information, and even of advanced students and faculty members. A few students have been exchanged, but mainly at the graduate level.

New Paltz has also trained Peace Corps volunteers for service in Sierra Leone and has welcomed student groups sent under the auspices of the State Department or the Experiment in International Living from countries such as Algeria, Morocco and Mexico. General convocations have been addressed by such well-known personalities as Tom Mboya of Kenya and G. L. Mehta, then Indian Ambassador to the U. S. A. A member of the faculty edits the quarterly *Literature East and West*, the newsletter of the Conference on Oriental-Western Literary Relations of the Modern Language Association of America.

## Conclusion

New Paltz now offers its students exceptional opportunities to learn in depth about various non-Western areas, especially Africa and Asia. It is perhaps unique among U. S. undergraduate colleges in requiring all students to take four courses dealing with the non-Western world as part of their general education program. The college has assembled a faculty remarkable for the number of its members who are specialists on non-Western areas. It is building up the relevant library resources.

One of the difficulties faced by the college administration has been the chronic problem of turnover among specialized faculty members. Another has been the continuing difficulty of deepening the commitment of serving faculty members to non-Western studies. Furthermore, both the pace of library development and the increase of opportunities for faculty members to extend their competence in non-Western studies have been slower than they might have been because the college has had to rely almost exclusively on its own funds.

Nevertheless, New Paltz has made notable progress in its drive to educate all its students in world understanding. It has been a pioneer among public colleges in providing non-Western studies for all students at both introductory and advanced levels and in encouraging other colleges, both in New York State and further afield, to build on its experience.

# 5

# WILLIAMS COLLEGE

## Rationale for Adoption of Middle Eastern Courses

Approximately three years ago a survey and content analysis of the Williams College liberal arts curriculum were made. The results, although somewhat startling, were not entirely unexpected on the part of those familiar with the academic content of the college. The three largest social science departments (history, economics and political science) then offered an array of 94 separate courses, of which 88 were properly classified as studies of problems, policies and events arising from a Western-European-American cultural context. Typical examples of these were History of 19th Century England, Principles of the American Economy and Comparative Western European Politics.

The six other courses then being offered in the social sciences included three courses which, to some minor extent, dealt with non-Western materials. But they were primarily international relations courses and their non-Western aspects were dealt with only in so far as they related to the main thrust of the courses—such as American International Trade or World Politics since 1900—with the result that the phrase "world politics," for

---

Williams College, Williamstown, Massachusetts. President John E. Sawyer. (Private; men; semester system; liberal arts to master's degree; 1228 students)

This statement was prepared by Professor Dwight J. Simpson for the conference of March 1964 on Middle East studies, reported in Item 19 of this Appendix.

instance, invariably meant the political relations among the major Western powers. The remaining three courses could at that time be legitimately classified as non-Western but these frequently were either "bracketed" out of actual existence or were offered as electives and at inconvenient schedule hours, with the result that they made small imprint on the over-all intellectual life of the college.

What was true in the social sciences was even more true in the humanities and letters sectors of the college. For instance, Williams offered instruction in seven languages, none of which was a non-Western language. The separate departments of the college, including philosophy, literature, art, drama, music, etc., had over the years constructed course offerings in such a manner as to reflect an apparent belief that the Western world was not only the center of the universe but was the universe itself. Indeed whatever was non-Western was non-existent in so far as the letters and arts curriculum was concerned.

This cultural bias naturally gave rise to serious distortions. Our students in letters and arts were given a view of a Western culture that apparently had arisen independently in a short time span in a tiny area at the western tip of the Eurasian continent. The non-Western roots of Western culture and the interaction of Western culture with other great cultures were only cursorily mentioned or left entirely unexamined. And in the social sciences it had become increasingly plain that we were turning out graduates in economics, politics and history who were un-equipped to understand the most pressing social problems of this era, most of which are now and will continue to be "non-Western."

In light of this and other considerations, the decision was made at Williams College to attempt some meaningful amount of curricular reform and modification with a view to introducing courses in non-Western studies judged to be consistent with the purposes of an undergraduate liberal arts college. Imme-diately, of course, Williams faced the question: what particular sub-areas of the vast field of non-Western studies might or ought to be chosen. Our approach was as follows: an area studies com-mittee was formed and was assigned the task of proposing the necessary structural changes in the existing curriculum while at the same time conferring with the disciplinary departments for the purpose of learning what new or existing courses might feasibly fit within the framework of an area studies program were it to be established.

Eventually the general faculty voted to establish an area studies program including the following four geographical regions: Latin America, Middle East and Africa, Russia, South and East Asia. From this it is plain why Williams dropped the term "non-Western," substituting "Area Studies."

Area studies courses are offered by participating departments as regular one-semester electives. Each is designed to be an analytical course applying the insights of a particular discipline to the societies under study. A student may register for any single area studies course after meeting the established prerequisites. A student who wishes to undertake a full area studies program, however, registers for a set of four complementary courses dealing with the same geographical region. The four courses will normally be in four different departments, assuming that the available course offering permits. This four-course program constitutes a set of electives supplementing a regular major in an established department. A student may register for such a program as a sophomore or junior by submitting to the department in which he intends to major and to the Committee on Area Studies a suitable plan of course elections for the following two or three years. In carrying through this program, he may be permitted to waive the prerequisites for at most two of his four area studies courses, by individual arrangement with the committee and the department offering a particular course, as for example by substituting a reasonable amount of preparatory reading.

A second form of area studies program includes a language of the area. A student registers for a four-course program *plus* a sufficient number of courses in an area language to attain useful command of it for speaking, reading and writing. This program with foreign language is especially desirable for students who may go on to graduate work in area studies. Study of any new language should if possible be started in the freshman year. The procedures and conditions of student registration are the same as described above.

A student registered for a four-course program may obtain honors credit for an area studies course by meeting requirements set by the department offering the course and approved by the Committee on the Honors Degree. The requirements will ensure that students seeking honors credit carry out sufficient individual work, at times distributed throughout the semester, to demonstrate honors performance and to maintain the distinctive honors character of their participation in the course. Honors credit can be obtained only in area studies courses for which a student offers the regular prerequisite.

At present there are 24 area studies courses at Williams, of which five are Latin American, five South and East Asian, eight Russian, and six Middle Eastern and African. Two of these area components (Russian and Latin American) include language instruction. Thus Williams College has a basic area studies program in general and a Middle Eastern studies program in particular. The enrolment of the College is 1200. Enrolment in the area studies program has been as follows:

|                        | 1962–63 | 1963–64 |
| ---------------------- | ------- | ------- |
| Latin America          | 19      | 54      |
| Russia                 | 88      | 86      |
| Middle East and Africa | 133     | 101     |
| South and East Asia    | 26      | 45      |
|                        | ───     | ───     |
| Totals                 | 266     | 286     |

Fundamentally the decision to add Middle Eastern courses was based upon the presence of teaching personnel who were both trained in the materials of the area and keenly interested in offering some course work. The college administration cooperated fully in this; no obstacles, neither policy nor budgetary, were encountered in this sector of the college. Some amount of opposition did arise, and continues to exist, among certain faculty members. Much of this was based upon what, quite frankly, must be called the innate conservatism or *status quo* mindedness of very many members of the teaching profession.

It quite clearly follows that the Williams faculty is not unusual in this respect.

From a very large number of conversations with skeptical or "oppositionist" faculty I perceived a common theme running through all the separate arguments: the teacher who has slogged his way through graduate school, conformed to the pressures of his chosen academic discipline, found security in a desirable teaching job, adapted himself to a particular academic environment and has his courses "set up" in a systematic manner tends to regard any substantive curricular change as potentially upsetting his personal and professional apple cart. Thus it was necessary to conduct a kind of campaign which attempted both to educate and to persuade. This campaign is still in progress; its full success will be necessary before further enlargements of area studies work at Williams can be undertaken.

Since our program in Middle Eastern studies is as yet a modest one we have not yet encountered the problem of scarce teaching resources. Should we attempt to expand our offerings in this field we would immediately confront the problem. I know of only one present staff member (a professor of religion) who has made an effort to "re-tool" in order to be able to offer course work in Middle Eastern studies. Hence any expansion of Middle Eastern studies here will necessarily require acquisition of new personnel.

## Scope of Middle Eastern Studies

It is difficult to describe exactly the degree of commitment, since the policy "line" on this matter sometimes seems to waver or to become partially obscured by other factors and considerations. Optimally I would estimate that the entire area studies program at Williams will be expanded and that Middle Eastern studies, revolving around an Arabic language core, will be the principal component. When, and indeed whether, this will occur depends upon several unknowns, one of the more important being finding means for financing such an expansion. In the judgment of the Williams College administration, such a program as described above would have to be financed by outside sources; Williams could not finance it from college funds.

We have not yet confronted the problem which naturally would arise: how to retain Middle Eastern specialists who may become dissatisfied because of the lack of opportunity for area research. Our resources (library holdings, documents, etc.) are not adequate to permit extensive Middle Eastern research, although we are acquiring more resources and, hopefully, we may begin to approach this point in the future. The great resources in the Boston and New York areas are near enough for periodic trips by any local Middle Eastern specialist who wishes to pursue his research. Some amount of college funds might be available to defray minor travel expenses. Inter-library loan is a very useful device in this connection and has proved most satisfactory. An imaginative and flexible leave-of-absence and sabbatical policy on the part of the college is obviously necessary if we are to attract and to hold high-caliber personnel in Middle Eastern studies.

Our original decision to effect a degree of Middle Eastern concentration was closely connected with the local availability of competent teaching personnel. The staff, quite by accident, was already here; what was needed was the decision to divert some of their energies into Middle Eastern courses. We decided on a single comprehensive introductory course and it is offered within the discipline of political science. Our instruction in Middle Eastern materials is devised so as to serve both purposes mentioned: enrichment of the general liberal arts training of the average student and a contribution to the pre-professional training of a potential Middle Eastern specialist. We regarded as minimal library requirements a collection in social sciences, philosophy-theology and literature sufficient to support the research for student term papers in various subjects. Our Middle Eastern periodical list in particular has been substantially enlarged.

### Instruction in Middle Eastern Languages

Our area studies instruction takes both of the forms already mentioned, i.e., with or without the student studying an area language. We do not see much merit in the argument as it is posed; that is to say, we intend to serve both groups of students:

the language learners and the non-language students. We are not now teaching a Middle Eastern language but, as indicated above, there is the possibility we shall offer instruction in Arabic provided the necessary arrangements can be made. We have conducted one survey of potentially interested students to see if there was any effective demand for Arabic language instruction. The response was favorable and from our study we concluded that there would probably be a sufficient number of Arabic language students to justify the introduction of the language at Williams.

Our tentative choice of Arabic rested on several grounds, including the decision that the two other major Oriental languages we were considering (Mandarin Chinese and Hindi) required a kind of commitment in terms of resources, diversion of student time, etc. we considered inadvisable. Arabic seemed to us to present the proper amount of challenge and opportunity we were willing and able to accept. It also promised the least amount of serious disruption of the normal pattern of education on the part of our students who would, as part of their undergraduate training, study the Arabic language. At present we encourage students who wish to study Arabic to think of beginning their studies by means of the Inter-University Summer program and/or the Princeton-Shimlan program.

## Special Interests and Problems

Williams probably has no so-called "special" problems in the field of undergraduate instruction in Middle Eastern studies. Our principal concern has been to integrate our area studies into a traditional curriculum, to alter the balance within that curriculum but without changing its basic liberal arts nature. The problems encountered—policy decisions, personnel problems, means of financing, expansion of resources, etc.—although important and at times difficult, doubtless by no means were unique to Williams. Any college comparable to Williams would surely have been confronted with all or most of the problems we face.

154

We are not at the moment sharing any Middle Eastern offerings with nearby sister institutions, although this is an attractive future possibility. Our nearest neighbors are North Adams State College, Berkshire Community College, Bennington College, Rensselaer Polytechnic Institute and Union College, and cooperation with them (meaning some form of student exchanges and sharing of teaching resources and library resources) is both feasible and desirable.

One problem, which again may not be a uniquely Williams problem, arises from consideration of our teaching resources in Middle Eastern studies. Since we have only a comparative handful of staff engaged in teaching Middle Eastern materials, we would have to go outside the college for replacements should any of our present teaching personnel in the area transfer or go on leave. We do not have any teacher here who has a Middle Eastern speciality and who is not currently teaching in our program. Hence any changes among our present staff would seriously jeopardize our Middle Eastern area studies unless replacements were found who were qualified to offer the same range of courses. This problem can be a difficult one in a small college, particularly unless there is planning well in advance intended to accommodate this quite real possibility of disruption of the Middle Eastern program.

## Evaluation of Instruction on the Middle East

Our objectives have remained the same since we first introduced Middle Eastern studies: the enrichment and strengthening of a liberal arts program which stood in need of re-examination and reform. There are probably many more things within the field of Middle Eastern studies we could do. We could expand the course offerings in the various existing departments as well as in disciplines (anthropology and sociology) not now taught at Williams. It is difficult to judge how far instruction in Middle Eastern studies at Williams might be further developed. Judgment about this would depend upon knowledge of two presently unknown variables: a policy decision to go ahead and the extent of potentially available resources to underwrite whatever commitment might be made. The Williams College administration would urge the seeking of funds from NDEA and/or foundation support.

## Summer Program

In cooperation with the American Association for Middle Eastern Studies, Williams held a summer faculty institute in Middle Eastern studies during 1962. This was one of a series of such summer programs sponsored by the association; others have been held at such institutions as the University of Illinois, University of Utah, etc. The purpose is to invite (on a full or partial scholarship basis) a highly selected group of college and university teachers who are not Middle Eastern specialists but who wish to begin a period of academic "re-tooling" in order to pursue research interests in the field or to offer courses in the field at their home institutions. At Williams we had twenty institute members from a wide variety of educational institutions that were also geographically dispersed. Teachers of sociology, history, geography, economics, politics and religion were represented. They came from both colleges and universities, including such institutions as Wellesley, Arizona State University, Vassar, Oberlin, Queens College, the University of New Hampshire and Yale. The program included intensive work by means of lectures and seminars conducted by a teaching staff of four professionally recognized specialists. The program was well supported by Williams College, which cooperated fully. It was judged to be both successful and a welcome event of the Williams summer program.

# 6

# HANOVER COLLEGE

Hanover College is one of the few liberal arts colleges where all students take at least two courses relating to the non-Western world. The decision behind this was part of the Hanover Plan adopted in 1961. The two courses are taken during the junior year, preferably in different terms. One is entitled World Literature. The other can be either Introduction to the Civilization of East Asia or Introduction to the Civilization of South and Southeast Asia. In addition, Hanover offers several elective courses relating to non-Western areas in various departments and instruction in Portuguese and Russian language, with a major in Russian studies. Some other courses, such as one in the development of drama and theater, includes some work in Oriental studies. A concentration (not quite equivalent to a major) in Latin American studies can also be arranged. These courses are supplemented by a number of college-wide annual institutes on non-Western countries, lectures, exhibits, plays, concerts and other opportunities for all students and faculty members to learn about non-Western cultures.

## Historical Background

The decision to incorporate non-Western studies into the curriculum at Hanover was made in part because the college has

---

Hanover College, Hanover, Indiana. President John E. Horner (Presbyterian; co-educational; semester system; liberal arts and teacher training to bachelor's degree; 827 students)

had a long tradition of interest in the Orient. This helped to create a climate of opinion among faculty and students which made them ready to accept the Hanover Plan recommendation that two of the fifteen general courses required for graduation deal substantially with the non-Western world.

Established in 1827, Hanover is a Presbyterian church-related college and was the first private, four-year college organized in Indiana. It has had many graduates who were missionaries in Africa, China, Japan, India, the Philippines and Korea. August Reischauer, father of Ambassador Edwin O. Reischauer and himself a student of Japan, where he taught for many years, graduated from Hanover in 1902. The late President Albert G. Parker, Jr, spent many years in China. Professor E. M. Tate, who served as dean from 1948-61, had spent ten years in Thailand as teacher and then president at Bangkok Christian College. He and three or four colleagues in the departments of English, history and political science encouraged initial efforts to introduce some attention to non-Western cultures into the curriculum.

In 1954 Hanover joined with fourteen other Indiana colleges in a joint program with Indiana University to enable a few students to study for credit in Mexico, Peru and Europe.

## Situation in 1958

When Professor John M. Thompson of Indiana University visited Hanover in 1958 to ascertain its interest in developing non-Western studies, as part of the statewide survey carried out by the university, there were nine faculty members offering as many courses relating to the non-Western world. Three of the courses were primarily concerned with non-Western areas, two in Russian history and one on Russian-American relations. Others devoting partial attention to the non-Western world were: one on Contemporary World Politics; two in economics; one on Asian and Pacific Geography; one on Comparative Religion and another on the Development of the Drama with some attention to Russian and Oriental theater.

At that time *only four members of the faculty had had much experience of the non-Western world.* One of these had taught

158

himself Russian and then studied Russian language and civilization at Indiana University; another had traveled in Latin America; a third had served in the Pacific during World War II, and the fourth was Dean Tate with his experience in Thailand. While no member of the faculty had had recent non-Western experience, and *none was a fully-trained specialist in any non-Western area,* a core of interested teachers, led by the dean, were already broadening the world view of the college.

Dean Tate estimated that *some sixty per cent of Hanover students were then receiving limited exposure to non-Western culture* through the nine courses named above. But he and his colleagues hoped to offer all students more serious opportunities to learn about other cultures. They particularly wished to introduce Russian language instruction and more systematic attention to Asian and Russian studies.

The faculty found support for these views in President John Horner, appointed in 1958. It was agreed that non-Western studies should be fitted into the over-all curricular changes then impending, with two foci. The first was to introduce more world perspectives and data into basic courses which are taken by most students, such as Western European History and the Principles of Economics. For example, units on Russia and European expansion into Africa and Asia were incorporated into the history course and data on the economies of India and Russia into that on economics. The second was to offer particular courses dealing more fully with non-Western areas, to be taken by a wider range of upperclass students than just those majoring in subjects such as history or political science. During the intervening years, these aims have been carried out, largely as a result of the study and discussion culminating in the Hanover Plan.

**The Hanover Plan**

The Hanover Plan constitutes a major reorganization of the college curriculum and calendar. It was designed to improve liberal education by reducing the number of courses taken by students and offered by the faculty, and to enhance the student's capacity to study and learn independently and creatively. The plan developed out of several years of faculty and administration review which began in 1957 and culminated in a *major self-study* by three full-time faculty members during the 1960-61 academic year.

Part of the rationale for the self-study derived from the recurrent need for "re-thinking our education." The committee also pointed out that "The challenges of the Soviet Union and Communist China make it impossible for us to be complacent about our achievements in education." From the start of his administration President Horner had informed the faculty that it was their prime responsibility to review and revise the curriculum of the college.

*The Self-Study Committee* consisted of three senior professors, none of whom had any special non-Western competence, and the president and the dean meeting with them *ex officio*. Dorothy Bucks, professor of English, was chairman; Arthur J. Porter, Jr, professor of economics, and John E. Yarnelle, professor of mathematics, were the other two members. Their duties were broadly defined to *focus on future plans* rather than on review of the past and they were to report to the entire faculty rather than to the Educational Policy Committee.

Their procedure was to establish a central office where they met together for an hour and a half each morning to review plans for the day and exchange the gist of their individual studies and their conversations with faculty members or students. The president and the dean usually met with the committee once a week. During the seven months of its work, the committee met at least three times for individual conferences with each member of the faculty, in addition to meeting periodically with teachers by departments and with many students, and making progress reports to general college assemblies, the faculty, students, trustees and members of the college constituency. They were thus able to encourage virtually every faculty member and many students to contribute ideas and to take some part in the study.

Consequently, when the committee presented its recommendations to the general faculty in the spring of 1961, some ninety per cent of the faculty voted to adopt its proposals, although this entailed the revision of every course and a major calendar change. The committee members reported that the plan represented a composite of many suggestions and involved some compromise. They insisted in their report that it was only because their work had involved such a large proportion of the college constituency, and was carried on with open channels of communication, that it was adopted with so little serious question. They were also the first to point out that, in the short run, the apparently beneficial aspects of the Hanover Plan may be due less to their ideas than to the well-known Hawthorne effect which suggests that change itself appears to improve morale, at least briefly, regardless of the character of the particular change.

Professor Tate reported in 1964 that when the Self-Study Committee was analyzing curricular changes there was a good deal of discussion of the role of non-Western studies. The usual problems of a lack of qualified personnel with specialist training to teach either disciplinary or language courses; how to attract students to take such courses if offered, and how to relate these to the rest of the curriculum came under review. In the course of their work the committee studied the experience of colleges such as Carleton, Dartmouth, Earlham, Kalamazoo and Lake Forest in reducing the number of courses. They visited Earlham to learn more about its three-term, three-course calendar, non-Western studies and new curriculum. They also invited five consultants to meet with them.

Of these five consultants, two were specialists on the non-Western world. John Thompson, a historian of Russia with considerable experience in Indonesia and other parts of Asia, was then directing the statewide program to strengthen non-Western studies, sponsored by Indiana University with support from the Ford Foundation. The other was Ward Morehouse, then educational director of the Asia Society, and a leader in encouraging non-Western studies in undergraduate education.

When the committee had to decide about required general courses, Miss Bucks' suggestion that every student should take at least one course dealing primarily with a non-Western culture and another on world literature, as part of the fifteen required courses, was accepted with little discussion. President Horner said: "If we don't put it in now, we'll be sorry five years from now." When the proposal was presented for faculty consideration, at was again accepted with little discussion about the principle. There were some questions about how to implement the requirement.

Fortunately, the committee could point out that Dean Tate was prepared to develop two courses on the Far East and South Asia, to relinquish the dean's office and to take the chairmanship of a new department of non-Western studies. The English department was also ready to organize the course on World Literature and to include more selections from non-Western traditions than are often offered in courses which bear a similar title. Dr Tate emphasized that:

> the objective of this requirement is not only to acquaint students with these reawakening cultures and their potential power, but to gain a new perspective on our own culture . . . through the study of Oriental contributions to civilization. A liberal arts education is not complete today with only a Western point of view being taught. We need understanding of another civilization to be liberally educated. We must, therefore, include the study of *both* Western and non-Western civilizations in the curriculum, and stress philosophy, religion, literature, art, economics and government as well as the basic subject of history.[1]

## Main Features of the Plan

The committee stated that the plan would provide "vigorous thrusts toward learning in depth as well as in breadth, toward a careful avoidance of overlap in each individual student's program, and toward a greater emphasis on independent, mature work." Other elements of the plan are:

1. Since 1962, each Hanover student takes seven courses a year, plus physical education in the first two years.
2. Of the 29 courses necessary for graduation, 15 are required of all students and two of these relate to non-Western cultures.

---

1.  Alumni News, Fall 1962, p. 7

3. The 33-week academic year is divided into three terms, the first two of fourteen weeks each, during which a student takes three courses per term. The third term lasts for five weeks, during which the student takes one course.

4. In addition, students may elect to carry quarter courses in such activities as band, choir, forensics, organ, piano, painting and play production.

5. Twenty-one of the 29 courses necessary for graduation must be in areas other than that of the major discipline.

6. The 15 required courses are to be taken in a carefully structured sequence.[2]

One result of these changes is that, when juniors take either course on the Civilization of East or South Asia, and the course on World Literature, their instructors know that every student has already taken certain courses in philosophy, science, European history and foreign languages, which have provided a common background as a basis of comparison and further learning. This enhances communication and the opportunities to relate elements in non-Western cultures to those in the West already familiar to students.

## Situation in 1964

*Every student at Hanover now takes a minimum of two courses dealing with the non-Western world.* He also has an opportunity to major in Russian studies or to take a concentration on Latin America. Eight and six students respectively availed themselves of these two opportunities in 1963-64. At least seventeen other basic courses and upperclass electives offer additional chances to learn about non-Western areas. Seven of the teachers offering such courses have considerably extended their competence since 1958.

By 1964 there were 900 students in the college. Thirteen faculty members, in eight departments, were teaching over twenty courses relating to non-Western areas—including four courses in the

---

2. Adapted from Hanover Plan booklet and catalogue

Russian language and one in Portuguese. There were *807 enrolments in these courses.* World Literature was being taken by 151 students; 59 were taking Introduction to the Civilization of East Asia, and 28 Introduction to the Civilization of South and Southeast Asia; 377 took a combined course in economics and political science which dealt in part with non-Western areas.

## Faculty

Hanover College has relied primarily on developing the interests and skills of serving faculty members. Only one new specialist has been appointed to teach about the non-Western world. His specialty is Russian language. Dr Hsueh-feng Poe, research chair professor at the National Chenchi University, Taiwan, who came to Hanover as a Whitney-Fulbright visiting lecturer, taught a course on the political thought of modern China during the first term of 1962-63 and acted as a consultant on the two courses on Asian civilization introduced that autumn.

Four of the thirteen faculty members mentioned above had had graduate training in non-Western area and language programs by 1963-64. There were two specialists on Latin America and two on Eastern Europe and the USSR. Two other teachers had taken substantial graduate training in East and South Asian studies but did not command a major language of these areas. While the remaining seven did not have this degree of special training in their areas, most of them had undertaken summer or year-long study of the region in the U. S. A., or had traveled for several months or taught for a year in the area since 1958.

For example, Professor Bowers, an historian, spent eighteen months studying Russian language and civilization at Indiana University and two summers in Eastern Europe and the USSR. Professor Bucks spent her sabbatical year traveling in the Orient, studying wherever possible the literature and drama of South and Southeast Asia. Professor Hill, in foreign languages, studied Brazilian literature for a semester at the University of Sao Paulo and traveled in the Orient. Professor Tate spent a sabbatical year in East Asian Studies at Harvard. He also joined a summer seminar at Stanford on Asian cultures and in a second summer studied in Japan. Professor Withey taught for a year at the University of Rangoon, studied Southeast Asian drama and collaborated in a study of a leading family of Burmese actors and producers.

This advanced study and field experience has been encouraged and at least partly supported by Hanover College. Additional support has been obtained from the NDEA post-doctoral fellowships in neglected languages for Professor Bowers; from a Fulbright appointment for Professor Withey to teach and do research in Burma; from NAFSA for the seminar which Professor Tate attended at Stanford; and from summer and academic-year faculty fellowships from the Indiana Non-Western Project awarded to Professor Tate to assist him to prepare his two new courses on the Civilization of East and South Asia, and to refresh and deepen his knowledge of Asian cultures. Each of these opportunities to extend their competence in a non-Western area has enabled the faculty members concerned to improve their courses relating to these regions. Their experience has also extended into all the courses they teach and into the general campus life by means of reports to college assemblies, participation in the annual institutes on Russia, India or Brazil, and publication.

## Students and Extracurricular Activities

Students at Hanover have taken an active part in helping to plan the non-Western studies program and in organizing annual institutes focusing on a world theme or an individual country such as Brazil or India. These institutes are participated in by most of the student body and faculty. Some classes are suspended for the institute, which is led by visiting American and foreign specialists and usually lasts from two to four days.

A particularly notable institute on "Christian Perspectives in Contemporary Culture" was held 8-11 March 1960. This institute had a great impact on the college community. It helped to pave the way for more attention to non-Western studies and world affairs which was incorporated into the Hanover Plan. Speakers at the Institute were: Eugene Carson Blake, Stated Clerk of the Presbyterian Church, U. S. A.; Andrew Cordier, executive assistant

165

to the Secretary-General of the UN; John Karefa-Smart, Minister of Defense and External Affairs of Sierra Leone; the author Dr Lin Yutang; Charles Malik, Lebanese Minister of Education and Foreign Affairs; Henry Margenau, Higgins Professor of Physics and National Philosophy, Yale University; and Robert E. Wilson, former chairman of the board, Standard Oil Company of Indiana.

An institute on "India: Problems and Perspectives" took place 21-22 March 1963. Four visitors from India and three Americans joined three members of the Hanover faculty as the main speakers. The Indians included a member of India's delegation to the UN, a political scientist, an artist and an educator. A State Department economist, a U. S. Information Service cultural affairs officer, who used to teach philosophy, and a sociologist comprised the visiting Americans with long experience in India. The Hanover faculty members spoke on "The American Image and India," "Education in India," and "India and Non-Alignment."

A special student contribution was the presentation of the traditional Indian comedy *The Clay Cart*, attributed to King Shudraka. Almost the entire college took part in this institute, which more than 300 students and faculty helped to organize. Student funds from the budget of the Public Affairs Forum and a subvention from the Indiana Non-Western Project helped to cover expenses.

Students and faculty state that the periodic reports of the American Universities Field Staff, supplemented by one or two visits from AUFS members each year, have proved effective adjuncts to formal courses on non-Western areas. Because of its fairly isolated location, Hanover College has been particularly glad to receive regular help in getting visiting speakers, artists or exhibits to the campus, or in sending students and faculty to conferences relating to non-Western regions. Visitors have come under the auspices of organizations such as AUFS, the Arts Program of the Association of American Colleges, and the Asia Society. Conferences have been sponsored by the Indiana Non-Western Project and the Cincinnati Council of World Affairs. The college also has an active international club.

## Student Exchange

Very few students study abroad for credit in non-Western areas. From two to four did so each year between 1961 and 1964. In 1963-64 there were five. Two at the American University of Beirut and one each in Japan and Nigeria were studying under the Presbyterian junior year abroad program. Hanover attracts few foreign students and in 1963-64 had only seven, four of them from non-Western areas. Two of these had scholarships from the college.

## Library

The library grew 32 per cent in the five years ending in 1963. Gifts from Lilly Endowment and the Kellogg Foundation have facilitated major additions to the library stacks and book purchases. The staff has increased to three professional librarians. In 1963-64 there were 73,000 volumes and the library received over 550 periodicals. It then budgeted $19,900 for books and $4,300 for additional accessions, exclusive of special grants. Roughly ten per cent of the books and periodicals then being purchased related to non-Western studies. Between 1962 and 1964 some 600 books on East and South Asia were catalogued.

The library holdings were rated as follows in regard to non-Western courses offered. In terms of instruction and student research, "good" for East Asia, Latin America and Slavic studies; "adequate" for Asia generally, South and Southeast Asia; "poor" for other areas. For purposes of faculty research, holdings were rated "good" for Slavic studies; "adequate" for Asia in general, East Asia and Latin America; "poor" for other regions. Hanover considered that its best collections were on China, Japan and Russia, and that it was "still weak in India and Southeast Asia." They identified their greatest needs as books and periodicals on Africa, the Middle East and South Asia, with back files of periodicals and major sets of references required for all areas. President Horner's annual report for 1962-63 noted that . . . "use of the library increased by fifty per cent over the previous year; and greater responsibility for the learning process was placed on the student."

## Future Plans

Hanover plans no immediate major changes in its non-Western offerings. There has been discussion about providing more opportunities to learn about Africa and the Middle East, probably by means of visiting lecturers from those areas or scholars competent to teach about them, in alternate years. In two or three years there may be another appointment made of someone who can assist with the required courses on Asian Civilization.

## Conclusion

The Hanover Plan's provision for two required courses in non-Western areas has thus far been implemented primarily by Professor Tate and two or three other members of the faculty. Excepting two courses on Russian history and two on Brazilian and Spanish-American literature, there are few specialized courses which interested students can take to follow up their introduction to non-Western cultures.

There appears to be some likelihood that faculty members in such fields as art, political science, philosophy, religion and sociology might respond to fresh opportunities to extend their competence to the non-Western world by taking part in a faculty seminar or related activity. This would in turn foster further infusion of non-Western perspectives into their courses. Unless present faculty members continue to extend their competence, or new staff members with non-Western specialization are appointed, there is obviously little prospect of either offering more advanced courses dealing with the non-Western world or introducing additional non-Western languages.

The plan's prospectus declared in 1961 that off-campus study might "very possibly be one of the most interesting directions in which the college can move." It suggested that:

> The five-week program away from campus can profitably be developed first, by study and research at university centers for advanced undergraduates and for faculty; second, by experimentation in correlating study on campus with work in metropolitan areas, especially in social, economic and political fields; and third, by more foreign study in

places such as Mexico, Brazil, Spain, India, Japan, Africa, and other areas. The possibility of faculty and student exchanges should be explored. There might be . . . semester or year exchanges with other United States colleges . . . and even year exchanges with foreign schools. . . . The present junior-year-abroad program should be examined and possibly expanded. . . . All of this would bring to campus other viewpoints and cultures and would help broaden the horizons of those on campus as well as those involved in the exchanges. . . . These proposals remain to be implemented, or modified by subsequent experimentation.

Hanover College's achievement in non-Western studies is unlikely to reach its full potential unless past progress is supplemented by further enterprise. Advances commensurate with the ideals of the administration and faculty depend on dynamic development along the lines proposed in the Hanover Plan, or in other directions that may be suggested by recent experience.

# 7

# MARIAN COLLEGE

Marian College illustrates what resourceful administrators and teachers can achieve in extending faculty competence and enriching the curriculum with non-Western perspectives by capitalizing on existing opportunities for faculty development. The initiative of a few teachers, the president and the dean has resulted in on- and off-campus opportunities for over a quarter of the faculty to extend their knowledge of non-Western areas. This has enabled them to infuse new perspectives into many courses, offer fourteen courses devoted primarily to non-Western areas and eight others dealing in part with them.

The college has accomplished this mainly out of its own budget, supplemented by various fellowships open to its faculty, and without any major financial assistance. The emphasis has been upon developing existing faculty resources and changing the character of the curriculum rather than on introducing many new courses. The Project for Extending the Study of Foreign Areas in Indiana Undergraduate Education has provided significant encouragement and help for faculty fellowships, for recruiting visiting specialists, for facilitating periodic visits by members of the American Universities Field Staff, for attendance at conferences and in other ways.

Marian College, Indianapolis, Indiana. President Francis J. Reine. (Roman Catholic; coeducational; semester system; liberal arts and teacher training to bachelor's degree; 787 students)

Marian College has also developed affiliations with three institutions in India, Japan and Peru, which provide for the regular admission of a few of their students to Marian annually. Another affiliation enables at least one Marian graduate each year to teach English in Kyoto for two years.

## Historical Background

These developments at Marian began to take shape in the spring of 1958 after a visit from John M. Thompson, associate professor of history at Indiana University, when he was collaborating with Robert F. Byrnes, chairman of the department of history at Indiana University, in a survey of non-Western studies in Indiana colleges. As a result of Professor Thompson's discussions with administration and faculty, the chairman of the history department at Marian was asked to review the prospects for non-Western studies for undergraduates in liberal arts colleges and to ascertain what Marian might undertake along these lines. Sister Mary Carol made a report at the North Central Liberal Arts Workshop held at the University of Minnesota in June 1958. She reported that the study of non-Western cultures as an integral element in the curriculum existed at very few undergraduate colleges. She added that Marian's curriculum was essentially traditional and Western-oriented, but that a few upper-class courses provided some information about Far Eastern history, Latin American history and literature, world religions and world geography.[1]

These preliminary inquiries led the administration to establish a *Committee on Non-Western Studies* in September 1958. Non-Western studies at Marian have developed out of a systematic survey of institutional resources which suggested action in four key areas. These have emphasized:

1. The professional growth of the existing faculty and the provision of opportunities for them to extend their competence to non-Western areas;

---

1. Latin American history and literature have been taught at Marian College for the last fifteen or twenty years and therefore were not covered by Sister Mary Carol's survey or by the report of the Committee on Non-Western Studies, mentioned below.

2. Curricular revision, with emphasis on infusing non-Western data and perspectives into established courses rather than on the introduction of new courses;

3. The modest expansion of library holdings relating to the non-Western world, primarily in close relation to courses taught;

4. Special co-curricular programs and activities open to the entire college and to the public as a supplement to regular courses or faculty seminars.

The aim of Marian's non-Western studies program has been to provide "in its formal course of studies and in its planned activities opportunities for all students to develop at least an awareness of and interest in peoples and societies other than Western, and if possible, to go beyond that to the attainment of an understanding and appreciation of these peoples and societies."[2] This aim began to be implemented through the four means listed above.

### The Institutional Inventory

The first stage in 1958-59 was mainly concerned with an institutional inventory. With the willing cooperation of the faculty, each department reported on the type and scope of non-Western materials used in each course and on any plans which it had to develop more attention to the non-Western world in its courses. This analysis confirmed Sister Mary Carol's impressions, but revealed that certain non-Western materials were used to illustrate points or to furnish comparisons in some courses in education, sociology, home economics, journalism, literature and art.

The survey also indicated that departments planned to introduce more non-Western materials into existing courses, mainly by broadening their scope. The department of English hoped to add a semester to World Literature in order to include examples of Asian and Middle Eastern literature. Sociology wanted to include more examples from Asia in the courses on Minorities and on Rural-Urban Sociology. The history department was the only one which recommended a new course designed to introduce non-Western cultures to lowerclassmen, so that they would have

---

2.   Report of the Committee on Non-Western Studies, 1962, p. 5

an early exposure to different societies and in the hope that some might continue such studies as upperclassmen.

This institutional inventory helped to consolidate faculty interest in non-Western studies. The intent was that these should "permeate the entire curriculum rather than be the interest of one department, and that this was to be accomplished primarily by altering the perspective in existing courses and by integrating the new materials into the courses rather than through the introduction of many new courses."[3] The lack of faculty competence in non-Western areas, of adequate library resources and finances, among other problems, were clearly recognized, but the committee, faculty and administration determined to move ahead on the four fronts mentioned above, concentrating mainly on the professional growth of serving faculty members. The college recognized from the start that it had little prospect of attracting and retaining teachers with non-Western area specialization, who are in short supply and great demand.

## Extending Faculty Competence

President Reine, Dean Sister Olivia, two members of the history department and a member of the foreign languages department took the lead in seeking out opportunities to extend the competence of faculty members by two chief means. The first was a series of annual faculty seminars dealing with major world areas in succession, which began in 1960. The second was summer or academic-year study at major university centers, sometimes coupled with travel abroad. Some teachers have also traveled in non-Western areas without prior advanced study relating to these regions. A quarter of the faculty has also learned more about non-Western societies by attending local and national conferences, lectures and exhibits.

## Faculty Seminars

There have been annual faculty seminars for in-service study of a non-Western area each year since 1960. In 1960-61 twelve

---

3. Ibid.

teachers studied the Middle East. The next year the focus was on China, the following year on Japan, and in 1963-64 on India. Planning for the next year's seminar usually takes place in the spring of the previous year. Particularly at the start, but also during each year, Marian staff have been assisted in their faculty seminars by specialists from Indiana University. The college also received a subvention of a few hundred dollars from the Indiana Non-Western Studies Project to assist with the expenses of consultants and visiting specialists for the first seminar.

Seminars meet about once a month for two to three hours. During the first semester, a *visiting area specialist* meets with the group to give a talk or read a paper and share in discussions of the topic or of outside readings. At the start the emphasis is on the historical and political development of the non-Western area being studied, in order to lead up to study of more contemporary issues during the second semester. Professor Vatikiotis of the department of government at Indiana University met with the first faculty seminar on the Middle East regularly each month during the first semester. Then a series of four specialists on the Middle East, representing different disciplines, and others with first-hand experience in the area took the lead in the seminars during the second semester. Each of the specialists met first with all interested members of the faculty and the next day just with members of the seminar.

William D. Schorger, associate professor of anthropology and Near East studies at the University of Michigan, spoke on village life among various ethnic groups in North Africa. Charles F. Stewart, associate professor of international business at Columbia, explained the characteristics of Middle Eastern economics and major economic issues of the area. Professor Majid Khadduri of Johns Hopkins spoke on the role of Islam in the modern Middle East and shared his knowledge of Islamic law. Dr Louis Dupree, an anthropologist specializing in Indo-European linguistic areas, explained the social organization of Afghan villages, during his visit as a member of the American Universities Field Staff. This visit was made possible by a special joint subscription arrangement between Indiana University, Marian and a few other Indiana colleges under the auspices of the statewide Non-Western Studies

Project. Gilbert Tutungi, a graduate of Cairo University and former teacher at the American University of Beirut, who had joined the English department staff at Marian College in 1960, gave two talks on urban-rural social relations in Egypt and Lebanon. The Reverend James Armstrong, pastor of a local church, reported on his recent visit to the Middle East and on political leaders in the Arab world. Rabbi Maurice Davis of the Indianapolis Hebrew Congregation discussed Israel's social problems.

Sister Mary Carol, chairman of the history department, served as coordinator of this first faculty seminar. The seminar was open to all faculty members. No additional remuneration or released time was made available to participants, who were expected to read widely and to prepare papers for the seminar. Sixteen faculty members took part in the seminar at first, and twelve of these were regular participants. This pattern has been used for subsequent seminars, although in 1963-64 there was less reliance on outside specialists and particular attention was given to the fine arts and music of India, mainly interpreted by Marian faculty members, with exhibits, slides and movies.

During the first three years of the faculty seminars, *sixteen teachers from eleven departments took part in one or more of the seminars.* This represents roughly one third of the full-time teaching staff. A core of eight faculty members from the departments of art, English, French, German, home economics, history, sociology and Spanish took part in all three seminars. Four other faculty members took part in two out of three seminars, and four more in one seminar. In addition to the departments listed above, teachers of education, Latin, philosophy and theology, and the librarian, took part in at least one seminar.

Marian College finds the faculty seminar an essential element in its continuing efforts to extend the competence of existing faculty to non-Western areas and plans to continue annual seminars. The college would like to find funds to provide for a visiting specialist to spend a semester each year on the campus. He would direct a *weekly* faculty seminar, teach a class in his discipline relating to a non-Western area and work individually with members of the faculty who wish to carry on more intensive non-Western study. A less satisfactory alternative would be to have a specialist visit the college twice a month to lead the faculty seminar and perhaps speak in classes or in public as heretofore. The college would have liked to provide for about one quarter released time from teaching for seminar participants but has not been able to find the necessary funds or part-time instructors for this purpose. Some administrators and faculty members believe that released time is less important and effective than summer or longer leaves of absence for more intensive study at a major university, and this is what Marian has encouraged in practice.

## Off-Campus Study and Travel

Nine of the participants in the faculty seminars engaged in further study or travel in non-Western areas, at major universities or in the field, between 1959 and 1964. Four other faculty members did likewise. They did so under a wide variety of auspices, primarily on fellowships supported by different agencies. Most of this study and travel was undertaken in the summer. Four faculty members studied throughout an academic year, and ten studied for at least a summer. Another spent a semester traveling around the world to study education in New Guinea, South Asia and the Middle East in particular. Two teachers have devoted three summers and an academic year to study of Russian civilization and language and to South Asia, Japan and China, respectively. The first has visited Russia and Eastern Europe twice. The second studied and traveled in Japan in the summer of 1961.

Fellowship support for this faculty study and travel has been furnished by a number of foundations, institutions and other organizations, notably: the Asia Society, the Carnegie Corporation of New York, the University of Chicago, Columbia University, the Ford Foundation, Project for Extending the Study of Foreign Areas in Indiana Undergraduate Education, the Japan Society and the U. S. Office of Education (under the National Defense Education Act of 1958).

As a result of these opportunities, and the initiative of individuals, by 1964 ten members of Marian's faculty had engaged in study and travel in one or more non-Western areas. Four had been in the Middle East, four in Latin America, three in the Pacific and South Asia, two in the Far East and two in Eastern Europe and Russia. Most of this study and travel was based on prior study in the faculty seminar or independently and was undertaken with specific curricular aims in view. Consequently, there has been a high degree of integration into existing courses of knowledge derived about non-Western areas through the faculty seminar, further off-campus study and travel.

## Participation in Conferences and Other Off-Campus Activities

Marian has found that administrators and faculty members have become more willing to support the development of non-Western studies as a result of participation in local and national conferences, workshops, exhibits and other activities designed to foster better understanding of the neglected areas of the world. Over a quarter of the faculty have been made more aware of the role of non-Western studies in liberal education by such activities. The national conferences held at Indiana University on Non-Western Studies in Undergraduate Education in 1958, and on Asian Studies and State Universities in 1959 spurred Marian College's representatives to seek ways to introduce such studies on their own campus.

Local conferences are said to have been more directly influential than national meetings in encouraging non-Western studies at Marian, because they suggested practical ways to implement plans and to compare experiences with other colleges. They also offered opportunities for Marian to extend its offerings on the non-Western world by cooperative projects with other institutions. A series of meetings in 1959 at which Indiana college and university teachers met to evaluate an experimental course on Russian history offered over TV for credit, and Sister Mary Carol's membership from 1960 onward in the state advisory committee for the Non-Western Studies Project in Indiana have been cited as examples.

In the spring of 1961 three members of the faculty took part in Western College for Women's Institute on China. The next year the dean and two members of the Committee on Non-

Western Studies attended a seminar at Earlham College on U. S. Education and Contemporary India. In June 1962 four Marian teachers participated in a conference on Oriental and Western Literary and Cultural Relations at Indiana University.

These formal and informal opportunities for the Marian faculty to enlarge their knowledge of non-Western areas have had a strong impact on the curriculum in two ways. First, a few new courses dealing with non-Western cultures have been introduced to broaden and deepen the curriculum. Second, non-Western materials have been integrated into several established courses.

## Curricular Change

The institutional inventory of 1958-59 showed that hardly any attention was being given to the non-Western world in lower division courses. At that time, Marian had only one course dealing solely with an Asian area—an upperclass elective in Far Eastern history—and three courses dealing with Latin America. A course on world geography and another on comparative religion touched indirectly on non-Western societies.

Two members of the history department began to correct this deficiency by offering an introductory course on Africa and the Middle East in the fall of 1959. A companion course on Asian Civilizations was offered in the second semester of the academic year 1959-60. The Asian course covers China, India and Japan, and both courses focus on traditional societies. Student response to these courses grew from 7 and 12 respectively in 1959-60 to 12 and 23 in 1960-61, and 29 and 26 in 1961-62. Enrolments have since leveled off close to the 1960-61 figures. The courses seem to have encouraged a number of students to take other courses on non-Western areas as they became available, to read more widely and, in some cases, to plan their careers in relation to one or other of these regions.

Since 1958 a total of twelve new courses dealing primarily with non-Western areas have been introduced: Oriental Art (offered through the Herron Museum of Art); three history courses, on Africa and the Middle East, Asian Civilizations, and

Russia since 1700; Eastern Literature; Latin American Culture; four courses in Russian language, and two in Russian literature. These are all semester courses.

In 1963-64, about a quarter of Marian's students elected one or more of 22 courses that deal in one way or another with non-Western cultures and are offered in the nine fields of anthropology, art, English, geography, history, religion, Russian, sociology and Spanish. Fourteen of these 22 courses were concerned mainly with a non-Western area—seven of them with Russian language, literature and history; the other eight were of the infusion type.

Infusion has been achieved mainly through the incorporation in courses of sections or units dealing with non-Western areas, or through illustration and comparison. Teachers who have taken part in one or other aspect of non-Western studies have become aware of such possibilities and have learned concrete ways of infusing new data into their own courses. Visiting specialists, particularly American Universities Field Staff members, have fostered this trend by their talks in class, their consultations with faculty and students and their published reports, to which Marian subscribes.

Comparative Religion and World Geography represented the first approach to infusion. While both were offered before 1958, these courses have now been enriched with further non-Western data and perspectives. In fact, so much attention is now devoted to Oriental religions in the Comparative Religion course that the department has considered changing its title to Eastern Religions. The introductory course in sociology and those on minorities and on rural-urban relationships have been broadened beyond their former focus on the United States to include examples and data from Southeast Asia and other non-Western regions derived from the chairman of the department's experience in the faculty seminar and study at the University of Hawaii. Lesser degrees of infusion have taken place in art, drama, education, home economics, history and political science courses. It is planned to develop units on Oriental philosophy for the course on the History of Philosophy.

## Library

There were 40,000 volumes in the Marian College library in 1963-64. It was receiving 272 periodicals and spending $10,200 for books and $1000 for periodicals per year. Some 16 per cent of the books and 6-7 per cent of the periodicals then being added to the library related primarily to the non-Western courses offered. The vital importance of the library to non-Western studies has been recognized from the start. One of the first steps in the institutional inventory was to ascertain that at the start of the academic year 1958-59 there were 232 volumes in the library on non-Western areas. The Committee on Non-Western Studies has worked closely with the librarian to secure basic bibliographies such as that issued by the American Universities Field Staff and to order key books. Faculty members and departments have been encouraged to obtain necessary books and periodicals dealing with the non-Western world. The departments of art, economics, history, literature, religion and sociology have taken the lead in making significant additions to the collections in their disciplines. About a sixth of the subvention for the first faculty seminar, amounting to $120, was spent for books on the Middle East.

The growth of the library's holdings on non-Western areas was at the rate of some 180 volumes annually between 1958 and 1963. Roughly $1000-$1500 has been spent for non-Western books and periodicals each year. These modest sums have been employed to purchase a core of essential texts, references and other works directly relevant to the faculty seminars and the courses being offered at Marian. The three areas of greatest need are Africa, South and Southeast Asia. While the staff acknowledges that "certain areas are still very weak," they believe that "on the whole . . . the college is making excellent progress in providing the essential tools for the proper development of the non-Western scholastic program."

## Co-Curricular Activities

The college has sponsored three types of co-curricular programs to extend awareness of the non-Western world to the entire college community and to supplement class and independent study. Guest lecturers from non-Western areas, experts on these regions, and cultural exhibits on Asian civilization have all made their contribution to global perspectives at Marian.

Membership in the American Universities Field Staff has been "the most important single force to make a favorable impact on the entire college community in support of the non-Western program . . ." according to the Committee on Non-Western Studies. The Indiana Project worked out an arrangement whereby five smaller colleges in Indiana joined with the university in subscribing to a membership in AUFS, with each college paying $750 per year and the university carrying the rest of the cost. In return, each college was to receive five copies of the reports of all AUFS associates in various non-Western areas and one two-day visit per year from a staff member. Marian elected to pay $1500 for two AUFS visits annually. AUFS specialists normally speak in classes and at college assemblies, lead seminar discussions, consult with faculty members and meet informally with students and teachers to share their up-to-date knowledge and insights about significant but often lesser-known peoples and regions of the world. They often speak in public as part of the community service of the college. When the administration proposed to delete the AUFS joint membership fees from the budget for 1963-64 as an economy measure, the student body protested, the faculty voted to continue the program, and the funds were restored to the budget.

*Cultural exhibits* have included some booked nationally by the Asia Society or the Smithsonian Institution and others organized within the state by the Indiana Project. They have ranged from Indonesian folk art to Thai sites and monuments, the culture and geography of the Mekong River Valley, early Chinese masters, and the sculpture, paintings and textiles of East India. Japanese students at Marian were inspired to prepare an exhibit on their country after they saw the one on the Mekong River Valley. The college believes that these co-curricular programs "have been very well received and have won for the non-Western program the strong and enthusiastic support of the student body and faculty."

## Overseas Institutional Affiliation, Foreign Students and Study Abroad

Marian is one of relatively few U. S. colleges which have a regular program to admit students from certain institutions in non-Western countries. Since 1961 it has admitted each year two new students from the Clarist Congregation, Chalakudy East, Kerala, India. In 1963 six Indian students were enrolled. Marian has also welcomed students from Religiosas Terciarias de San Francisco de Asis, Lima, Peru since 1961 and three were enrolled in 1963. One new student every other year comes from Fugi Women's College, Sapporo, Hokkaido, Japan. Two students from there were enrolled at Marian College in 1963-64. Each year, at least one Marian graduate goes to teach conversational English at Notre Dame Jogakuin, Kyoto, Japan for a two-year period.

Marian also welcomes students from abroad on an individual basis. There were 21 from non-Western areas in 1963-64. Sixteen of them were granted scholarships by the college. Such students are used occasionally as resource persons in classes and on panels, radio, TV or civic information programs and they sponsor exhibits on their countries from time to time.

No Marian students have yet studied in a non-Western area for credit during the academic year, although the college welcomes such a prospect under proper supervision. In 1963 three students received credit for summer study in Mexico.

## Conclusion

Marian College has made considerable progress toward its goal of extending the competence of at least a third of its faculty in order to integrate non-Western studies into the curriculum and general life of the institution. President Reine and the Committee on Non-Western Studies plan to continue their fourfold emphasis for the next few years. They will be able to draw upon some continuing assistance from the Indiana Project, at least until 1966. They hope to encourage more faculty members to take part in seminars and to take advantage of other opportunities for study and travel, in order to learn more about non-Western areas. They also hope that teachers already engaged in this process can deepen their knowledge and refine their courses. They would like to accelerate these trends with the help of special funds, but if these do not materialize, they are determined to carry on with their own resources.

Meanwhile Marian has proved that much can be accomplished within the normal budget of a small college provided that the commitment of key members of the faculty and administration can be enlisted to support the growth of non-Western studies.

# 8

# MILLS COLLEGE

"Each Mills student, whatever her special field of interest, must become accustomed to thinking in world perspectives and intercultural terms. It is our hope and intention that no student will graduate from Mills who has not achieved a reasonable working insight into at least one culture other than her own." In these terms President C. Easton Rothwell recently stated the goals of the new program for the understanding of non-Western cultures upon which the college has embarked. The program carries into effect an aspiration he had expressed shortly before assuming the presidency of Mills in 1959: "for the college in the years just ahead . . . there will be more emphasis upon comparative civilizations than upon only western civilizations. This should affect the teaching of history, literature, philosophy and the arts. It should also influence the study of society and of political institutions. One can foresee the stirring of the imagination and the release of new creative energies."

By 1961 the faculty and administration began to implement an improved program of non-Western studies. They moved into action to extend the competence of existing faculty members by means of faculty seminars and other study and travel opportunities, and to appoint a small number of new, key faculty members with special competence in non-Western cultures.

Mills College, Oakland, California. President C. Easton Rothwell. (Private; women; semester system; liberal arts and teacher training to master's degree; 761 students)

## Historical Background

The aspirations expressed by President Rothwell have long been shared at Mills. They are as old as the founders, Cyrus and Susan Mills, who had been educational missionaries in Ceylon and the Sandwich Islands before acquiring in the 1850's the young seminary that grew into Mills College. The rich heritage they left was both cherished and developed by their successors. President Aurelia H. Reinhardt visited China and Japan in the 1920's, encouraged students from the Orient to attend Mills and fostered the development of courses to help American students learn more about the Far East.

Dr Lynn T. White, who followed Dr Reinhardt, stressed the importance of Asian studies in his 1943 inaugural address on "The Reconstruction of Humanism" and subsequently developed the theme in *Educating our Daughters* (1951):

> . . . we Americans limit our horizon with the blinders of a North American education, which gives us no understanding of the ancient, proud and in many ways sophisticated peoples whom we face across the Pacific. . . .
> The cure will not be complete until, in the minds of educated Americans, Tu Fu and Li Po are as inseparably linked as Shelley and Keats, until the names of Ashoka, Abu Bekr and Shi Hwang Ti ring no more strangely to our ears than those of Caesar or Charlemagne. . . .

There has also been a strong foundation of faculty support at Mills for the study of Asian civilizations. There was enthusiasm for President Reinhardt's early introduction of courses on the Asian region. The first undergraduate course in Oriental art was introduced in 1927 by Anna Cox Brinton, who served as dean of the faculty. Katherine Caldwell, lecturer in the history of art, has taught Chinese and Japanese art and a survey of Oriental art at Mills since 1951. She has done field research in India, Japan and Europe and is a founder-director of the Society for Asian Art in San Francisco.

Courses on Oriental philosophies and religions were introduced by Professor Elliot Diller in 1939. He is a former student of Pratt at Williams and of Hocking and Whitehead at Harvard. He was a delegate to the International Congress for the History of Religions in Tokyo in 1958 and spent several months studying and traveling in Japan, Southeast Asia, India and Nepal. He has done research on the effects of World War II on religion in Japan and the subsequent disestablishment of Shinto. He teaches semester courses on the religions of India, China, Japan and the Near East.

During the 1950's courses relating to the non-Western world were also available in comparative politics, the government of the USSR, Spanish American literature, the development of economic thought, and current economic problems. These courses then provided the only opportunities for students at Mills to learn about non-Western regions.

Two summer programs that gave further expression to the interest of the college in cultures other than those of the traditional West came into being soon after President White assumed the presidency in 1943. The first was the *English Language Institute* whose goal was to offer foreign students newly arrived in the United States opportunities to improve their command of English and to learn something about American history, culture and folkways before the start of their formal academic training on various campuses in the United States.

During and shortly after World War II, most of the students attending this institute came from Latin America. After the war the emphasis was on Asian students, with the majority since 1950 coming from the Ryukyu Islands. The English Language Institute was most recently directed by Evaline Uhl Wright, associate professor of dramatic arts and a member of the 1963-64 faculty seminar on non-Western studies. Miss Wright spent a semester in 1962-63 on sabbatical leave studying Far Eastern theatre in Asia and was a member of the seminar on Southeast Asia convened by the Center for South and Southeast Asian Studies at the University of Michigan in the summer of 1964.

The second enterprise was *a center for Chinese studies* called Chung Kuo Yuan. This was planned in 1943 and began in the summer of 1944. Courses in Chinese language, art and history were offered. Participants were expected to speak Chinese as much as they could and were housed in what is now called Alderwood Hall, which the Mills catalogue claimed "was perhaps the only academic building in the United States essentially Chinese in its architectural style." This summer program in Chinese language and culture studies had to be discontinued after three years because, probably as a result of the war and its aftermath, not enough students applied for the program.

Thus, when Mills College decided to broaden and deepen its non-Western studies after 1959, it was able to build on these faculty resources and on courses leading to majors in the history of art and religion which included established offerings in Asian art and religion.

### Faculty and Administrative Initiative

In the years since 1959 the college, availing itself of past achievements, has taken steps to strengthen and give coherence to its teaching about cultures other than those of the West. These steps were aided by a systematic analysis of the resources of the college, a reorganization of the faculty and a careful review of the curriculum. The curricular review, touching all aspects of the work at Mills, was begun in 1958-59, when the faculty Committee on Educational Policy appointed an interdisciplinary *ad hoc* committee of five to make searching inquiry into what was being done and what should be done. In September 1960 the *ad hoc* committee, having considered the needs for more consistent but selective emphasis upon non-Western civilizations, reported in part as follows:

> There are many areas which in the contemporary world call for attention: Latin America, Sub-Saharan Africa, North Africa and the Middle East, and the various areas of Asia. These are too many and too varied for comprehensive attention in a college the size of Mills. It would be self-defeating to attempt to spread our resources so thinly. Our goal should be the provision of the opportunity to explore with some thoroughness two or three of these areas, which in turn will enrich our traditional emphasis on the cultures of Western Europe and North America. It will doubtless prove most practicable to build on our existing offerings in languages, religion, art history and government

(Latin America, the Middle East, India, China, Japan, Soviet Union), but the Committee believes this question can best be resolved by the faculty, and only calls attention to the need for supplementation in the fields of anthropology, the arts, economics, government, history, literature in translation and sociology. Owing to the smallness of the college we do not recommend the addition of any of the "esoteric" languages or even of the major but more difficult languages such as Hindi, Chinese or Japanese.

The faculty supported this view, as did the president and the dean of the faculty. Accordingly, four specialists joined the faculty between 1960 and 1963. Dr Robert Anderson, associate professor of sociology and anthropology, was appointed in 1960. Dr Edward LeFevour, an historian of China who knows Chinese and has resided in the Far East, was appointed in 1962 and began teaching courses on the history of East and South Asia and of Russia in 1963. Lawrence Shrader, a specialist on Asian comparative government and particularly on the politics of India and Pakistan, joined the staff in 1963-64.

In 1961 the college invited Professor Harold H. Fisher, former director of the Hoover Institution and professor of history at Stanford, to join the faculty as a John Hay Whitney visiting professor. He was asked to teach a course in international relations and another on Russian history and to conduct a faculty seminar. The college also decided to provide one quarter released time out of the regular budget of the college for six of the seven faculty participants in the proposed seminar.

It was only after these decisions had been taken that the Asia Society supplied modest funds to assist in providing outside consultants for the 1961-62 seminar. The Mills drive to establish Asian studies was then facilitated by a grant of $132,000 from the Ford Foundation for a three-year period from December 1962. The grant was to help Mills to carry forward the faculty seminar, assist in the development of a new course on the "styles" of culture, provide for faculty study and travel abroad, and strengthen library holdings on non-Western areas.

After receipt of the Ford grant, Professor Charles Larsen, then chairman of the division of social sciences, was appointed coordinator of non-Western activities. Various groupings of faculty members and administrative officers have been convened to deal with such matters as the handling of faculty applications for travel and study grants and the feasibility of study in Asia for selected Mills students.

## Faculty Seminars

The two faculty seminars, held in 1961-62 and 1963-64, have been crucial in developing faculty interest and extending the competence of participants to Asia. The membership of the seminars has been widely representative of the various disciplines and divisional groupings of the faculty. A majority of the participants from thirteen departments have been fairly senior members of the staff with tenure. As Professor Fisher led both seminars and Dr Anderson also took part in both, there has been substantial continuity. Moreover, all but two of the participants in these seminars are still teaching at Mills.

The first seminar met for two hours weekly during the 1961-62 academic year. It reviewed non-Western programs in operation on other campuses and analyzed how the curriculum at Mills could be revised in order to

> increase the use of non-Western materials and emphases, and provide the participants the chance to study non-Western materials in their own fields and to learn from their colleagues the ways in which such materials were already being employed. It was from this group that the recommendation for an interdisciplinary course emerged.

Participants represented a broad range of disciplines.

| | | |
|---|---|---|
| Dr Robert Anderson | — | Anthropology |
| Mrs Katherine Caldwell | — | Art History |
| Dr Elliot Diller | — | Religion |
| Dr Robert Johnston | — | Government |
| Dr Charles Larsen | — | History |
| Dr Marion Ross | — | Economics |
| Dr Allan Wendt | — | Literature |

During the year between faculty seminars, Dr Fisher and his research associate, Mrs Rosemary Hornby, developed the broad outlines of an interdisciplinary course concentrating on India. They were assisted by Drs Anderson, Larsen and Ross, who had spent the summer in Asia, and other members of the original seminar. In the fall semester the second faculty seminar was organized. The seminar began by studying the Indian experimental course and later assisted in applying the same concepts to China and in developing a program of study for the new course. Members of the first seminar met from time to time with this second group during the spring sessions.

The second seminar met, also for two hours weekly, throughout the 1963-64 academic year. The members "took" the course and contributed to its further development. The syllabus for the new "styles of culture" course was developed by members of the following departments in this seminar:

| | | |
|---|---|---|
| Dr Robert Anderson | — | Anthropology |
| Dr Dorothy Babcock | — | Education |
| Dr Darl Bowers | — | Biology |
| Mr George Brown | — | Mathematics |
| Dr Robert Edgren | — | Psychology |
| Dr Esther Lee Mirmow | — | Psychology |
| Mr Morton Subotnick | — | Music |
| Miss Evaline Wright | — | Dramatic Arts |

The new course rests upon the premise that in analyzing the "styles" of culture in any civilization, it is important to understand the ways in which religious beliefs have influenced and continue to influence people, and how values and norms affect modernization, particularly in contemporary Indian or Chinese civilization where one is dealing with the problem of different types of transition from a traditional to a modern society. The following list of six problems faced by traditional Asian societies in transition illustrates the kind of issues studied in the second faculty seminar.

1. How do the people of the village or small community in the traditional societies being studied cope with problems of providing for their material wants? In what respects are the nature of the wants and the modes of providing for them distinctive or characteristic of these societies?

2. How have the people of a small community of a traditional society dealt with problems of living together and cooperating in a social system? What is characteristic or distinctive in the societies being studied in regard to these matters?

3. How do the people of small communities in traditional societies cope with the problems arising from the human need for an explanation of man and his environment and the desire for objects of worship?

4. How does the nation state, the entity into which the small and large communities of the society being studied are incorporated, deal with the problems of the scope and organization of state power, the rights and duties of citizens, national unity and international relations?

5. How is the nation state dealing with problems of economic and social development?

6. How are the policy decision makers and the leaders in the arts and intellectual expression coping with the problem of reconciling the cultural heritage with the new concepts and ways of life now being introduced?

## Faculty Study and Travel Abroad

Opportunities for faculty research and travel in Asia are given high priority in developing non-Western studies at Mills. The administration hopes that by the end of 1965 at least one third of the faculty will have had an opportunity to travel, study, teach or do research in Asia and that key members of the administration will also have had first-hand exposure to Asia. In pursuit of this goal, two participants in the first faculty seminar spent the summer of 1962 in India and another in Nationalist China. A fourth seminar member studied in India in the summer of 1963 and a fifth plans to be in India for the summer of 1965. The administration has assisted interested faculty members to win awards for the Fulbright summer institutes in Formosa and India and subsidized the four winners in 1962 and 1963. Two other faculty members have recently spent leaves in Asia. In the spring of 1963 President and Mrs Rothwell attended the first American Assembly in Asia at Kuala Lumpur, Malaya, and then visited alumnae and educational institutions in nine Asian countries.

### Effects of Seminars and Travel on Teachers and Courses

The results of seminar participation and travel and study in Asia have already found concrete expression in new approaches and data introduced into existing courses. The comments of participants illustrate their recognition that the experience has improved their competence as teachers in their disciplines in addition to helping them to learn a good deal about Asia. Seminar members who have been able to follow up with field experience in Asia seem to have derived the most benefit from these cumulative opportunities.

Examples of the resulting infusion appear in such courses as Mr Larsen's on the diplomatic history of the United States; Miss Ross's in economics; Mr Wendt's on the contemporary novel; Mr Anderson's in anthropology; Mrs Caldwell's in art; and Mr LeFevour's in Asian history. Mr Larsen took part in the Fulbright Institute on Chinese Civilization in Taiwan in the summer of 1962. He reports that this experience gave him a feeling for the Orient "which no amount of reading could equal." It also gave him a chance to revise course materials and look at them in a new light. Consequently he has introduced Asian materials into his course on American diplomatic history which he is now able to present in broader perspective.

Dr Ross's course on the development of economic thought has benefited from her participation in the Fulbright Institute on Indian Civilization in the summer of 1962. Miss Ross also teaches the course on the elements of economics required for the major in sociology and economics and is developing new data and approaches to this course as a result of her Asian experience.

Mr Wendt had been teaching a course entitled the Contemporary World Novel dealing with French, German and Russian novels in translation. This was a sophomore-level, one-semester course offered in alternate years and taken by about fifty students. As a participant in the 1961-62 faculty seminar he was "delighted to find out about Indian novels." He developed his interest while on a summer Fulbright grant to India in 1962. After his sabbatical leave in France in 1962-63, he utilized his course on the world novel to introduce a semester of study devoted exclusively to the contemparary Indian novel and focused on nine novels written in English. This course was offered for the first time in 1963-64 with thirty students enrolled. A student who took the course wrote: "I've learned more from this one course this semester—more about a people, a religion, a way of life—than I would have thought possible at the beginning of a class . . ."

Professor Wendt hopes that "eventually a student will be able to major in literature—not just in English literature or in French literature—for a well-founded understanding of the written expression of many countries, taught in a joint effort by faculty members who are familiar with the works in their original languages. In the meantime, Indian novels, since many of them are written in English, are a good beginning." He is also sharing his new knowledge. Thirty-five teachers came to hear him describe his new course at the Modern Language Association's annual meeting in Chicago in December 1963.

Dr Robert Anderson is an anthropologist whose previous specialization was in European culture. During the summer of 1962 he did field research on voluntary associations in Hyderabad and in nearby villages. This was an extension of his interest in voluntary associations in European urban centers and peasant life in Europe. Before his participation in the seminar and his study in India, he had had "minimum exposure to the Orient." Professor Anderson has found that his initial extension of competence into Asia has been highly fruitful. It has enabled him to deepen his research and to broaden his courses both on the ethnology of Europe and the ethnology of India.

## Curricular Changes

Mills has three major curricular emphases to strengthen non-Western studies. These are (1) the infusion of world perspectives into introductory and upperclass courses in several disciplines, particularly anthropology, art, economics, education, government, history and religion; (2) the addition of new elective courses on non-Western cultures; and (3) the development of the one-semester course on "styles" of culture at the junior-senior level. These are to be the curricular means whereby every Mills graduate will shortly have at least an elementary understanding of a non-Western society as an integral part of her liberal education.

Infusion is already substantial, as is shown by the examples cited in the preceding section. By 1963-64 Mills students could take fifteen courses dealing primarily with non-Western cultures, not counting two years of Russian language and two courses on Spanish-American literature.

The new one-semester interdisciplinary course for juniors or seniors will be a noteworthy experiment. It is designed to help students gain a useful understanding of other societies by identifying the distinctive elements of each which go to make up what the anthropologists call its style of culture and then to contrast and compare these elements. The styles of culture course will be offered to undergraduates for the first time in the autumn of 1964, concentrating on India and China. It is hoped later to include the study of Islamic civilization.

## Language

Mills has long had a reputation for effective teaching of languages. Traditionally the modern European languages have been taught by native speakers. Intensive audio-lingual techniques have not been used. But a pilot laboratory was established in 1963-64 for advanced phonetics in French and in Spanish and a language laboratory is included in a projected new classroom building. Aside from two years of Russian introduced in 1961-62, the college at present offers no instruction in non-Western languages. It is willing to grant credit to students who learn such languages elsewhere. Mills offered instruction in the Russian language during World War II and subsequently in Chinese, but registrations were low and the courses were dropped.

Considerable thought has been given to instruction in various non-Western languages, and members of the faculty, the coordinator of non-Western studies, and the administration are open to the possibility of introducing certain major non-Western languages into the curriculum at a later stage if funds and personnel to do so can be found. Meanwhile the college acts on the assumption that high-quality substantive instruction relating to non-Western cultures can be offered without teaching non-Western languages at the undergraduate level.

## Library

The Mills library is relatively large for a college of 750 students. There were 132,000 books in the library in 1963-64 and it was receiving 414 periodicals. The library was then spending $17,600 annually for accessions, of which $12,000 were allocated for books and $5,600 for periodicals. The Mills librarian estimated that ten per cent of the books and five per cent of the periodicals currently being added to the library related primarily to non-Western studies. For example, in 1963 the library purchased 150 books on South and East Asia, about two thirds of them devoted to India and Pakistan and one third to China and Japan. During the next three years the college plans to spend some $5,000 annually from the Ford Foundation grant to build up its non-Western holdings, particularly in relation to Asia.

The staff at Mills evaluated present library holdings for instruction as "good" on Asia in general and on East and South Asia. They rated holdings for instruction and student research "adequate" on Africa in general, Southeast Asia and the Middle East and for Slavic and East European studies, but "poor" for Sub-Saharan Africa, North Africa and Latin America. The library was considered "adequate" for faculty research on Asia in general, East Asia and South Asia, but "poor" for all other non-Western areas.

Mills College students buy and presumably read more books from the college book store than most other collegians. According to a recent report of the National Association of College Stores, the Mills College book store did more business with students than any of the other 1800 members of the Association in 1962-63 and earned greater profits than any comparable stores that have a standard operation and staff. The Indian novels being read in Professor Wendt's new course and beautifully illustrated works on Indian and Oriental art were on exhibit in the crowded book store in January 1964.

## Cooperation

Although Mills College is not developing its courses and programs in non-Western studies on the basis of formal sharing of faculty or courses with neighboring institutions, the college has drawn widely on the experience of other institutions. In 1961-62 specialists and consultants from the University of California, Stanford, Washington and Chicago were invited to visit the campus in order to help plan the faculty seminar and curricular revisions. Each of the consultants and two other visiting specialists on Asia spoke in a general college assembly lecture series on the non-Western world during 1961-62. Subsequently, highly qualified visitors from the University of California at Berkeley have lectured to various classes in the non-Western fields.

Mills College is willing to grant credit for courses in non-Western subjects or languages taken at other accredited institutions. It has an agreement with both the University of California and Stanford which would permit its students to take courses at those institutions in non-Western and other subjects under certain conditions.

## Students and Extracurricular Activities

Thirteen students from non-Western areas were enrolled at Mills in 1963-64 and five of them held scholarships granted by the college. In recent years between five and eight students from non-Western areas have held scholarships and been in residence at Mills annually. In the last five years no student has received credit for undergraduate study in any part of the non-Western world. But a faculty committee is now investigating the possibility of study in Asia for a small group of Mills undergraduates.

The college art gallery is used constantly for exhibits and instruction, some of it relating to non-Western cultures. The gallery has substantial holdings of Oriental art and has presented many special exhibits of Asian art during the past three decades. Faculty and students benefit from the many opportunities to visit other galleries which exhibit non-Western art in the San Francisco Bay Area and also from informal contacts with teachers and students specializing in Asia at neighboring institutions.

Students take an active role in three annual intercultural activities undertaken by the Associated Students of Mills College: an International Relations Institute, a World Affairs Conference, and a model United Nations. Each involves some study of non-Western materials as, for example, when Mills represented Burma in 1962 and Ghana in 1964 in the model United Nations.

## Conclusion

Mills College's efforts to develop a new awareness of the world and particularly Asia throughout the college community are already achieving success. By early 1964 roughly a quarter of the faculty had had some direct experience of study, teaching or travel in Asia; four teachers with special competence in non-Western societies had been appointed; at least five courses had been modified by the infusion of non-Western data; several new courses relating to the non-Western world had been introduced and were attracting good enrolments; and two groups of trained, highly interested faculty members were planning a new key course in the social sciences and the humanities, which will endeavor to introduce all freshmen to world cultures, and were deeply engaged in devising the new junior-senior level course on styles of culture.

Mills still faces unanswered questions, such as how to extend faculty competence in Asia still further and how best to enable students to study in Asia, and might try additional approaches to non-Western studies. But its enterprise has already brought it a good distance toward its goal of having both a faculty and a student body "accustomed to thinking in world perspectives and intercultural terms."

# WESTERN COLLEGE FOR WOMEN

At the start of Western College for Women's second century in 1953, the trustees adopted a resolution based on faculty proposals which set out to make Western an *international college:*

> To offer through the formal program a systematic presentation of the world's major systems of culture; to encourage through the shared experiences of international life on the campus general attitudes of goodwill toward all men and appreciation of the values of all civilizations.

Western College has adopted an institution-wide approach which endeavors to integrate world perspectives into all major aspects of campus life including faculty, student body, curriculum, library, extracurriculum and dormitory activities. It is one of the few colleges in the U. S. A. where almost all students have a chance to graduate with an informed understanding of both their own and at least one other major world culture. They learn from teachers who, as a group, speak eighteen foreign languages and have lived, studied, taught or traveled in every major world

---

Western College for Women, Oxford, Ohio. President Herrick B. Young (Private; women; semester system; liberal arts and teacher training to bachelor's degree; 446 students)

region. From ten to twelve per cent of the students come from abroad. Out of a full-time faculty of fifty, twenty have had first-hand experience in non-Western societies. Three are specialists on the Far East, Latin America and Slavic areas. The president taught for ten years in Iran.

Intercultural studies have become an integral part of the curriculum. Major world cultures are studied in annual rotation under the guidance of a visiting lecturer from the area. Each summer a group of students led by faculty members familiar with the area makes a study tour of the focal region. Consequently, between 90 and 100 per cent of the students in recent graduating classes have taken one or more courses focusing on non-Western cultures and ten per cent of the 1962 and 1963 classes took part in a summer study tour of a non-Western area.

Western has developed this program primarily out of its own modest resources. After the new plans had been put into effect, the college received a grant of $60,000 from the Carnegie Corporation to assist intercultural studies for the five year period 1956-61.

The college appears to be unique in its efforts to test scientifically the effects of the international program on its students. In the spring of 1964, the faculty established an interdepartmental committee to evaluate the total international program and recommend guidelines for its future development.


## Historical Background

Western College was originally chartered in 1853 as Western Female Seminary in what was then frontier Ohio. True to its model, Mount Holyoke Seminary, and to the pious intentions of its founders, Western encouraged its graduates to dedicate their lives to Christian service anywhere in the world. At the 25th anniversary of the seminary in 1878, the catalogue recorded that 36 former students were missionaries in such countries as China, Persia, India, Ceylon, Turkey, Burma, Siam and Syria. In succeeding years, a growing number of graduates went overseas as missionaries, and earlier ones sent their daughters back from abroad to study at their alma mater.

Western's interest in other countries took a new turn in 1902 with the enrolment of the first foreign student, Suzono Yukuyama of Tokyo. Kiku Ishihara studied at Western in 1909-13, then returned to Japan where she founded a kindergarten and a famous school for kindergarten teachers. These students started a trend which has continued ever since. In recent years an average of from ten to twelve per cent of the students at Western have come from 55 different countries.

Late in 1942, a faculty committee headed by Miss Jeremy Ingalls of the English department drew up a tentative plan for the curriculum of "a liberal arts college in world crisis." This plan provided a "blue-print for a post-war curriculum which in many ways anticipated the plan adopted in the college's centennial year. It proposes a major in 'world culture' to which various departments would contribute . . . closer correlation of departments and concerted effort to gain 'a broader and deeper appreciation of cultures outside the United States'."[1] This plan could not at once be adopted but some of its recommendations were put into effect on a trial basis in the following two summers.

During the summers of 1943 and 1944, Western held a six-week summer school with courses grouped into four major categories: The World Today, Man and the Physical World, War-Time Skills, and The World of Tomorrow. The departments of history, sociology, theater, English, religion, modern languages, biology, chemistry, home economics, mathematics, psychology, and education collaborated in these offerings. The plan took effect in modified form after the new emphasis on intercultural studies was introduced in 1954.

After World War II, President Henderson encouraged foreign students to attend Western by increasing the number of scholarships for the assistantships in modern languages established in the 1920's, and appointing a faculty committee to cooperate with the Institute of International Education and other organizations to secure students from abroad.

---

1.   Nelson, N., *The Western College for Women*, 1853-1953, Oxford, Ohio, 1954, pp. 208-211

Professor Edward W. Pohlman, a sociologist with long experience in India, was appointed dean of the college in 1952 and served as acting president from July 1953 to January 1954, when President Herrick B. Young assumed office. Under their leadership, and building on expressed faculty wishes, Western set out to become more effectively international. The original faculty recommendation urged "that changes be introduced gradually and experimentally and as need arises . . . that general education be an integral part of the curriculum . . . but that . . . the core of the curriculum remain the liberal arts. . . ."

The plan to build Western into an international liberal arts college for women had three main features. The first was "to create an international life on campus." The second was to transform the curriculum into an "interculturally-oriented program of higher education." The third was "that the number of foreign students be increased gradually towards a possible proportion of 50-50 in the student body." Experience has shown that this optimistic goal is hard to attain and not necessarily desirable for the time being. Western began to implement these recommendations of the faculty and trustees in 1954. The faculty has been internationalized: forty per cent are natives of other countries or have studied, taught or traveled abroad and speak one or more foreign languages. The curriculum has been enriched by infusing new materials into established courses and adding certain key courses such as the Development of World Civilizations. International life on the campus is fostered by the substantial proportion of students from abroad, who represent 25 to 30 countries and about one tenth of the total enrolment. Each year intercultural studies focus on one of four major world areas: Africa, Latin America, the Middle East and the Far East.

## Faculty Resources

Western has concentrated on three main methods of developing faculty recources for its intercultural studies. The first has been to provide means by which members of the faculty may develop and deepen their knowledge of other parts of the world. The second has been the appointment of a small number of new faculty members with specialized skills and experience relative to the non-Western world. The third has been the regular use of visiting scholars from the world region under particular study for the year, who teach and act as resource persons.

Each spring a *faculty seminar* meets weekly for about six weeks for discussions, papers and movies relating to the world area which is to be the main focus during the next academic year. Attendance at these seminars is voluntary. Lists of suggested readings are supplied but homework is not required. Faculty members or visiting experts on the area prepare talks or papers as the basis for discussion, which is not specialized but aims at an interdisciplinary approach and a general introduction to the region.

For example, in the spring of 1963, the faculty seminar on the Middle East met on six Monday evenings. Attendance averaged 20-22 faculty members out of a total of 50 full-time teachers. President Young led the discussion twice. Professor George Scherer, chairman of the chemistry department, who had taught in Jordan in 1956-58, showed a film and led a discussion on the Arab refugee problem, Arab-Israeli relations and their implications for the area. One session was led by Charles Hulac of the American Friends of the Middle East. Another reviewed the influence of classical Arabic and Persian literature, particularly the work of the mystical Sufi poets. Former Ambassador Rives Childs spoke on Arabia.

Another means of developing faculty interest and competence has been the *summer seminar tour* to the area which has been studied during the preceding year. This study tour enables some two or three faculty members and about 25 students to get first-hand experience of the people whose culture they have begun to learn about at Western. Sixteen members of the staff from twelve departments, the registrar, the dean of students and the president had been on one or more of the summer seminar tours by 1964. Six of the teachers were chairmen of their departments —home economics, intercultural studies, physical education, political science, religion and sociology. The other departments represented were biology, economics, English, foreign languages, mathematics and music.

Faculty members have also extended their competence in the non-Western world by *formal study* both in the U. S. A. and abroad. The college has assisted by providing summer pay for reading and preparing new course materials, or released time during the academic year to develop a plan for a new course. Faculty study of non-Western societies, however, has usually taken the form of year-long or summer research and travel to a given area, sometimes under the Fulbright-Hays Act, occasionally with the help of the college, or at the expense of the individual faculty members. In the summer of 1963, Professor Fred Sturm of the department of philosophy was assisted by the college to take part in the Fulbright program's special institute on Chinese civilization at Tunghai University, Taiwan. Other faculty members have studied at a major university for the summer, to increase their competence in Russian for example.

In *appointing new members* to the faculty, Western has adopted two criteria. First, all other qualifications being equal, the condidate who has lived for some time in another country, especially for the purpose of teaching, study or research, or who is a native of another land, is to be preferred; and second, preference is to be given to the candidate who is articulate in another language as well as in English. Two recent examples of such appointments are: Joseph Backor, assistant professor of history appointed in 1961, a graduate of the University of Slovakia with further study at Ohio State and Indiana Universities; and R. Frank Fulton, associate professor of religion appointed in 1963, with both a B.D. and Ph.D. from American universities, but long experience in teaching and study at the College of Chinese Studies, Peking, and at the Inter-American University in Puerto Rico.

Western College has supplemented the resources of its own staff by inviting a *resident visiting specialist* from abroad for a year at a time in order to provide the particular combination of disciplinary training and intimate, recent knowledge of another culture, including language, not always possessed by members of the faculty of a small liberal arts college in the U. S. A. Thanks primarily to the cooperation of the Committee on International Exchange of Persons of the Conference Board of Associated Research Councils, and a network of alumnae and other friends overseas, a visiting scholar has come to Western each year for the past decade. Western has learned to fit each one productively into the curricular and extracurricular programs of the college by careful advance planning and close cooperation with regular members of the staff familiar with the visiting scholar's culture. The following scholars have served as visiting professors from non-Western areas:

1954-55    Latin America year. Dr Angelica Mendoza, originally from Argentina and on the staff of a UNESCO project in Mexico
1955-56    Middle East year. Dr M. Safwat, Egypt, history
1956-57    Asia year. Professor T. A. Bisson, Sinology
1957-58    Africa year. Professor Wyn Rees, South Africa, history
1958-59    Latin America year. Senora Maria Liona de Guzman, Chile, Spanish-American literature
1959-60    Middle East year. Mr Sohrab Dustdar, Irian, philosophy
1960-61    Asia year. Mr Baldev Raj Nayar, India, political science
1961-62    Africa year. Dr Johannes Jansen, South Africa, geography
1962-63    Latin America year. Mr Washington Vasquez, Uruguay, sociology
1963-64    Middle East year. Dr Sevkiye Inalcik, Turkey, Arabic and Islamic culture and history

An incidental factor of some importance has been the help which visiting professors have given to foreign students, especially those from their own language and culture area, to whom they have been able to offer mature reassurance not otherwise available.

The cumulative effect of these and parallel attempts to develop a more international faculty has been significant. Professor Sturm's report of 1962 on the international program at Western College for Women pointed out that:

Of the 58 full and part-time members of the teaching faculty listed for the 1961-62 academic year, 21 have had some educational experience outside the United States of America; 12 being natives of another nation (Chinese, Filipino, Chilean, German, Austrian, English, Japanese, etc.), 20 having studied on the university level or conducted advanced research in another nation, and 11 having taught on the university level in another nation.

## Curriculum

The pattern of curricular development at Western College for Women has been determined by the considerations summarized in Professor Sturm's report as follows:

Western is a small (450 students in 1961-62), private college with neither denominational support nor a large endowment. The program of intercultural studies needed to be developed within the framework of the curricular pattern already established and largely under the direction of existing personnel. The decision not to expand through the establishment of separate area study programs was not motivated by economic necessity, however. The goal was not to provide specialized education through Institutes of African, Asian, and Latin American Studies, for example, but rather to produce regular liberal arts graduates working in the traditional disciplines of study who would be conversant with the living cultures of the world and prepared to assume responsibility as well-informed citizens of an increasingly interdependent community of nations. Transformation of a typical liberal arts curriculum concerned with the heritage of Europe and the United States of America, into an interculturally-oriented program of higher education was what the objective envisaged.

In short, there has been no attempt to provide for concentrated study of any particular non-Western culture. The aim has been to give a global perspective to the whole curriculum, partly through the infusion of non-Western data into courses in the conventional disciplines, partly through the provision of courses dealing wholly or mainly with non-Western experience and achievement or with issues of intercultural scope.

Examples of infusion cited by Professor Sturm are:

(a) The freshman-level introduction to music was retitled "Survey of World Music" with appropriate changes in course description and syllabus;

(b) The corresponding course in the theatre department was titled "A Survey of World Theatre, Ancient and Modern";

(c) Introduction to the History and Criticism of Art added to its syllabus a section on Chinese art;

(d) The course description of Twentieth Century Music was changed to read "Representative works by composers of all nationalities are studied and analyzed in detail . . .";

(e) The History of Philosophy courses were expanded in content to include developments in philosophic thought in India and China as well as in Greece and Europe, during the four periods covered: ancient, medieval, modern and contemporary;

(f) American Philosophy became "A history of philosophic thought in the Americas . . .";

(g) To the content of three philosophy courses (Ethics, Aesthetics, Philosophy of Religion) was added the thought of men and movements from the Chinese and Indian traditions;

(h) Instructors of courses in mathematics and the physical and biological sciences make references to original contributions made to development of work within the discipline with which they are concerned by men and schools from non-Western areas, and frequently use material from those areas for illustrative purposes.

By 1963-64 the college was offering upwards of twenty *courses of predominantly non-Western or intercultural character*. Some of these predated the adoption of the new program in 1953. They included: in the department of religion, Comparative Religion and Religious Thought in the Orient; in the department of sociology, Cultural Anthropology and Population Problems; in the department of political science, Comparative Government, International Law, International Organization and International Politics. New courses, such as Comparative Education, International Economics, Masterpieces of World Literature in English Translation, and Teaching English as a Foreign Language, have been developed as faculty competence permitted.

In 1956-57, an interdepartmental committee of the faculty developed a basic course on Development of World Civilizations, normally taken by sophomores. It offers:

A survey of the major cultural achievements of the world's civilizations. Broad and varied in topical range, but historical in general approach. Members of various departments contribute to the course instruction . . .

In 1958, a department of intercultural studies was established. The first majors in this field graduated in 1960. Courses in this department have two chief aims: first, to introduce students to the historical development and cultural achievements of those areas of the world that contrast most markedly with the Western civilization predominant in modern times; and second, to study the complex of contemporary issues that has recently emerged in Asia, Africa and Latin America as the peoples of these areas seek to reach a footing of equality with the Western nations.

Courses in the department of intercultural studies include Social and Economic Geography, offered annually, and the following courses offered in alternate years: the Middle East in Modern Times; Africa in Modern Times; Latin America in Modern Times; North Asia; South Asia; the United States and the Far East; and a senior seminar. Courses on contemporary civilization, focusing on the major world region for the year, are taught by the visiting lecturer from the area.

In addition to fields of concentration relating to other world areas, the department offers a major in United States civilization, which has proved of particular value to foreign students but is also important for U. S. citizens. The faculty endeavors to relate introductory and advanced courses on non-Western areas and intercultural studies to the American and Western European cultural traditions. This concern is implicit in the name of the department.

This program has had a cumulative impact on the student body that does not appear to have been equalled by any other college covered by the present survey. Between 90 and 100 per cent of the graduating seniors in each of the classes from 1959 through 1963 had taken the basic course on Development of World Civilizations, and an average of 37 per cent of the same classes had taken at least one advanced course on a non-Western area.

Language instruction has benefited from the interest aroused by the general atmosphere of the college and sharpened by student and faculty participation in annual summer study tours to various parts of the world. Up to the present, however, this interest has been reflected in increased study of Western European languages alone. Although courses in elementary and intermediate Russian have been offered since 1958, only five students were taking Russian in 1963-64. The introduction of other critical languages has been deferred until there is more demand for them.

## Library

Western College's library is of moderate size and cramped for space. In 1963-64, it had 56,000 volumes and received 272 periodicals. The budget for book accessions was $9800 and for periodicals $2000. The staff estimated that ten per cent of the books and fourteen per cent of the periodicals currently being added related primarily to non-Western studies. The growing number of books, periodicals and documents relating to Africa, Asia, Latin America, the Middle East and Slavic areas are readily available on open stacks in a special reading room. The librarians evaluated library holdings for instruction as "good" for Asia in general, "adequate" for Africa, Latin America and the Middle East, and "poor" for Slavic studies. For student research the evaluation was that the collections on Asia in general and on Latin America were "adequate," but that they were "poor" for other areas. For faculty research holdings were rated "adequate" on Asia in general but otherwise "poor."

Western College identifies its priority needs for the library as: first, materials for Slavic Studies; second, for Africa; and third, for the Middle East. Holdings were improved with the help of some funds from the Carnegie grant mentioned earlier.

Faculty and students from Western College have ready access to the library of Miami University, located within a few minutes' walk from the Western campus. The Miami library contains 376,000 volumes, subscribes to 1600 periodicals, houses over 200,000 government documents and is a depository for U. S. government publications. It is building up its holdings on world affairs and non-Western areas under the impetus of new programs for international studies.

## Cooperation

Western College has developed its emphasis on intercultural studies primarily on its own initiative, although it has shared faculty and library facilities with its neighbor Miami University for many years. Thanks to its substantial experience in non-Western studies Western has, particularly in recent years, been called upon to share its knowledge with other colleges and institutional groups. Interaction with other scholars and institutions is also stimulating the staff at Western to evaluate and improve their own program.

The college has been a member of the *Regional Council on International Education* since it began in 1959. The council is a membership association of 28 colleges, within a radius of 300 miles of Pittsburgh, in Western Pennsylvania, New York, Ohio and West Virginia, which are cooperating to further international and non-Western studies on their campuses and which annually attract some 1500 students from abroad. President Shepherd Witman directs the council's work from an office at the University of Pittsburgh. The council has sponsored annual conferences, workshops and study tours for administrators and faculty members, and has provided clearinghouse facilities to schedule visits by foreign scholars and to exchange information. In February 1964 it received two grants from the Ford Foundation: one for a foreign student orientation center, the other for a four-stage faculty development program.

Western College is one of a dozen women's colleges which, under the leadership of Randolph-Macon Woman's College, have developed a *faculty exchange program with six women's colleges in India*. Plans call for six teachers from each country to take part in the exchange each year starting in 1964-65. Three administrators from each country will also exchange visits of about one month. President Young of Western will revisit India as one of the three U. S. administrators in the autumn of 1964. A biology teacher from St Mary's College, Bangalore, will spend part of her time in the U.S.A. during 1964-65 lecturing at Western. The departments of music and sociology are planning to take advantage of her skill in Indian music and her knowledge of

Indian family life. Western College hopes to arrange for one of its faculty to spend a year at one of the Indian colleges within the next two years.

## Students and Extracurricular Activities

Western College had a diversified student body from forty foreign countries in 1963-64. The college does not normally admit more than two students from a given foreign country at once, and seeks to secure students from all economic and social classes, and especially from emerging countries. It has also made special efforts to attract American Indian, Negro and Puerto Rican students to increase the ethnic diversity of its U.S. constituency. Close to ten per cent in 1963-64 were international students. Thirty-two of the foreign students held college scholarships. In order to stress the dignity of labor, foreign students are encouraged to accept at least some of the financial aid they may need in the form of work grants. This broadens their experience and helps them to acquire useful skills which facilitate their obtaining summer employment. Foreign students are expected to live with U. S. room-mates, who are carefully selected and are encouraged to invite them to their homes for visits, particularly at Christmas and Easter.

The administration considers all of its students as scholars first. It then recognizes individual differences and needs, and has devised a comprehensive set of policies and procedures for meeting the most important needs. For example, it has organized a two-week orientation program before the start of the academic year to assist all incoming foreign students to learn about the college, take placement tests in English language, and get acquainted with students, faculty, the local community and American institutions. Courses in English as a foreign language are offered throughout the year by the foreign student adviser, who has special training in this field. An academic adviser helps each international student plan her study program in accordance with the regular academic standards of the college and her own particular needs. Head residents in the dormitories have, during the past ten years, included a Chinese and two Indian ladies particularly able to assist American and foreign students to understand cultural differences and to adjust effectively to them.

In addition to regular counseling services, the foreign student adviser and the dean of students keep in close touch with foreign students. Particular attention is given by them and the placement office staff to: (1) summer employment that provides valuable experience as well as financial support; (2) opportunities for graduate study and practical training; and (3) reverse orientation in preparation for return home, including suggestions on possible employment.

Foreign students are encouraged to preserve and represent their own cultural traditions while becoming integrated into the total life of the college. They have responded with imagination and vigor. They have been leaders in the active cosmopolitan club serving both Miami University and Western College. They have enlisted many of their American friends in the annual production of an international students' show. It has become commonplace for them to assume positions of responsibility in a wide range of extracurricular activities. The cosmopolitan character of extracurricular activities at Western College is also illuminating to U.S. students and adds cultural variety and intellectual stimulus to programs which formerly lacked this international dimension.

For American students, perhaps the most important single extracurricular opportunity is offered by the *summer seminar tours*. Those who wish to take part in a seminar tour prepare for it with the visiting scholar from the area and with professors in their major department—first, to be adequately informed and oriented so as to derive maximum benefit from the trip, and second, in order to concentrate on some topic of field observation and research during the summer seminar. This field study is reported on in an independent paper after the student returns to campus the following autumn.

An *annual area conference*, held each spring, focuses on the culture and region which have been emphasized throughout the academic year, and is usually the culmination of a series of lectures and other programs offered at least once a week to supplement the formal curriculum. It brings to the campus authorities on the region who lecture, lead discussion and workshop sessions and meet informally with students and faculty. It is customary to include the visiting professor and students from the region as chairmen or rapporteurs for discussion panels. Faculty members and students preparing to visit the region as members of the summer seminar find this annual conference and its leaders particularly helpful in consolidating their earlier study and focusing on particular issues which they will explore on the spot some weeks later.

Other extracurricular programs, such as assemblies, Sunday chapel, concerts and exhibits regularly include speakers or artists from non-Western areas or persons with expert knowledge of them.

## Self-Evaluation

Much of higher education rests on assumptions which have not been or cannot be subjected to scientifically conducted tests to ascertain their validity. Courses or programs of non-Western study, scholarly exchanges, and study abroad appear to be even less susceptible to testing than other aspects of higher education. Psychologists at Western College for Women, and the trustees of the college, have tried three times since 1956 to measure the effectiveness of the international program in terms of changes in attitude among students. While these endeavors at evaluation have not proved definitive (in part because the involvement of the entire college community in the program left no control group on campus), they indicate some significant positive changes in favor of the international emphasis and in attitudes toward foreigners. No means have yet been devised to ascertain what proportion of these changes should be credited to the international program or to other factors. Perhaps the faculty committee set up in the spring of 1964 to evaluate the program will find more satisfactory methods to check on its influence on students during the past decade. And, as relatively few tests endeavoring to measure the impact of an intercultural program of this sort have been conducted in colleges, the inquiries at Western may stimulate further research and testing in this area of learning and attitude change.

## Future Development

Western College for Women appears to have had substantial success with its ten-year endeavor to internationalize the whole institution. These changes have been brought about by the united efforts of the administration, the faculty and the students, with the backing of the trustees. Many alumnae who were originally skeptical about the international program now give it their support.

Western's pioneer enterprise rests, however, on limited resources. The college needs broader and deeper faculty competence in non-Western areas. It would like to obtain at least one specialist, with command of at least one major language, for each of the principal non-Western regions, particularly Africa and the Middle East. It hopes to develop regular opportunities for serving faculty to engage in more intensive study of other cultures, both in this country and abroad. This is particularly desired for the member of the faculty directing study of a given area, who should be able to revisit the area, at least once every four years, during the summer before the year emphasizing his particular area. When more specially-qualified teachers can be employed, the curriculum can be further enriched.

Western College hopes to obtain funds for the appointment of a coordinator of intercultural affairs, to give better focus to the program than is practicable for the chairman of the department of intercultural studies, who has a very heavy teaching load, or for the dean and the president, who cannot give as much time as they would like to the administration of the international program. The president would also like to employ retired foreign service officers or people with comparable international experience to lecture and assist in the program on a regular basis as a supplement to the standard courses.

The administration wants to provide more scholarships for foreign students and aid for both students and faculty members to participate in the summer seminar tours to non-Western areas.

It hopes to enrich the program by attracting more visiting speakers, artists and exhibits to the campus and to find means to enable more students and faculty members to extend their study off campus at other universities, in Washington, at the United Nations and in field situations where learning and observation can be enhanced by direct participation. The college would also like to improve the audio-visual and language teaching aids available, and to find funds to support research and experimentation, more careful evaluation of the program, and preparation of teaching materials to supplement those now available.

Consideration has been given to extending the informal faculty seminar held each spring. One plan calls for it to meet weekly throughout the year, with more reading and preparation required of participants and more use made of visiting specialists. Another suggestion has been made to transfer the area conferences held each spring to the autumn, in order to develop interest earlier in the academic year in the non-Western culture under study.

Professor Sturm urged in an article in the college paper in May 1963 that, early each autumn, every new student and faculty member should take part in a special orientation to the international aims and character of Western College. He believes that this would help to create a more concrete vision of "what it means to be a responsible member of a nascent international community" and elicit more general and understanding support of the program.

The action taken by the faculty in the spring of 1964, establishing an interdivisional committee to evaluate the intercultural program, was a logical result of the original faculty proposals of 1953. These called for future experimentation and periodic evaluation. The new faculty committee is:

> charged with the responsibility of studying and evaluating the total scope of the program in both its curricular and extra-curricular dimensions, including also such semi-curricular aspects as area conferences, summer seminars, lectures and recitals programming, library purchasing, faculty recruitment, admissions policy and public relations. In addition the committee is to assume responsibility for the preparation of a series of recommendations designed to strengthen the program as presently conceived, and especially to provide guide-lines

for its future development. It is expected that the committee will terminate its work and issue a final report within the space of one year from the date of its appointment.

The trustees also planned to review the program in 1964. This broadly-based interest reflects one of Western College's greatest assets—the strong, institution-wide commitment to developing an effective program of intercultural studies in the liberal arts.

# 10

# CALIFORNIA STATE COLLEGE
# AT HAYWARD

California State College at Hayward is a new institution created in 1959-60. In order to accommodate graduates of the numerous junior colleges in the state, the college (known as Alameda County State College until July 1963) was organized to teach only junior and senior courses until September 1963, when its first freshman class matriculated. The 1964-65 academic year will be the first in which Hayward is conducting a four-year program.

Cal-State at Hayward's significance lies in the fact that, as a new four-year, non-residential college, it is starting out with a commitment to global perspectives in the curriculum. Its future plans provide for area and language majors on South Asia, Africa, Latin America and the Middle East, with additional offerings on the Far East and Russia. It already requires every sophomore in the creative arts, humanities and social sciences (except psychology) to take a course on Comparative Studies in Asian Cultures.

California State College at Hayward, Hayward, California. President Fred F. Harcleroad. (State; coeducational; quarter system; liberal arts and teacher training to bachelor's degree; 1897 students)

## Historical Background

This new college began with a special opportunity to develop innovations in the curriculum. Its president, Fred Harcleroad, formerly dean at San José State College, came determined to build a college with a world outlook. From the start, he and his key associates have planned the curriculum with this aim in view and have recruited faculty members with special competence in non-Western areas because, as President Harcleroad wrote in a letter on 3 February 1964,

> . . . I am committed to the idea that a person obtaining a liberal education in the last part of the twentieth century has been cheated unless his education provides him ample opportunity to learn from scholars from other countries, and the opportunity to truly understand the way of life and culture of Asiatic, African and Latin American peoples.

President Harcleroad has had a lifelong interest in the non-Western world, growing out of Methodist church associations and long contacts and correspondence with missionary friends in China and India particularly. His studies and friendships with scholars from abroad at Stanford further stimulated this interest. Ever since World War II he has felt uneasy about "the insularity of so-called liberally educated people of the United States . . ."

At San José State College, in 1954, he helped to introduce a two-year humanities program in general education "which was supposed to include some world-wide perspective . . ." and a junior year elective course on Asian cultures taught by four qualified instructors. He found that the humanities program did not retain its intended intercultural content but "was rapidly narrowed to cover only Western culture." The course on Asian cultures never attracted more than forty students out of a student body of 10,000. Dr. Harcleroad thinks that the humanities program soon focused on Western culture because most of the men teaching it had virtually no experience with any other culture and over-emphasized their traditional disciplinary orientation. The course on Asian cultures was by-passed because faculty advisers "never sent any students into it" and it was "kept elective

217

and met very little of the general education requirements." He decided to avoid these pitfalls in developing new approaches to liberal education with a world view at Hayward.

## Early Plans for Non-Western Studies

From the first year of the college's existence its leaders sought expert advice on how to implement their determination to "provide a world-wide approach to liberal education, rather than the narrow approach limited to Western culture." Their plans are still developing, but they are based on guidelines suggested in the Morrill Report of 1960 and by consultants on Asian studies in 1961, and on the experience of the president and several of his colleagues.

Early faculty discussion of the Master Curriculum Plan dealt with various ways to provide a more globally oriented curriculum. These included revision of regular courses already being offered to include international perspectives; broadening a Western into a world civilization course; and the organization of area study courses and programs centered on one or more regions of the non-Western world. During this first year of study in 1959-60, Dr Charles Merrifield was appointed head of the social sciences division. He took the lead in arranging with the Asia Society for assistance in holding a short faculty seminar led by visiting specialists in non-Western studies. The report of the Morrill Committee on *The University and World Affairs* appeared, late in 1960, at the same time as plans for the faculty seminar were taking shape. This report was reviewed carefully by the administration and faculty at Cal-State at Hayward. The planners found it helpful in clarifying issues and in its emphasis on the importance of closely relating existing courses to the new intercultural and non-Western offerings being developed.

## The 1961 Faculty Seminar

The culmination of the college's initial efforts to define the problems of non-Western studies and to find solutions took place in a seminar, open to all faculty members, held on the campus,

10-11 February 1961. The theme of the seminar was "Asiatic Cultures and Liberal Education." It was planned by a faculty committee composed of Arnold Biella, professor of English and head of the division of the humanities, Floyd Erickson, director of libraries and college archivist, and Charles Merrifield, professor of social science and head of the division of social and behavioral science. The visiting consultants were Wm. Theodore de Bary, historian, director of the East Asian Institute at Columbia; Peter Gosling, specialist on Asian geography, from the University of Michigan; Merrill Goodall, expert on India and Nepal, chairman of the department of government at Claremont Graduate School; and Ward Morehouse, educational director of the Asia Society. Each consultant spoke before the entire seminar, which then discussed the topic. There were also panel sessions devoted to curricular development in general education, to regional or area studies, and to enriching existing course offerings.

Consultants at the faculty seminar urged that students be well grounded in knowledge of their own cultural heritage before concentrating on the study of a non-Western culture. As specialists on Asia, they also argued convincingly for Asia as the first area to be studied. Hayward teachers, with and without non-Western area competence, agreed with this recommendation. There was, however, some skepticism among certain members of the faculty about the role of non-Western studies in general education in an undergraduate liberal arts college.

A full report of the proceedings, edited by Arnold Biella and Charles Merrifield and imaginatively illustrated with sketches in Oriental style by Professor Howard Slatoff, was published by Alameda State College Foundation, as Higher Education Curriculum Series Publication Number 1, 1962. The report and a summary of the seminar were made available to each faculty member.

As a result of this seminar and the work of the Oriental Studies Committee the following guidelines were adopted:

1. Non-Western dimensions might be introduced into the curriculum as part of general education courses or as enrichment of single departmental courses.

2. These changes have broad implications for library development, staff recruitment, staff utilization, in-service staff development, language course expansion and general integration with other courses.

3. The initial approach should be to make Oriental studies a part of the general education program: more advanced courses on the non-Western world should be introduced later.

4. Faculty members with Oriental studies interests and competence should be appointed within the regular departments and divisions.

5. Primary planning and responsibility should center in the humanities and social and behavioral science divisions, with participation invited from other divisions.

6. It appeared feasible, within the broad general education framework, to develop two year-long courses in Western Studies and Oriental Studies as a way for some of the freshmen and sophomores to meet humanities and social and behavioral science requirements, including institutions, history and government.

7. A year-long course, covering the ancient Oriental world, contacts with European cultures, and contemporary problems and issues of the Non-Western World, was envisaged. An interdisciplinary team, utilizing both historical, topical and case-study methods, seemed desirable.[1]

## The Master Curriculum Plan of 1962

Discussion of the Master Curriculum Plan continued during 1961-62. The faculty agreed that a sound understanding of current world issues depended on a substantial course on Western civilization for freshmen. An interdivisional committee on Western culture met and developed a course of that name during 1962-63. They also planned this course as preparatory to the proposed complementary course at the sophomore level on Asian cultures, with both courses viewed as important offerings in the general education sequence. When the entire faculty reviewed and accepted the Master Curriculum Plan late in 1962, they also decided to increase general education requirements from 68 to 76 quarter units and to allow greater weight in credits for the two courses on Asian and Western cultures and additional

---

1. Adapted from memo. by Dr Jon Peters and letter from Dean Lepore, 3 March 1964.

courses on non-Western areas. The Master Plan further provided for the future development of undergraduate majors in Middle Eastern, South Asian and Latin American studies.

The freshman course on the History of Western Culture was introduced in September 1963. Some 180 out of 600 freshmen enrolled in this course in 1963-64. It was expected that most of them would continue with the new, interdivisional general education sequence on Asian Cultures in their sophomore year.

With a rapidly expanding enrolment, the addition of a freshman class in 1963-64 and a sophomore class in 1964-65, and the possibility of allocating three full-time staff positions relating to the Asian Cultures course to the general education budget, the college had unusual latitude to appoint new teachers. During 1962-63, a number of key appointments of staff with non-Western competence were made. After the 1961 seminar on non-Western studies, however, no systematic effort was made to encourage serving faculty members to develop their interest and competence in non-Western areas. In relative terms, the small proportion of faculty members with such competence was reduced as new appointments, though including some specialists in non-Western fields, primarily involved teachers without such qualifications.

### The Interdivisional Committee on Asian Studies, 1963-64

At the start of the academic year 1963-64, the president appointed an interdivisional Committee on Asian Studies with the following members:

William L. Thomas, Jr, professor of anthropology and geography, chairman
David Chan, assistant professor of history
Glenn Glasow, assistant professor of music (part-time)
Mrs Ellen Gumperz, assistant professor of history (half-time)
Baldev Raj Nayar, assistant professor of political science
Jon Peters, professor of education and associate dean of instruction
Howard Slatoff, associate professor of art and dean of men

With the exception of Professors Peters and Slatoff, all members of the committee were new members of the faculty. Only

Professor Slatoff had taken part in the 1961 seminar on Asian cultures. Four members of the committee were specialists on Asia, had had field research experience there, and were products of graduate non-Western area training centers. These were Chan from the University of California at Berkeley and the University of Pennsylvania, Gumperz from Cornell, Nayar from Chicago, and Thomas from Yale.

The Committee on Asian Studies was charged by Dr Lepore, dean of instruction, with responsibility for developing new courses on Asia, recommending changes in existing courses relating to the Orient, working with divisions and departments in regard to changes in or additions to staff, dealing directly with the librarian or with audio-visual services on book, film or slide requests, ordering the necessary texts and reference materials, and preparing syllabi, examinations, course descriptions and schedules. The committee was to report directly to the dean of instruction.

The work of the committee was complicated by the fact that the chairman and most of its members were new to the college and were primarily oriented to their respective disciplines. They came from large institutions with different approaches to scholarship and undergraduate liberal arts education. They were also at a disadvantage because most of the rest of the faculty had little experience with non-Western studies. On the positive side, members of the committee had special qualifications and it had strong administrative backing.

## A Disciplinary or Interdisciplinary Approach?

The committee's first task was to devise the proposed general education course on Asian Cultures. The group met roughly once a week between September 1963 and February 1964. At the first regular meeting, Professors Biella and Merrifield reviewed the background of the college's plans for non-Western studies and reported in detail on the 1961 faculty seminar. Some members of the committee were doubtful about the efficacy of the "survey" or interdisciplinary education approach to Asian studies. There was also a feeling that particular disciplines deserved more emphasis in the proposed course and that the methodology to be used should derive primarily from this or that academic tradition.

The proponents of the first view thought that the proposed general education course on Asian Cultures was not the best way to use faculty or student time and skills. They preferred to organize and teach concrete courses such as Indian Art, the Politics of Japan, or the Geography of Thailand. Adherents of the second approach were persuaded that it was pedagogically unwise to follow any methodology except that of their own discipline—for example, that of the historian or the creative artist. Part of their concern may have been linked to the fact that the greater amount of time devoted in the course to a given discipline, the more teachers trained in that discipline and inclined to follow its methodology would be likely to be instructing in the course. Some proponents of the second thesis were willing to consider modifications involving comparative courses in particular disciplines. These natural differences, reinforced by the dedication of highly trained and specialized scholars to their disciplines, complicated the work of the committee.

Some of the preliminary course outlines in which the committee sought to resolve these differences faced similarly contrasting views in the general faculty. Late in the autumn of 1963 it appeared that one division might be unwilling to recognize the proposed course unless the syllabus were revised to include more material which they considered essential. Further discussions in the Committee on Asian Studies, with the dean, divisional heads and members of the committees on courses and on educational development, and in the Representative Assembly of the Faculty eventually reconciled the differing views. It was agreed that during the first year of the course on Asian Cultures all students majoring in the humanities or the social sciences, with the exception of psychology, should be advised to take this course in fulfillment of general education and divisional requirements.

As President Harcleroad's experience at San José suggested, the commitment of faculty advisers in various departments to the importance of non-Western studies may be crucial to the success of this effort to encourage most sophomores to take the course

223

on Asian Cultures. Unless special, continuing efforts are made to develop and strengthen general faculty interest in non-Western studies, advisers may remain lukewarm in their counseling and thus limit the potential benefit of the course.

## The New Course on Asian Cultures

In February 1964, the Representative Assembly gave unanimous approval to the new course, Comparative Studies in Asian Cultures, to be introduced in 1964-65. This integrated, inter-divisional, general education series is made up of three term courses taught in sequence, as follows:

ASIA 2001. *Patterns of Asian Cultures*

The significance of contemporary Asia; approaches to the study of Asia through various disciplines; physical, biotic and social patterns of the major regions of Asia; Asian prehistory. Four units; Fall quarter.

ASIA 2003. *Development of Traditional Asian Cultures*

Major traditions of Southern, Southeastern and Eastern Asia, including political, economic and aesthetic developments. Prerequisite: Asia 2001. Four units; Winter quarter.

ASIA 2005. *Asian Societies in the Modern World*

European expansion in Asia; the rise of nation states; problems of modernization. Prerequisite: Asia 2001 and 2003. Four units; Spring quarter.

Henceforth, all non-transfer students in the divisions of creative arts, humanities and social science (excepting psychology) at Cal-State at Hayward will have the two year-long sequences in Western and then Asian Cultures as an important part of their general education during the freshman and sophomore years. Students will also be able to elect from at least 25 more advanced courses relating primarily to non-Western cultures in all major world regions.

## The Junior and Senior Symposia

During their final two years at Cal-State at Hayward, students will also take required junior and senior symposia which are to include materials on non-Western societies. These symposia are special interdisciplinary courses in which, according to the catalogue, "the student examines and relates selected ideas in . . . the fields of biological and physical science, humanities, and social science" by means of lectures, readings, papers and discussions. Thus, the college intends to provide liberal arts students with both introductory and more advanced courses of an interdisciplinary character to encourage their capacity to correlate and integrate learning at the same time as they study a chosen major field in greater depth.

## Faculty Resources

A core of the senior teaching faculty and administration have taken part in planning for non-Western studies at Hayward since 1959. Faculty participants in the 1961 faculty seminar on Asiatic Cultures and Liberal Education included professors of chemistry, mathematics, social science, geology, political science, art and education, the dean of instruction and the associate dean of students.

Cal-State at Hayward has not depended on visiting scholars to serve as teachers or coordinators of one or more courses. Nor has it planned systematic methods to extend the competence of serving faculty members to non-Western areas. Instead, its recruitment policy has stressed the previous international experience and competence of new staff members, particularly those appointed to help teach the new comparative course on Asian cultures.

The college does not plan to cooperate with neighboring institutions to share faculty members or courses, partly because it has so much flexibility in employing staff with the desired competence in non-Western studies and world affairs.

In addition to the members of the Committee on Asian Studies and seven teachers competent in Latin America, Cal-State at

Hayward has faculty members in several other departments with more limited knowledge of non-Western areas. They teach in the departments of anthropology, art, economics, education, foreign languages, geography, history, music, political science and speech. Their courses now deal with all major non-Western regions except the Middle East, which is to be covered later.

In developing the non-Western studies program the Committee on Asian Studies has thus far drawn primarily on the experience of major graduate centers which offer general courses on all or parts of Asia to undergraduates in their liberal arts colleges. They now wish to explore further the experience of other undergraduate colleges, such as Antioch, Earlham, New Paltz and Portland State, to ascertain if their experience may be more relevant to Cal-State at Hayward's needs than that of major universities.

## Library

The library has been built up rapidly to over 90,000 volumes. In 1963-64, $31,000 was budgeted for book accessions and $8,000 for periodicals. The library then received annually 750 periodicals, including eight newspapers from non-Western areas. The librarian estimated that five per cent of the books and three per cent of the periodicals being added in 1964 related to non-Western studies. He considered library resources for undergraduate teaching relative to the non-Western world reasonably adequate for then current needs, and hoped to be able to keep ahead of growing faculty and student demands for such materials. The college rated its library holdings for instruction on India and the Middle East as "good;" "adequate" for Asia generally; and "poor" for African, Latin American, Slavic and East European studies. For student research, the same rating applied, except to the Middle East, which was rated only "adequate." Library resources for faculty research were rated "poor" for all non-Western areas excepting Indian philosophy, which was considered "adequate" thanks to the recent purchase of a private library from an Indian scholar.

In February 1964 the college purchased most of the library of the former West Coast office of the Institute of Pacific Relations from the World Affairs Council of Northern California. This collection includes "over 1000 out-of-print books and monographs, several hundred . . . pamphlets, and about 200 unbound periodicals (including a 15-year run of *Amerasia.*)"[2]

The library's most urgent needs to support the non-Western courses are, first, more books and journals on Asia, particularly Southeast Asia, and secondly, art collections and books illustrating the arts of Asia. The college is fortunate, however, in being able to draw on the major libraries and art collections of the San Francisco Bay area. Members of the faculty hope that the librarians at Hayward will develop an inventory or check list of holdings in neighboring libraries which are particularly relevant to non-Western studies at the college. With few exceptions, teachers have been able to obtain essential books for reserve shelves or assigned readings for courses relating to non-Western cultures offered in 1963-64.

## Students and Extracurricular Activities

During 1963-64, there were about 1700 full-time students and 800 part-time students at Hayward. The college expects a very rapid rate of growth, with possibly as many as 800-1000 new students enrolling annually during the next few years.

Students are organized into divisional councils for recreational and other extracurricular activities. The chief programs relating to world affairs are the annual United Nations Day in October, and Law and Freedom Day, celebrated on May 1. Both are under student direction, and in recent years they have focused on the emerging nations. In the spring of 1964 the library presented an exhibit of Asian books and artifacts.

Students and faculty at Hayward suffer from the disability of many non-residential institutions in that there are few opportunities for informal conversations and contacts between them outside classes. The administration has tried to mitigate this

---

2.   Memo. from Dean Lepore, 3 March 1964

difficulty by providing lounge and commonroom facilities in each building, and by means of the divisional councils, in which students and teachers in major divisions can meet periodically to discuss mutual interests. These councils are linked with the faculty-student counseling arrangements. But the fact remains that commuting students and faculty have difficulty meeting informally outside the classroom.

It is an explicit aim of the college to attract students and teachers from abroad and to encourage its own students and faculty to study in non-Western and other foreign areas. There have been foreign students at Hayward since 1960. In 1963-64, 28 students from fifteen foreign countries were enrolled. No students or teachers were studying abroad in 1962-63, but in 1963-64 the chairman of the sociology department was on leave in Egypt, and the head of the humanities division will be there on a Fulbright grant in 1964-65.

## Conclusion

At the start of the 1961 faculty seminar on non-Western studies, President Harcleroad stated his views, which have been decisive in subsequent developments, in these terms:

> The content of liberal education in Western Europe and North America has never been constant. A major addition to a liberal education of American college students in the last half of the twentieth century must be the ideas and the knowledge necessary to achieve a better . . . understanding of the cultures of Asia and Africa . . .

> A truly educated citizenry in the United States, knowing the values and the responsibilities of freedom and the cultural differences of which other people are so justly proud, can make a significant contribution to improving the lot of millions of people living in these new developing countries. What could be more appropriate than giving careful attention at a new American college to the ancient philosophy, evolving culture and dynamic political efforts of these new countries? Our Western heritage is one of several great traditions. Only by understanding these other traditions, as well as understanding our own, can we hope that the American example can eventually find its rightful place in the larger world community. This is the underlying idea which leads Alameda State College to explore the

extension of liberal education in the direction of world affairs. In particular this is true of Asian Studies . . . it will be true of African studies, as it is fast becoming true of Latin America. Eventually we may look forward to the time when to be educated in the American college system will itself be an education in world outlook.

California State College at Hayward has begun to implement these goals. It is one of relatively few public, four-year, non-residential institutions to introduce non-Western studies to most of its undergraduates from the start. Within five years, it has recruited five specialists on Asia and seven on Latin America and has introduced over 25 courses relating to the non-Western world, which are offered in six departments. Its sophomore level, interdivisional, year-long course sequence in general education, entitled Comparative Studies in Asian Cultures, provides one way to meet graduation requirements for the creative arts (3 units), humanities (philosophy, 5 units), and social science, exclusive of the California Code requirements in U. S. history and institutions (4 units). It complements the freshman interdivisional sequence on the History of Western Culture, which also fulfills various graduation requirements.

In 1962 President Harcleroad recommended that Cal-State at Hayward should be the state college in California which would pay particular attention to the development of Middle Eastern, South Asian and Southeast Asian studies. The recommendation has been tentatively accepted by the State College System. Cal-State at Hayward also plans to offer courses on the Far East, although San Francisco State College is expected to take the lead in that area.

The college's plans call for additional non-Western courses. Its decision to organize a major in Latin American studies in 1964-65 is based on the fact that in 1963 it had seven members of the faculty with substantial competence in the economy, geography, language and literature of Latin America. By 1968-69 the college intends to offer majors in Middle Eastern and South Asian Studies. These are to be preceded by the introduction of instruction in Arabic, Russian and probably Hindi between 1966 and 1968. During the next eight or ten years, the college plans to organize institutes for more specialized study of one or two non-Western areas and to undertake faculty and student exchanges with colleges or universities abroad.

Cal-State at Hayward's careful planning, substantial institutional commitment, specialized faculty competence and growing library holdings relating to the non-Western world may offer useful guidelines to other public institutions, in California and elsewhere, that would like to provide the majority of their students with a serious introduction to one or two major non-Western cultural traditions.

The main obstacles are the threat of sheer size and, possibly, dwindling faculty commitment to these aims. As enrolment expands rapidly and continues to hinder administrative attempts to encourage informal contacts between students and teachers, Hayward's character as a non-residential liberal arts college may be altered. Hence, it may face complications similar to those of the University of California at Riverside, which was intended to remain relatively small, in order to foster closer student-faculty relationships, but is being gradually forced to abandon that policy by the pressure of rising enrolments. Much as they might like to do so, the California state colleges seem unlikely to be able to resist comparable pressures.

If, however, in spite of rapid growth, Cal-State at Hayward can maintain a substantial core of its faculty committed to general education requirements centered on non-Western societies and languages, and to majors in these areas and cultures, its ambitious plans may provide its students with exceptional opportunities for intercultural understanding.

# 11

# OCCIDENTAL COLLEGE

Occidental College introduced a comprehensive interdepartmental program in diplomacy and world affairs in 1964. It emphasizes political, economic and cultural studies or, under the category of regional studies, concentrations on Asia, Latin America or Europe within the major in diplomacy and world affairs. The program grows out of an earlier major and the college's long and substantial interest in the Far East and Latin America. In 1942, Occidental became one of the first colleges in the U.S.A. to offer courses in Russian language.

An advisory council and program director bring into focus the 42 courses which, offered in eight departments, deal with every major non-Western area. The program draws on the talents of 24 members of the faculty with experience in one or more non-Western societies. Ten of these teachers are specialists on such areas.

Every Occidental student gets an introduction to non-Western cultures in a required two-year sequence on the History of Civilization which, particularly in its first and sixth terms, devotes some attention to non-Western civilizations and their interac-

Occidental College, Los Angeles, California. President Arthur G. Coons. (Private; coeducational; quarter system; liberal arts and teacher training to doctor's degree; 1530 students)

tion with the West. Over a third of the students also take advanced courses in which they can learn more about the non-Western world and intercultural relations.

## Historical Background

The international interests of Occidental College have long been a significant element in its institutional life in and out of the classroom. They spring in part from the Christian, ecumenical character of the college. Its early concern with missionary service in the Orient and the Student Volunteer Movement shifted to a more scholarly basis under President Silas Evans (1917-20). Under the presidencies of Remsen Bird (1921-46) and Arthur G. Coons (1946-    ), the international element in the college's program underwent dynamic development.

K. S. Inui became a faculty lecturer in 1918 and introduced courses on Oriental history and culture which were among the first offered in any of the smaller liberal arts colleges. The departments of history, economics and political science have since provided the central academic base for study of non-Western areas. Professor R. G. Cleland's courses on Mexican history and Hispanic-American affairs, initiated in 1922, were buttressed by the Norman Bridge Professorship in Hispanic-American Affairs endowed in 1923. Dr Cleland was joined in the same year by Dr Osgood Hardy who taught courses on the history of Latin America and the Pacific Basin and led frequent student study tours to Latin America during the next thirty years. The tradition of Hispanic-American studies was continued from 1940 until 1957 by Dr Glenn S. Dumke, and in subsequent years by Professor Clifton Kroeber and other members of the faculty.

In 1944 Dr P. K. Mok, former dean at Peking National University, was appointed professor of Oriental history and culture. Currently chairman of the history department, he has taught many courses on the history of China and the Far East, Southeast Asia, Oriental literature, philosophies and religions, and cultural relations between Orient and Occident.

Dr John P. Young became professor of economics in 1926 and Dr Arthur G. Coons joined the department in 1927. Both men were specialists on international economics and had practical experience of the Far East. Dr Laurence de Rycke, another expert on international finance, joined the staff in 1943.

In political science, President Bird named Thomas R. Adam to the faculty in 1930. He inaugurated the study of issues in international relations which Professor Raymond G. McKelvey, appointed in 1939, and others continue to develop.

On the extracurricular front, Presidents Bird and Coons encouraged many steps to make Occidental "the college with a world view." These included visits and lectures by representatives of various cultural, religious and national groups, foreign student exchanges, and a series of annual conferences on Hispanic-American affairs.

The Remsen Bird Lectures, endowed in 1948, have brought to the campus such men as Charles Malik, Lebanese cabinet minister and delegate to the United Nations, Edmundo O'Gorman, professor of history at the National University of Mexico, Lin Yutang, Chinese philosopher and author, and Alexander Kerensky, prime minister of Russia in 1917.

Student exchanges were developed in the 1930's with Lingnan University in China and the University of Hawaii. An affiliation with Yenching University was frustrated by war in 1937 and all such relationships were broken by World War II. Soon after the war, Occidental students helped to raise $11,000 for a war memorial scholarship endowment to honor their fellows who had died in the conflict. A joint student-faculty committee decided to use the income for international student contacts. From 1947 to 1958 student-financed exchanges were arranged between Occidental and institutions in Egypt, Greece, India, Japan, Korea, Mexico, Pakistan, the Philippines, Sweden and Turkey. During the same period foreign students came independently or under various auspices from a score of countries, including Brazil, Denmark, Formosa, Honduras, Hong Kong, Iran, Jordan, Korea, Lebanon, Nigeria, Okinawa, Rhodesia and Saudi Arabia.

In recent years, Occidental College has organized a series of annual conferences on Mexico and Hispanic-American affairs which provided fresh stimuli to the faculty and student body by drawing distinguished participants such as J. Frank Dobie and

Miguel Luis Leon-Portilla to the campus and focusing national attention on issues such as Mexican-American intellectual and economic relations, and on profitable channels of research in this field.

## Faculty Development Since 1957-58

By 1957-58 Occidental had developed a solid base in its faculty and curriculum for further attention to non-Western areas and world affairs. The establishment of the Chevalier Program in Diplomacy and World Affairs in 1957, endowed by a gift from the widow of former trustee Stuart Chevalier, enabled the college to add a professor who would strengthen the college's offerings with particular relation to non-Western and less developed areas. This and other special funds were also devoted to building up library holdings in these fields and to supporting a major in diplomacy and world affairs administered by the department of political science. The Chevalier program has been developing its long-range plans as part of a broader review of the curriculum.

From 1957 to 1962, three incumbents served in turn as Chevalier Professor. The first was Dr Graham H. Stuart, former professor of political science at Stanford University, who taught a seminar on United States diplomatic and consular practices and courses in United States and Latin American relations and in international law. He was followed for a year by Dr Arthur N. Young, a graduate and trustee of Occidental, who lectured on problems of underdeveloped countries, and Far East rivalries. From 1959-62, Dr J. Cudd Brown taught courses on African politics. Dr Edward W. Mill, a specialist on Southeast Asia, has served as Chevalier Professor since 1962.

Between 1957 and 1964 the administration continued to strengthen faculty competence on non-Western areas in two ways. First, it made thirteen new appointments in six departments. By 1964 new appointees had added to the staff varying degrees of competence in the following disciplines: three in *economics*, each specializing in a non-Western area; two in *foreign languages*, one in Russian and one with Middle Eastern experience; one in Russian and East European *history;* two in *philosophy and re-*

*ligion,* one familiar with the Middle East and the other with Russian experience; four in *political science,* all with international orientation and three of them specializing in Africa, Southeast Asia and Eastern Europe respectively; and one in *psychology* who has Indian experience.

Second, it enabled eighteen teachers already on the faculty to learn more about these regions by research, teaching abroad or travel. They represented nine departments: a professor of *art* who did research in India; two *economists* who taught or studied in Colombia and Iran respectively; three persons in *English and comparative literature* who visited Eastern Europe, South Asia and Taiwan; three in *foreign languages,* of whom two did research in Latin America and the third visited Russia and East Europe; one in *geology* who did field research in the Middle East; four in *history,* of whom two studied the USSR, another did research on China, and a fourth taught and traveled in Latin America; two in *music,* one who studied in Eastern Europe and one who performed and studied on tours to Asia and Latin America; two in *philosophy and religion* who did research in the Middle East, and one in *speech and drama* who spent his sabbatical leave in Scandinavia.

The additional study undertaken by these faculty members was assisted in one way or another by the following organizations in addition to the college itself: Beirut College for Women, the Brookings Institution, the Ford Foundation, the Fulbright-Hays Fellowship Program, the Guggenheim Foundation, the Hebrew Union College Biblical and Archaeological School, the Rockefeller Foundation, the Government of Thailand, the University of Guadalajara, Mexico, and the United States Government (Departments of State and Commerce).

As a result of these initiatives on the part of the administration and faculty, and despite the loss of three teachers competent in Chile, China and Iran, 24 members of the staff in eleven departments, besides President Coons, have had experience in one or more non-Western areas. This represents a quarter of the full-time teaching faculty at Occidental.

These 24 professors are affiliated in the numbers indicated with the following eleven departments: history 5; economics 4; foreign languages and political science 3 each; English and comparative literature, and philosophy and religion, 2 each; art, geology, music, psychology, speech and drama, 1 each. In terms of non-Western areas there were four staff members with competence in the Far East; two in Southeast Asia; six in South Asia; five in the Middle East; five in Eastern Europe and the USSR; two in Scandinavia; and nine in Latin America. (The total of 33 is accounted for by the fact that several of the 24 faculty members are competent in more than one non-Western area.) Eight of these teachers are area specialists. Two more have such extensive experience in Asia, Latin America or elsewhere that they might be classified as specialists in international economics and development.

The participation of seven of the chairmen of the eleven departments represented in this extension of faculty competence on non-Western areas, the high proportion of professors and associate professors who have availed themselves of these opportunities, and the caliber and variety of their sponsors suggest how much importance is attached to this enterprise at Occidental College. The established and developing knowledge of the faculty is reflected in the recently revised curriculum and in the courses on the non-Western world which many of them teach.

## Curriculum

Occidental College made major administrative and curricular changes between 1960 and 1962. These were designed to improve the educational life of the college by enabling faculty members and students to focus on fewer, more relevant learning tasks. In order to improve the internal coordination of faculty and curriculum, the nineteen departments were grouped under three divisions of the humanities and fine arts, social sciences, and natural sciences and mathematics. The three new divisional chairmen, a representative of the faculty at large, the dean of the faculty, and the registrar constituted an Educational Policy and Curriculum Committee.

After over a year of study by this committee and careful review by the faculty, a new three-course, three-term program was adopted to replace the semester system, in the autumn of 1963. A summer session of two terms of five or six weeks each, combined with a concurrent eleven-week term, was also established to permit qualified students maximum scope for independent study and other learning opportunities not available during the normal academic year. President Coons has stated that the introduction of the three-course, three-term program included a general pruning of the curriculum, resulting in a reduction in the number of courses offered from well over 400 to less than 300. This consolidation also facilitated reduction of the teaching load from an average of four courses and 10-12 hours per week to two courses and 8-10 hours per week. The changes have led to a better integration of courses and did not necessitate an increase in the size of the faculty.

By 1964, Occidental College offered 42 courses relating to the non-Western world in the following eight departments: art, 1; economics, 4; English and comparative literature, 1; foreign languages, 8—6 in Russian and 2 in Spanish-American literature; history, 12; philosophy and religion, 3; political science, 7; sociology and anthropology, 6. Thirty-two of these courses devoted over half of their content to one or more non-Western regions. The remaining ten were of the infusion type. Thirteen of the courses concerned several areas. Nine related to Eastern Europe and the USSR, six including the Russian language. Seven dealt with Asia in general, four with South and Southeast Asia, and two with the Far East. Six focused on Latin America and one on Africa.

The basic, integrated two-year History of Civilization course required for all freshmen and sophomores *introduces all students at Occidental to every major non-Western region.* The focus of this sequence is on the emergence and development of Western civilization. But in the second year approximately fifteen per cent of the lectures and two of the ten books on reserve deal specifically with non-Western areas. During 1963-64, 23 instructors from nine departments collaborated in teaching this course. The chairman was a historian specializing on Latin America and eight of his colleagues had had first-hand experience in one or more non-Western areas. Two were experts on Southeast Asia and Slavic studies. Nevertheless, several of the staff have expressed the hope that a considerably greater proportion of this basic course will soon be devoted to non-Western cultures and world affairs.

There are administrative as well as substantive problems involved in shifting the focus of such an integrated course taught by a large number of instructors from several departments. Each lecturer leads a discussion section of the course as well as addressing the entire class. Hence participation in this single course represents half of the teaching load of an instructor. Experience at Occidental suggests that it may be better for a specialist in a non-Western culture to concentrate on particular courses than to use a large proportion of his time in a more general, basic course such as History of Civilization. Occidental is fortunate in that it has built up a corps of teachers who have varying degrees of competence in the non-Western world, so that it can include in the staff of History of Civilization instructors with such experience and have others who devote most of their time to more advanced courses dealing with non-Western cultures.

When the new Chevalier Chair in Diplomacy and World Affairs was endowed in 1957, a broadly based advisory committee was established to develop and guide its policies and administration. After five years of experiment and some shifts in emphasis and leadership, the Chevalier curriculum was reorganized and consolidated in 1963 into an *Interdepartmental Program in Diplomacy and World Affairs* leading to the B.A. degree in diplomacy and world affairs. The new program offers a number of optional emphases along disciplinary or regional lines. It builds on Occidental's strength in economics, history and political science with special reference to Asia, Latin America and Europe, including some attention to Eastern Europe and Russia.

The Interdepartmental Program in Diplomacy and World Affairs requires ten courses: two each in political science, economics and history, and one in anthropology, plus advanced competence in one foreign language and demonstrated ability in English prose writing. A number of the required or elective courses recommended for the emphases on political or economic studies deal with non-Western areas. The cultural studies emphasis has no special required courses, but several of those suggested for this concentration relate to non-Western cultures. While Russian language may be taken to fulfill the special language requirement of the Chevalier program, it is only one of several options along with French, German and Spanish. Consequently no non-Western language is required for this program in any of its emphases.

Under the regional studies emphasis, students can concentrate on Asia, Latin America or Europe, including Eastern Europe and the Balkans with some attention to Russia. The fifteen suggested elective courses in six departments—economics, 1; English and comparative literature, 1; history, 6; philosophy and religion, 2; political science, 4—all deal primarily with Asia excepting the two on U.S. Foreign Policy and International Organization.

Students concentrating on Latin America have to take five additional required courses and so have no electives within the major, although three of the required courses offer options. The list of required and elective courses is as follows:

*Economics*—one of the following two courses required:

    109. International Economic Systems
    120. Economic Development

*History*—two of the following three courses required:

    145. Mexico and the Caribbean
    146. Argentina, Brazil and Colombia
    144. 20th-century Latin America

*Political Science*

    111. United States Foreign Policy (Highly recommended)
    112. International Organization (The United Nations)

*Sociology and Anthropology*

    124. Intercultural Relations
    150. Language and Culture

*Spanish*—both of the following courses required:

    107. Spanish-American Literature I
    108. Spanish-American Literature II

No courses were required for the emphasis on Europe, although seven in history, five in political science and two each in economics and in English and comparative literature were suggested as electives. This means that, in effect, students taking this concentration can ignore the several offerings relating to Eastern Europe and the USSR. They nevertheless get considerable exposure to non-Western areas in the ten courses required of anyone taking the interdepartmental major in diplomacy and world affairs.

## Library

The Occidental College library is comparatively large for a student body of about 1500. It is a central depository for California and U.S. publications and purchases United Nations materials as they are issued. In 1963-64 its holdings included 175,000 catalogued volumes, 25,000 documents and 20,000 periodicals. The library received 886 periodicals and newspapers. It has above-average collections on world affairs and non-Western cultures, particularly Latin America and Asia. The annual budget is $26,300 for books and $8,800 for periodicals. Roughly five per cent of both books and periodicals currently being added to the library, and ten per cent of total operating expenditures relate primarily to non-Western studies. About 6000 volumes have been added to the collections annually in recent years.

The staff rated holdings as from "adequate" to "good" for purposes of instruction and student research, but uniformly "poor" for faculty research on all non-Western areas. The greatest areas of strength were Asia and Latin America, with fair strength on Africa, the Middle East and Slavic studies. The three greatest library needs for non-Western studies were stated to be: (1) primary source materials and historical works to supplement current publications; (2) books, periodicals, newspapers and documents published in non-Western countries; and (3) more funds to buy current books on non-Western areas. The librarian has asked the administration for an increased budget to obtain more books and periodicals, particularly on Asia and Latin America.

The library has the following special collections on world affairs and non-Western areas: the Booth Collection in Economics and the Social Sciences, the Martin Fund for Training in Foreign Service and Diplomacy, the Cleland Collection on Latin America, the Osgood Hardy Fund for History of Latin America, the William W. Cumberland Fund and Browsing Room (which commemorate an alumnus of 1912 who served as general receiver and financial adviser to the Haitian government from 1924-27 and whose name still signifies economy to Haitians), the Mary Lou Fife '50 Fund for books on Southeast Asia, and the William B. Pettus Collection of Chinese paintings.

## Study Abroad

A growing number of undergraduates engage in study abroad for credit as part of their degree program. Between 20 and 26 students have done so among recent graduating classes. A few have studied during the academic year in non-Western areas, particularly Latin America and the Middle East. Three did so in 1958, five in 1959, three each in 1960 and 1961, ten in 1962 and five in 1963. They attended such institutions as the American University of Beirut and Mexico City College. Two students studied at the University of Guadalajara, Mexico, under the University of Arizona program, in the summer of 1962.

Several years of study by a faculty Committee on International Studies, which considered effective ways of encouraging carefully planned study abroad for qualified students, culminated in the establishment of a new program in international studies to take effect in the fall of 1964. The interdepartmental committee consists of Professor John Rodes of the department of history as chairman and representatives of the departments of economics, English and comparative literature, foreign languages and physics. This program offers each year a limited number of Occidental International Fellowships to selected juniors or seniors for six months' study during the summer combined with either the spring or the autumn term. Students from any major may apply to study at any appropriate place outside the U.S.A. Those accepted will register for two course credits in International Studies I and II taught by the staff. The new program in international studies will henceforth also supervise the work of any student seeking credit in the summer term for participation in the annual European History Study Tour. Nineteen students applied for the first six international fellowships, including two who wished to study in Latin America, and one each in Egypt and Lebanon.

In the fall of 1961 Occidental College joined the European cooperative program of summer research administered by Princeton University on behalf of Colgate, Columbia, Princeton and Rutgers Universities and Swarthmore College. The project was established in 1960 under a grant from Carnegie Corporation and has proved so successful that its scope may be extended to other areas such as Africa, Asia or Latin America.

In recent years a number of undergraduates have spent the summer in non-Western countries under the auspices of the Experiment in International Living. For example, in 1962 there were two in Nigeria, and one each in Greece and India.

## Foreign Students

In recent years the student body at Occidental College has become more diversified and cosmopolitan, with representatives from most of the states of the Union and fifteen to twenty foreign countries on campus in any given year. The catalogue expressly states that "As part of the total program in international education at Occidental, the college admits each year a number of students from foreign countries." Joint student-faculty committees concerned with international student exchanges have been active on the campus since the end of the First World War. Since World War II the students have taken more responsibility in these matters. This is partly the result of the activities of the Political Science Forum established in 1954, the International Club, the model United Nations and the International Students Committee. This last group is part of the International Development Council which raises funds for student exchanges and scholarships.

The college welcomes qualified foreign students and has set aside funds for the financial aid of those in need. Income from the David R. Faries International Scholarship fund of $31,500, established in 1958, and the War Memorial Fund of $11,350, set up in 1947-48 to honor the 39 students who died in World War II, is designated for this purpose. Additional funds to assist international students are included in the budget for the multi-million-dollar, fifteen-year capital gift campaign launched in 1961.

There were twenty undergraduates and six graduate students from abroad at Occidental College in 1963-64. Twelve of the undergraduates and all six of the graduates were from non-Western areas. Six of the undergraduates held scholarships ranging in value from $900 to $1800 and totaling $9475. Since 1958 the college has granted scholarships to forty undergraduate students from non-Western countries: four each in 1958 and 1959, seven in 1960, nine in 1961, ten in 1962 and six in 1963. These students serve occasionally as resource persons in classes and often take part in debates, forums, radio and TV panels and other extracurricular activities in which they can interpret their cultural traditions to the campus and the community.

## Extracurricular Activities

Many extracurricular activities reflect the college's interest in world affairs and non-Western cultures. The model United Nations, the International Club, the Political Science Forum and the International Students Committee have already been mentioned.

The name "Crossroads Africa" was coined by Occidental students in 1957 after they heard the Reverend James Robinson speak about his plans for African work projects. By the summer of 1963, 24 Occidental students had been chosen to serve in Operation Crossroads Africa. In February 1964 Dr Robinson stated that Occidental College had made the most remarkable contribution to this grassroots movement of any of the 32 cooperating schools and colleges.

Students and faculty have frequent opportunities to learn about non-Western cultures through lectures, artistic performances and other programs. For example, in recent months they might have heard Carlos Romulo, president of the University of the Philippines, or watched Uday Shankar's Hindu Ballet, or taken part in the annual Diplomacy and World Affairs Day for high school students and their counselors, or met with James P. Grant, Deputy Assistant Secretary of State for Near East and South Asian Affairs.

## Conclusion

The global dimensions of the international program at Occidental College are apparent in its administration, faculty, curriculum, library and extracurricular activities. The college catalogue explicitly expresses this world view. The annual reports of the president have special sections devoted to international study and international students. The report for 1957-58 devoted ten pages to Occidental and World Affairs and mentioned over a hundred alumni engaged in international service abroad.

Occidental College has developed substantial faculty competence in non-Western areas. Its curriculum, library and extracurricular activities combine to offer many opportunities to learn in some depth about non-Western cultures. All of its students get a brief introduction to them in the required History of Civilization course. Many others get further exposure through more advanced electives and Russian language study. In less than three years the number of courses dealing with the non-Western world (exclusive of History of Civilization) rose from 26 to 42, and enrolment in these courses from 582 to 1,043.

The administration and faculty recognize that the international emphasis must move forward. Professor Léon Dostert, who formerly directed the Institute of Foreign Languages and Linguistics at Georgetown University, hopes to develop more attention to such critical languages as Arabic and Chinese. Support from the Vocational Rehabilitation Administration has already been received to underwrite a special program to teach Arabic and Chinese to selected groups of well-qualified blind college students. These students will be in regular degree programs, and these languages will be available for study by other students at the college. Faculty members hope to infuse more material on non-Western cultures into the History of Civilization sequence. Occidental may experiment with a continuing faculty seminar to interest an even larger proportion of its staff to extend their competence to non-Western areas.

The pace of advance in non-Western studies has been fairly rapid since 1957. The Chevalier Interdepartmental Program in Diplomacy and World Affairs, the international studies programs and the broad effort to extend the world view of every student indicate that this enterprise is being consolidated and extended. Cooperation with neighboring institutions may add other dimensions to these programs. Occidental College has a remarkable tradition and unusual strength in non-Western studies and world affairs. With such a base, the college may soon achieve its objective of providing every student with a world view founded on substantial appreciation of his own and at least one non-Western culture and language.

# 12

# ATLANTA UNIVERSITY CENTER

Spelman and Morehouse Colleges initiated a non-Western studies program on behalf of the six institutions of the Atlanta University Center in 1961. This cooperative enterprise was undertaken to help selected faculty members from participating colleges to extend their competence to China, India and Africa by means of an intensive weekly seminar, and to integrate their new knowledge into their existing courses. It was also hoped that a

Atlanta University, Atlanta, Georgia. President Rufus E. Clement. (Private; coeducational; semester system; liberal arts and teacher training to master's degree; 681 students)

Clark College. President James P. Brawley. (Methodist; coeducational; semester system; liberal arts and teacher training to bachelor's degree; 770 students)

Interdenominational Theological Center. President Harry V. Richardson. (Interdenominational; coeducational; semester system; theology to master's degree; 105 students)

Morehouse College. President Benjamin E. Mays. (Private; men; semester system; liberal arts to bachelor's degree; 810 students)

Morris Brown College. President Frank Cunningham. (African Methodist Episcopal Church; coeducational; semester system; liberal arts and teacher training to bachelor's degree; 921 students)

Spelman College. President Albert E. Manley. (Baptist; women; semester system; liberal arts and teacher training to bachelor's degree; 596 students)

few new courses focusing on these non-Western civilizations would be added to the curriculum, primarily at Spelman and Morehouse but open to qualified upperclass students from the other colleges.

The rationale expressed in the proposal of 10 April 1960 requesting support from the Ford Foundation stated that:

> . . . college curricula and the specific course content of academic work are still, in large part, dominated by a focus on the United States and Western Europe. Although there is a trend towards greater emphasis on non-Western civilizations, the gap between the real world and the academic reflection of it remains enormous. This is probably more true in the South, with its traditional emphasis on local and national history, than in other parts of the country. . . . After weighing several possible approaches, the two colleges have concluded that the most effective way of bringing about a lasting change towards greater emphasis on Asia and Africa is to give key members of the faculty an opportunity for intensive study of non-Western civilizations.

The plan provided for an administrative committee composed of faculty members in the social sciences from Morehouse and Spelman, with the presidents of both colleges serving *ex officio,* and a program director competent on the area under study in each of the three years (first China, then India and finally Africa). The program director was to have four main duties: (1) to organize and lead the weekly faculty seminar; (2) to teach an undergraduate course on the civilization of the region being studied that year; (3) to arrange for two- or three-day visits about once a month by a series of specialists on the area of study; and (4) to supervise the building of a library, including books, periodicals and audio-visual materials on the area of study. This library was to be housed in the centrally-located Trevor Arnett Library of Atlanta University, which serves all five affiliated institutions. The program began to be implemented in 1961 after the Ford Foundation granted $200,000 for its support for the initial three-year cycle ending in 1964. Three significant but unforeseen outgrowths of this program have been: (1) an annual series of weekly television programs based on the undergraduate courses on China, India or Africa and sometimes featuring members of the faculty seminar, students and visiting specialists; (2) a workshop for high school social science teachers in Atlanta; and (3) the initiation of non-credit classes in Mandarin Chinese and Hindi respectively during the first two years of the program.

## Historical Background

Spelman, Morehouse and other colleges in the Atlanta University Center have had long connections with Africa, although most courses dealing with that continent have been offered at the graduate level by Atlanta University. The considerable African experience of numerous faculty members in the affiliated institutions has not yet been brought to bear on the development of many undergraduate courses on Africa. Since 1946, however, three courses have provided some opportunities for undergraduates to learn about China, Japan and India. For about ten years after the Second World War Dr Paustian, who had spent some twenty years in the Orient, offered a course on the History of the Orient; one semester dealt with China and Japan, and another with India. From 1952 until 1954 Mr Wong-Quinsey, a Chinese who had studied at Oxford, offered a course in the English department called Classical Chinese Culture. In the late 1950's a course on Non-Western Civilizations was offered in the department of history at Spelman. There has also been a course on world geography which includes some study of non-Western areas.

Neither Spelman nor Morehouse College had a specialist on China, India or Africa among their faculties when they began to plan for the program in 1959. But Professor Robert H. Brisbane of Morehouse had taught political science at Patna University, India, as a Fulbright senior professor in 1958-59, and Professor Howard Zinn spent the year 1960-61 as a post-doctoral fellow at Harvard University's Center for East Asian Studies. Dr Zinn returned to Spelman to serve as the first director of the non-Western studies program in 1961-62 and as chairman of the history department. Dr Brisbane succeeded him as program director for the India year in 1962-63. Dr Arthur C. Banks, Jr, professor of political science at Morehouse, became program director for the year 1963-64 when the focus was on Africa.

## Administration and Faculty

The Committee on Non-Western Studies makes basic policy decisions, selects the program director and seminar members for each year, reviews reports and assists the director. The committee consists of two members of the faculty in the social sciences from each of the two colleges, Morehouse and Spelman, and the presidents of both colleges, to whom the committee is responsible. The director is appointed in the spring of the year before he conducts the seminar so that he can plan ahead for the visiting specialists, library acquisitions, books which seminar members are to receive and read, and similar matters. Funds are available for about fifteen members of the seminar each year. These provide the college with $2500 to assist in obtaining a replacement for the faculty member, who is granted about one-third released time in order to read and do research for the seminar. Each participant also gets an allowance of $500 to purchase a small library of books or periodicals relevant to the area being studied and to cover attendance at conferences, travel for observation of other non-Western study programs, or research. The publications purchased with these funds remain a part of the individual's library. The grant also provides $5000 for library materials and audio-visual aids and covers the entire salary of the director and the costs of administration. Spelman College serves as fiscal agent.

The faculty seminar meets one evening a week throughout the academic year. Morehouse and Spelman Colleges usually designate four members each from their social science departments. Clark and Morris Brown Colleges, the other two undergraduate institutions affiliated with the Atlanta University Center, normally have two members each. The Interdenominational Theological Center and Atlanta University are usually invited to have one participant each. Associate members from the neighboring institutions, who are not automatically eligible, have been admitted by special arrangement each year. For example, a historian from Oglethorpe University took part in the first three seminars, a philosopher from Georgia State College attended the first two, and a historian from Emory University the second and third.

During the first three years of the seminar there were 21 official participants representing eleven departments. Eight of the members were in all three seminars (one from Clark, two from Morehouse, one from Morris Brown, two from Spelman and one each from Atlanta University and the Interdenominational Theological Center); five attended two seminars (two from Spelman and one each from Morehouse, Morris Brown and Atlanta University); and eight took part in the seminar just one year (four from Morehouse and one each from Clark, Morris Brown, Spelman and I.T.C.). The numbers of representatives from the various departments were: philosophy and religion 6, history 3, political science 3, art 2, and anthropology, economics, education, English, French, geography and sociology 1 each.

Morehouse College had the most seminar members with seven from six departments. Corresponding figures for the other institutions were: Clark 2/2, Morris Brown 3/3, Spelman 5/5, Atlanta 2/1, and I.T.C. 2/1. Although it was expected that participants would remain in the service of their institutions long enough for them to derive some benefits from the knowledge which faculty members acquired in the seminars, four teachers who took part in the first or second seminars had left by 1963-64. This attrition of faculty members who have gained certain degrees of competence in non-Western areas is a serious loss, especially since one of these professors played a significant part in planning the program and taught the two new courses on China.

About thirty seminar meetings are held each year. In the first semester the traditional culture and historical background are examined. More modern developments and the contemporary scene are accented during the second semester. The coverage is broad and topical, with a chronological framework, but an attempt is made to delve in some depth into significant subjects such as philosophy, art, religion, law and political modernization. This process is assisted materially by the contributions of the eight visiting specialists who spend a few days on the campus at intervals of about a month and lead the seminar, speak in undergraduate classes and in public as well as meeting informally with faculty and students.

The pattern of seminar meetings has usually included an hour of presentation followed by an hour of discussion in an informal atmosphere. The presentation, usually in the form of a paper, is made either by a member of the seminar, the visiting expert, a specialist from another Atlanta institution, or the director. Experience has shown that it is wise to schedule the first reports by seminar members fairly late in the first term so that they have a better chance to get their bearings in a new civilization before presenting their findings to the group.

In order to prepare more adequately for the seminar, participants have been provided with book lists and some thirty essential books ahead of time and asked to read at least three or four of the books during the summer. For example, during the seminar on China in 1961-62, they were assigned J. K. Fairbank's *The United States and China,* F. S. C. Northrop's *The Meeting of East and West,* and E. O. Reischauer's *Japan, Past and Present.* While the seminar focused on China, it was thought important to do some reading about Japan; so five of the thirty basic books concerned Japan rather than China. The two main source books recommended for the seminar were: *Sources of Chinese Tradition,* edited by De Bary, Chan and Watson, and Feng Yu-Lan's *A Short History of Chinese Philosophy.*

Aside from the on-campus faculty seminars and some travel to other colleges such as Haverford and Earlham, to learn more about their non-Western programs, and to professional meetings, the faculty of the cooperating Atlanta institutions have used relatively few other opportunities to extend their competence in non-Western areas. Professor Brisbane spent the summer of 1962 at the Center for South Asian studies at the University of Pennsylvania, in preparation for his duties as director of the seminar on India during 1962-63, and the summer of 1963 studying political change in several African countries. Professor Banks spent the summer of 1963 in intensive study of Africa in preparation for directing the 1963-64 seminar. The impact of the seminars and non-Western studies program on faculty members is hard to evaluate concretely, but conversations with participating teachers indicate that it may be considerable.

## Curriculum

The chief curricular change effected by the program has been the initiation of two semester courses each on China, India and Africa, originally taught by the director of the program for the given year. A course on Latin American history is intended to be introduced in 1964-65.

The new courses on China, India and Africa are primarily upperclass electives purposely restricted to 15-20 specially interested and qualified students. A few sophomores and auditors have been admitted. The courses are primarily historical and political in orientation. The emphasis has been on seminar-type discussions, with frequent student reports, students leading discussions of selected topics, and unusually heavy outside reading assignments. Normally students have had to prepare one or two major research papers chosen from a list of some thirty topics each semester. A feature of these courses has been that each visiting expert has spoken in class and met with the students in the course of his campus stay, and that interested students may attend faculty seminar meetings. Students have also helped to prepare for, and taken part in, some of the weekly television programs, sometimes discussing their own research topics.

Faculty and student interest has been aroused by the new courses. The decision to keep the classes small and select has helped to maintain a high academic standard. On the other hand, the number of students reached by these courses is correspondingly small. It is therefore helpful that infusion of non-Western materials is taking place in ten other courses which together attract over 300 enrolments a year. The titles of the six new semester courses on China, India and Africa and of the nine courses in which infusion occurs are as follows:

| *New Non-Western Courses* | *Infusion Courses* |
| --- | --- |
| China—Past and Present | History and Appreciation of the Arts |
| China—Communist China | Introduction to the Fine Arts |
| India—Prehistoric, Ancient | Comparative Economic Systems |
|    and Classical India | Humanities 161-2 and 251-252 |
| India—Medieval and Modern | History of Civilization |

| *New Non-Western Courses* | *Infusion Courses* |
|---|---|
| Africa—Introduction to the Civilization of Africa | International Politics |
| | Problems in International Relations |
| Africa—The Politics of Freedom | Religions of the World |
| | Social Theory |

Each of the new semester courses carries three semester hours of credit, but none is as yet required for majors or for graduation.

None of the colleges taking part in this program offers formal instruction in any non-Western language. But non-credit classes in conversational Mandarin Chinese and in Hindi, organized in the first and second years of the program respectively, drew 18-25 participants for Chinese and 6-10 for Hindi. The interest shown in these informal courses may lead to more regular instruction in one or both languages as the program becomes consolidated. Both of these language courses came into being through the initiative of the program directors and the availability of people with the requisite knowledge.

The course in Chinese was organized because it was learned that a graduate student from China at Atlanta University had experience in teaching the language and that one of the Morehouse undergraduates in the new course on China had learned to speak Mandarin and had spent two years in Taiwan as an Air Force interpreter. The director arranged for the Yale series of texts and tapes on Mandarin Chinese to be supplied and provided a modest subvention from program funds. The course met regularly for one evening each week with 18-25 students and faculty members in attendance. Unfortunately, as the Chinese graduate student left the following year, the course had to be abandoned, but a few faculty members and students have expressed the hope that it may be reinstated and become a regular part of the curriculum.

The Hindi course was organized in comparable fashion by arranging with a visiting professor from India at Atlanta University to conduct the class. This and other aspects of the program led to friendly contacts with the local Indian Association. Both classes used modern instructional materials. The fact that they were organized suggests that there may be people able—perhaps with intensive additional study at a major center—to give at least elementary courses in critical non-Western languages in more colleges than now offer them. Such introductory study might be followed up by the more serious students through the Princeton University Cooperative Undergraduate Program for Critical Languages and in intensive summer institutes.

Faculty members from the cooperating colleges report that they not only learned much about China, India and Africa, but that their intellectual horizons were broadened by regular contact with scholars in other disciplines engaged in examining common topics. The following examples of the infusion of non-Western data were reported by the four undergraduate colleges of the Atlanta University Center. Clark has integrated materials into the survey course on philosophy and religion and hopes to include units on the non-Western world in the humanities sequence; Morehouse has changed the Western civilization course to one entitled History of Civilization and found that the seminars have helped faculty members to synthesize Western and non-Western materials; Morris Brown has added units on China and India to its World History course and gives more attention to Oriental influences in Western culture in the Humanities sequence; at Spelman the faculty has gained enough confidence from the seminar to overcome earlier hesitation and has decided to replace the course on the History of Western Civilization with one on the History of World Civilization and to introduce a course on World Religions.

An associate member of the seminar from Oglethorpe University reported that its Survey of Civilization course had been enriched by non-Western material as a result of his association with the cooperative program and that his university planned to introduce a sophomore-level course called Introduction to Oriental Literature. He added that Oglethorpe's summer institute for gifted high school students would have special classes on China and that the Atlanta school system was interested in developing a pilot project in the humanities for gifted twelfth-grade students which would use non-Western materials. He credited these initiatives to the influence of the non-Western study program at the Atlanta University Center, and said that a number of high school students had been following the television series.

## Library

The Trevor Arnett Library which serves the Atlanta University Center had 272,000 volumes in 1963. Its total budget was $209,000, with $55,500 allocated for the purchase of books and the 2184 periodicals received annually. The staff did not give an estimate of the percentage of recent acquisitions relating primarily to non-Western studies. The faculty rated library holdings for instruction and student research as "good" for Africa, "adequate" for Asia and Latin America, and "poor" for other areas. Holdings were considered "poor" for faculty research in all areas except Africa. The library has had strong collections on Africa for many years. Its greatest needs in relation to the undergraduate non-Western studies program were for critically selected and out-of-print books directly relevant to the needs of the faculty seminars and the new courses on China, India and Africa.

The following numbers of books and periodicals had been acquired for the program by the end of 1963:

|  | | Books | Periodicals |
|---|---|---|---|
| China phase | (1961-62) | 409 | 17 |
| India phase | (1962-63) | 287 | 7 |
| Africa phase | (1963-64) | 157 | 1 |
| Totals | | 853 | 25 |

This compilation was made in the middle of the Africa phase of the program, hence the lower figures for publications on Africa.

These figures reflect another difficulty, which is that many important works, including some published fairly recently, are out of print and hard to obtain. For example, even in the case of books on China, which are more plentiful than those on India, which in turn are probably more numerous than those on Africa, the Atlanta program ordered over 700 publications but actually acquired just over 400. Nevertheless, these accessions, coupled with the existing collections in the library, have provided a reasonable base for the program's needs.

From the start a special alcove in the library was set aside for books and periodicals relating to the non-Western program. Students in the class and faculty members in the seminar were allowed to remove these books from the shelves for three days. Otherwise they were held on reserve. As there tended to be a big demand for certain publications whenever the topic of the seminar, class or visiting specialist was covered in particular books, the library had to get multiple copies of some works which are still in print. Program directors have learned that library funds can be used more efficiently if they are expended over a few years rather than in any given year. This means that the library has reserve funds from the grant for additional purchases.

A tape recorder, texts and tapes for Chinese, Japanese and Hindi language instruction, maps, slide collections, teaching aid packets, and other materials have been acquired and used in class, in the seminar and on loan to other institutions in the city. Tape recordings of most of the seminar meetings, public lectures and television programs, and of a few class sessions, have also been made and used periodically.

## Students and Extracurricular Activities

The four undergraduate colleges of the Atlanta University Center had a total of 21 students from non-Western countries, all on scholarships, in 1963-64. The numbers in previous years had been six in 1958-59 and 1959-60, and 21 each year thereafter. No students had studied abroad for credit, but two who were in the India course in 1962-63 won scholarships for study in India. Both were sophomore honor students at Spelman. One was given a scholarship by the Indian Studies Center of the University of Wisconsin to study community development at Osmania University, Hyderabad. The other won a Merrill traveling scholarship and planned to spend two years in social science study at the University of Delhi.

Students from non-Western countries, mainly in Africa, are encouraged to learn all they can about American civilization and how their study in the U.S.A. can be adapted to the different needs and situations at home. International students have been used occasionally as native informants in language classes and as resource persons in courses. They have often taken part in informal foreign language groups and spoken on radio or television, in debates and at forums. This type of activity has been fostered by the active International Relations Club.

Public lectures and other events, such as the performances of the Ceylon National Dancers and of the Phakavali Dancers of Thailand, the Atlanta-Morehouse-Spelman presentation of the Chinese drama *Lute Song,* and the UNESCO exhibit on "2000 Years of Chinese Painting" have attracted considerable interest from the Atlanta University Center constituency and from many others in Atlanta who have not been in the habit of attending lectures or performances at the center. *The Atlanta Constitution,* radio and TV stations have given these events and other aspects of the non-Western studies program favorable coverage. Educators in Atlanta have proposed various forms of cooperation with the program. Professors at Emory University and at the Georgia Institute of Technology have requested bibliographic help; the Fulton County and Atlanta Boards of Education planned a summer seminar on China for gifted high school students; and a private school consulted the director of the program on plans to establish a course on the non-Western world.

In 1963 the center arranged with the Asia Society to co-sponsor an all-day workshop on non-Western civilizations and institutions for high school teachers in the social sciences in the Atlanta area. The workshop was held at Atlanta University. About fifty teachers and principals attended. They were presented with special materials prepared by the Asia Society, and then divided into groups for individual workshops on East, South and Southeast Asia. The response to the workshop was encouraging and it may be repeated periodically.

## Conclusion

Members of the Committee on Non-Western Studies reported at the end of 1963 that they were gratified with the development of the program. They hope to provide opportunities for from three to six members of the faculty of each cooperating college to spend a year on leave studying some non-Western culture in depth in order to acquire more specialized competence than is now available on their own campuses. Presidents Manley of Spelman and Mays of Morehouse hope that the program can include faculty members from a broader range of disciplines. It may be necessary to broaden the membership of the supervisory committee to include representatives of disciplines other than those in the social sciences (three of the four faculty members on the committee in 1963-64 were political scientists) and of at least two more colleges—Clark and Morris Brown, the other two undergraduate colleges of the center.

It may also be necessary to encourage more rotation in the membership of the faculty seminar, particularly as the first three-year cycle has been completed. Much will depend on future financing, for it was uncertain in March 1964 whether further foundation support for the program would be available after the end of the 1963-64 academic year.

The Non-Western Studies Program has broken new ground in the deep South. It has added significant dimensions to the competence of over twenty faculty members at center institutions plus three or four others not formally related to the cooperative program. It has created new interest among students, introduced six new courses on China, India and Africa and led to the infusion of non-Western materials into other courses. The library has been enriched and the community has been stimulated by the program. The faculty seminar was the first of its kind to bring together negro and white faculty members from all of the Atlanta institutions of higher education on a regular basis. Public lecturers under the program have attracted large audiences of both races.

The program's many achievements have depended heavily on a small core of interested administrators and faculty members and on large amounts of external support. Unless this is continued or unless the cooperating institutions can rapidly absorb the costs of the program into their regular budgets, it may have to be modified or even curtailed. Much useful experience has been gained and perspectives have been broadened, but the program is still affecting directly only a limited number of faculty and students. It needs to be consolidated and to find ways to serve a greater proportion of its potential constituency.

258

# 13

# THE GETTYSBURG GROUP

Not least of the countless problems faced by the small liberal arts college today is its inability to offer extensive area programs in non-Western studies comparable to those now being included in the curriculum of large universities. The worth of such pro-

---

Dickinson College, Carlisle, Pennsylvania. President Howard L. Rubendall. (Private; coeducational; semester system; liberal arts and teacher training to bachelor's degree; 1217 students)

Gettysburg College, Gettysburg, Pennsylvania. President Carl A. Hanson. (Lutheran; coeducational; semester system; liberal arts and teacher training to bachelor's degree; 1852 students)

Hood College, Frederick, Maryland. President A. Randle Elliott. (Private; women; semester system; liberal arts and teacher training to bachelor's degree; 670 students)

Mount St Mary's College, Emmitsburg, Maryland. President Robert R. Kline. (Roman Catholic; men; semester system; liberal arts to bachelor's degree; 791 students)

St Joseph College, Emmitsburg, Maryland. President Sister Rosemary Pfaff. (Roman Catholic; women; semester system; liberal arts and teacher training to bachelor's degree; 579 students)

Western Maryland College, Westminster, Maryland. President Lowell S. Ensor. (Methodist; coeducational; semester system; liberal arts and teacher training to master's degree; 983 students)

This report is drawn from an article by Sister Hilda Gleason, D.C., former president of St Joseph College, published in *The Catholic Educational Review*, LXI, 7, October 1963, and a paper prepared for the Association of American Colleges by Professor Norman E. Richardson of Gettysburg College, coordinator of the six-college program.

grams is recognized, the need for them is well understood, but the small college realistically faces the fact that it cannot expand its offerings without considerable financial support from outside sources. Competition for this financial aid is so keen that the administrators of such colleges hold little hope of being among the recipients. They do not blame the foundations for investing their funds where they will reach the largest number of people, but they wistfully dream of the day when some stroke of good fortune will enable them to open up new avenues of culture to their students and new areas of study to their self-sacrificing faculty members whose projects must so frequently be shelved because financially they are unattainable.

It was perhaps as the result of such a dream that the administrator of a small college brought into being this non-Western studies program. He was well aware that concern for non-Western studies was a normal part of the liberal arts tradition and that such studies have taken on considerable importance in view of world events. The curriculum of his college, like that of other small colleges, was Western-oriented and, at best, he could only hope to add a few courses in non-Western areas. With this he could not be satisfied. How could he prepare his students to cope with problems that were front-page news when he could not afford to have separate departments for non-Western studies nor the specialists who drew big salaries at large universities? In the fall of 1960, General Willard S. Paul, then president of Gettysburg College, deeply concerned about this problem, decided to try to solve it at the cooperative level.

Within a 35-mile radius of Gettysburg were five other small colleges which would represent a sizeable unit if they could be brought together to work out the project. Together these six colleges, Dickinson, Gettysburg, Hood, Mount St Mary's, St Joseph and Western Maryland, have a total enrolment of about 5500 students and a combined faculty of 455 members. What each could not accomplish alone might well be done by a joint effort and a pooling of funds. Moreover, a foundation would be more apt to contribute funds in view of the number of institutions being served, provided that the proposal was academically sound and intellectually of high caliber.

## Planning

A meeting of the college presidents decided to turn the planning over to a committee of faculty from the colleges, while assuring the committee of the interest and backing of the administrations. A faculty committee was accordingly set up to try to gather the best information possible and then to tool that information to our needs. Many of these needs we discovered as we went along.

The Asia Society was most helpful at this point, sending us four consultants who both gave talks at different colleges and met with the committee. Not all were completely enthusiastic about the direction which our thinking was taking. These consultants were: Kenneth Morgan of Colgate, Theodore de Bary of Columbia, Robert I. Crane of Michigan—later Duke, and Wing-tsit Chan of Dartmouth.

The planning committee did not leave each college in a position of trying to solve unaided the many problems created by participation in the program. It worked diligently to propose solutions for these common problems. It asked the librarians to work together in obtaining and circulating books and arranged for a cooperative pool for specialized and rare books. It sought a cooperative solution for the replacement of faculty members who would be on part-time leave. It arranged the location of seminars among the colleges so that no one college would be inconvenienced. It planned a schedule so that the visiting lecturer could talk to the students of all the colleges while he was in the area. It investigated the possibility of a cooperative solution to the problem of specialized non-Western languages for the cooperating colleges.

By the spring of 1961 a tentative program had been drawn up, with Dr Norman E. Richardson, chairman of the philosophy department of Gettysburg College, as coordinator. In an attempt to guard against superficiality, it was decided to limit the scope of the program to the study of China and India. Concentration was to be on the intensive training of faculty members chosen by each college rather than on an immediate change in curriculum.

## Presentation to the Ford Foundation

Not the least of the problems undertaken by the committee was the drawing up of a proposal to present to a foundation for financial assistance. Each college declared itself willing to back the project while aid was sought and to continue to contribute its share of funds during the whole program. Exploratory conversations were held with John Everton of the Ford Foundation. When he became the United States Ambassador to Burma, his place at the Foundation was taken by George Beckmann with whom the negotiations were finally concluded. The announcement of the Ford Foundation's approval of the project was made on 22 March 1962, and a grant of $180,000 was received. It had been established that the cost to the six colleges would be about $75,000 over a two-year period. None of the colleges would have any trouble meeting this demand, and they were deeply grateful to the Ford Foundation for the financial assistance.

## Structure of the Cooperative Plan

The running of the program was the responsibility of an executive committee, whose rulings were to be carried out by the coordinator. Gettysburg College was to serve as financial agent, and the moneys were to be paid directly to the other colleges for such things as books and released time. Stipends were to be paid directly to the participants. The program was then able to act autonomously within the limits of its franchise.

Each of the two parts of the program was to have a consultant. Wing-tsit Chan served as consultant for the China part and Robert I. Crane for the India part.

The colleges were to maintain their independence with regard to the men they chose for the program and the use they were to make of the results. Since the seminar meetings were to be held at different colleges they took over the details of arrangements for the seminars for which they were hosts twice a year.

It should be emphasized that the separate colleges backed the program from the start, and without this cooperation between them and the committee any success that we may have had would have been impossible.

## The Program

Each part of the program covered three phases. The first phase was summer reading from a list of books drawn up by the consultants. For this the men and women were paid a modest sum to relieve them of teaching in summer school. The books were general in nature and served to give the participants a common background of information. Before the summer reading started, the consultants met with the participants to go over their individual programs. This enabled those who had already done some reading to work further in the direction of their own specialties and yet to remain within the framework of the whole group.

In the second phase, twelve seminars were held during the year, covering the main stages in the development of these cultures in historical fashion. Bibliographies for these seminars were mailed out well in advance so that the participants could get their homework done. And, because they were teaching only half time, they were expected to do it. The seminars did not regularly include a public lecture—it tended to be a waste of time for the participants.

The format of the seminars was usually to start with supper on Friday night. This gave the committee a chance to clue the visiting specialist in to exactly where the program was, as well as enabling people to get to know one another. There followed a rather formal presentation of an hour and a half or two hours. The following morning there was another two-hour-long session. Lunch, and then a wrap-up session such that we were usually through by 4:00 P.M. The seminars varied with the topic, of course, but this was the general pattern.

The consultant took four of the seminars throughout the year, which enabled him to keep in close touch with the work of the participants. In both cases the two consultants, Chan and Crane, have also carried on a considerable correspondence with the participants with regard to their own work and their plans for summer school.

Thirdly, the second summer was an attempt to follow up the work of the seminars with still further study, mainly in the field

263

of the participant's own discipline. While many of the participants stayed in this country, several of them on the China program were in Taiwan and Hawaii. As India is more open to such summer work, seven of the thirteen India participants will be in India this summer.

## Personnel

The original idea was to have two participants from each school, but it worked out at eleven for the China part and thirteen for the India part. In addition to this group an almost equal number of interested faculty members were usually present as auditors.

The 24 participants represented the following disciplines: sociology, 2; history, 5; languages, 2; art, 4; psychology, 1; political science, 2; English, 3; religion, 2; philosophy, 2; and economics, 1.

## Results

The direct and immediate results focus mainly on the academic enrichment of the faculty participants, the spirit of cooperation which has been generated by the program, and the addition of books to the college libraries.

The enrichment of the faculty can be gathered from the following facts: (1) five of the group have been awarded summer Fulbrights; (2) three of the India participants will spend an additional year in India with Fulbright, NDEA and American Institute of Indian Studies grants; (3) two of the China participants are adding another year to their training, one at Columbia and the other at Harvard. The program, therefore, has been a significant stimulant for even further training, and a good deal of this has been in the languages.

It is impossible to describe accurately the results of having a group of faculty people, with such a wide spread of disciplines, meeting regularly together, both for planning and for participation in such a program. Add to this the fact that four major religious traditions, Catholic, Lutheran, Reformed and Methodist, are represented and there it is even better. Suffice it to say that these meetings have spilled over into further meetings of all sorts in which there has been a lively exchange of ideas and concerns. The ground work has been laid for still further cooperation.

An additional direct result has been the addition to the libraries of books of sufficiently high quality and quantity to be able to mount the kind of additional courses that we want to offer in the near future.

The indirect results—exactly where to draw the line here is hard—would include the following:

(1) enrichment of the courses which are already offered, and of courses which otherwise might never have had any non-Western dimension at all.

(2) the addition of new courses in each of the colleges.

(Here a comment needs to be made. Since the program does not end officially until September 1964 and, as can be seen from the above, several of the participants will be abroad for still another year, it is almost impossible to come up with specifics here and now. This much we are sure about: new courses in non-Western areas are being proposed to the various curriculum committees at the colleges now. Then, in the very near future, we *hope* to have our whole group working on a cooperative course in Asian Civilization, which would be given at each school. With the large number of disciplines which we have represented among the participants, this seems to be the thing that we might be able to do best. In addition, and this is still in the talking stage, we hope that we can do something with the problem of the confrontation of these various cultures.)

(3) With this spread of personnel, as well as with such a number, we hope that we will be better able to influence the curricula of individual colleges.

(4) A most welcome addition to our program has been the presence, through the Whitney-Fulbright cooperation of four visitors from colleges and universities in Taiwan and India on four of our campuses both this year and next, for a semester each.

These visitors have offered two courses each on the campuses as regular parts of our curricula. The courses will go a long way toward building up interest among the students.

(5) Because of this program, other sources have been tapped and channeled into this work: individual teachers have located still further fellowships; sources of funds for still more books have been located; and student exchange has been greatly enlarged in some places.

(6) Already we are sending students into graduate schools with the purpose of training for work in non-Western fields.

As the cooperative program of Asia studies progresses, the six colleges will gain new strength and stature with the intellectual community. They have shown that by combining their resources they can give advantages to their faculty and students equal to those given by large universities. They have brought to their students exceptional contacts with a culture other than their own. Already recommendations are being made for new courses, and the revision of the present curriculum is being considered. Cooperation among these colleges in future Asian course offerings is a possibility under investigation, as well as the extension of the program to retrain high school teachers in the area who are required to teach courses in world culture. Whatever major changes may unfold in the near future, the bond of unity which now cements the friendship among this group of colleges can surely be expected to effect desirable improvements for all.

# 14

# GREAT LAKES
# COLLEGES ASSOCIATION

## Constitutional Questions

The Great Lakes Colleges Association is both new enough and old enough to present constitutional questions. Their resolution may determine the fate of the organization.

Like all federations, the Association has to decide what to do at the center and at the periphery, through the whole and through the parts. Two critical decisions have been made—to decentralize and to use certain member colleges as agents for all others. Although one full-time and several part-time officers have been added to the staff, no one has been added in the headquarters office. All but one have come from within the faculties of the member colleges and have remained on their home campuses or temporarily moved abroad to a GLCA study center there. In undertaking the difficult task of establishing overseas study centers in Japan and Latin America, a carefully considered decision was made to delegate each task to a member college acting as agent for the Association. Therefore, Antioch College, using its own staff, administrative facilities

The Great Lakes Colleges Association is an association of twelve colleges in Indiana, Michigan and Ohio: Albion, Antioch, Denison, DePauw, Earlham, Hope, Kalamazoo, Kenyon, Oberlin, Ohio Wesleyan, Wabash and Wooster. This text is excerpted from the report of the Association for 1963.

and experience, has undertaken the promotion, establishment and operation of the overseas program in Latin America. It has done so *for the Association.* Earlham College has undertaken the same in Japan. Both these decisions affecting staff and operations reflect a high degree of decentralization, with obvious advantages and obvious risks.

This pattern of administration fits the philosophy under which the Association began—that a growing central secretariat would be a warning sign. It recognizes that officers must be added as joint functions are assumed but enlists their aid without removing them from their home campuses. The use of the agency principle, or members as agent colleges, in operating overseas study centers capitalizes on existing experience, available specialized competence, and established administrative procedures rather than starting afresh or duplicating at the center. Also, controls for safeguarding the interests of all member colleges are employed through such devices as payment of salaries by the Association and approval of personnel and budgets by officers of the Association.

The risks are apparent. An agglomeration of colleges takes time to become something more substantial and cohesive. Is extreme decentralization a technique for making progress or simply for living with tradition? Will persons both inside the Association and outside it regard the overseas study centers as those of the agent colleges or those of the Association? Will home-based staff happily combine the old loyalty to the member college and the new loyalty to a common cause? One consequence is certain: the pattern embarked upon will accentuate the problems of communication, which are necessarily already formidable. Yet common understanding is the *sine qua non* of effective cooperation. Therefore compensatory machinery may have to be devised, or compensatory effort exerted, to offset this hazard.

**The Main Thrust**

In keeping with the original idea that attention would be focused on "the new and the few," the Association has sought to be highly selective in its choices for action. Much that might be done is not being done. Much proposed is not undertaken. Likewise, some choices now being pursued may give way later to higher priorities. The "good thing" psychology of cooperation, which breeds projects by the score, has to be offset by hard decisions about one use of Association personnel as compared with another. The results are salutary.

The main thrust is as last year. It is aimed at the provision of greater intercultural experience for all students at home and for some students abroad; increased professional opportunities for the faculty; educational research, particularly for the improvement of teaching; clarification of objectives and exploration of cooperative programs in graduate education; and enrichment of cultural life through additional lecturers. The first three have been launched with substantial progress to report. The last two are on their way in a more restrained sense— the first because of the seemingly intractable problems of promoting advanced study in the liberal arts college tradition and the second because of the high ratio between time and effort and success.

## International Education Program

The plan for international education worked out last year has come to some fruition already and the financial support required for greater progress is assured for the immediate future.[1] Effort is being made to retain the wholeness and balance of the original plan, although financial support for some components is not yet assured.

The objective is to infuse into education a larger international component, to emphasize the intercultural dimension and to surround the student with opportunities both at home and abroad to understand a culture quite different from his own and, as a by-product, to understand his own better. As a result the emphasis is on non-Western cultures. Two interrelated attacks are planned: an advance across-the-board for all mem-

---

1. Early in 1964 the Ford Foundation made GLCA a grant of $500,000 for a three-year period.

ber colleges, with each using, as it wishes, curricular modification, library resources, student or faculty exchanges and extracurricular life; and a selective advance of greater penetration by five or six of the member colleges, with each concentrating on language, staff, library and other resources relevant to a particular non-Western culture for its own benefit and for the shared benefit of all other Association members. These two home-front developments are given point and outlet through a third development: overseas centers for student instruction and faculty research—one in each of the great cultural areas corresponding to the five or six campus concentrations alluded to above. The interlacing, mutually sustaining possibilities are clear.

So far the overseas study centers are moving faster than home developments, with funds provided by the Association itself. With the Ford Foundation grant for faculty fellowships, the domestic re-tooling can begin in some places and be accelerated in others. The five or six campus cultural concentrations are without outside support so far and therefore without the central impetus desired and required for the service of all the colleges. What has been begun will require patient extension and shoring up.

Three overseas study centers are advanced to the point of actual operation or assurance of operation in the next academic year.

*Japan Program.* Twenty-five students from Earlham, Antioch and Kalamazoo inaugurated a pilot program for the Association in Japan in the summer of 1963, with continuation through the current academic year. Some returned at mid-year, some stayed the full year. These beginnings grew out of a joint Earlham-Antioch program in Japanese studies, involving both students and faculty members. The students who went to Japan studied the Japanese language at Earlham in the preceding term, including the Kalamazoo student who transferred to Earlham for that particular purpose. All studied the language intensively in Japan during the summer also. In the fall, they enrolled, as previously planned, in the international division of Waseda

University in Tokyo. Instruction was in English. Meanwhile, acquaintance both with the language and the culture was intensified by living in the homes of Japanese families.

Professor Jackson H. Bailey of Earlham College, a specialist in Japanese studies, represented the Association in its relations with Waseda while also serving as executive associate in the International House in Tokyo. Professor Joseph Whitney, a British geographer, was employed as coordinator for the student group.

Later in the year Earlham was asked to take responsibility and leadership in planning and setting up a cooperative program between the Association and Waseda University, whose representatives had meanwhile visited most of the GLCA colleges. Still later, Earlham was formally named agent for the Association in this entire enterprise, and Miss Yasuko Kakegawa was employed in Tokyo to serve as resident liaison representative of the Association in its dealings with both students and the university. She will function under the general supervision of a GLCA faculty member who will go to Tokyo each year both to teach (or do research) and serve as coordinator of the program. In addition, someone at Earlham College will serve as administrator of the program in the United States.

Under these arrangements a Japan program is in being and plans for 1964–65 are well advanced. Students who have returned from the pilot experience are enthusiastic about what they learned, corroborating the appraisal of possibilities as viewed firsthand by several GLCA faculty members who have visited Japan in the last two years. These include Association board chairman, President Landrum R. Bolling of Earlham, and Professor Lewis M. Hoskins of Earlham, chairman of the Committee on International Education.

*Latin America Program.* The 1962 feasibility study in Latin America was supplemented in 1963 by another on-the-scene survey. The latter suggested a concrete program, with concrete means to the desired ends. It was done by Professor Raymond L. Gorden of Antioch College, accompanied by Lic. Enrique Romero-Yllades from Antioch's Mexican study program in Guanajuato. It culminated in a report subsequently used to shape the emerging program. The salient features are these: a flexible program fitting different student needs and preparations and different academic calendars; a three-phase study opportunity concentrating on one or two semesters in Colombia, with a preliminary summer in Mexico for those who need further language training (the first GLCA-organized and operated and the second dependent upon classes in three Bogotá universities); tailor-made orientation and "comparative civilization" courses required of all students; and a physical facility owned or rented by the Association in Bogotá as an academic, social and administrative center.

The preparation of this report, entitled "A Proposal for a Latin American Program," reflects that Antioch College had been asked to take responsibility and leadership in planning and establishing a program in Latin America, following the lines of the 1962 report. Later Antioch was formally named agent for the Association in the Latin America Program, and Professor Gorden was named administrator. A faculty representative will serve as coordinator in Bogotá and a Colombian will be chosen as resident assistant there.

The Mexican prelude to Colombian study, for students who need more Spanish or for those who want a longer and more varied Latin American experience, led to utilization and modification of Antioch's previous relations with the University of Guanajuato. As a result the summer session there will be taken over and operated as part of the Association's Latin America program, and since it was formerly open to students from other colleges and universities, this part of the Latin America program will so continue. A dean, or equivalent, will represent the Association in Mexico each summer.

Plans are carefully laid for the admission of students for the Mexican phase in the summer of 1964 and for the Colombian phase in the fall.

Mounting a successful program in Latin America is more difficult than in many other areas and perhaps therefore more important. That is why time has been taken and plans have been drawn so carefully, on the basis of recommendations from two survey teams and on the basis of Antioch's experience in

Mexico and Ohio Wesleyan's experience in Colombia. In addition to some support from the Ford Foundation and the Department of State for the first survey, the Association has voted to underwrite the considerable promotional and developmental costs until the program is launched and becomes self-supporting. Beyond reliance on Colombian universities in Bogotá, the Association will organize a complementary program of its own, using GLCA faculty and faculty chosen from the Colombian universities. Independent study and research will also be fostered to maximize the use of informal means of learning in and through a foreign culture. In all these ways the Association hopes to enhance opportunities for its students and faculty and to contribute to intercultural understanding in Colombian universities, where North American students are almost never seen. For the several hundred Colombian students who have studied in the United States each year recently, United States students going to Colombia have not much exceeded a dozen annually. The Latin America program offers promise, in other words, of being a pioneering effort, significant to the colleges of the Association and the universities of Colombia alike.

*Near East Program.* Ten students are currently enrolled in a cooperative program with the American University of Beirut in Lebanon. The arrangement was concluded late in the last academic year—too late for proper planning on many campuses. Hereafter approximately 25 students will be chosen each year. In return for the reservation of places for qualified GLCA students in this manner, the Association provides the American University of Beirut with a part-time faculty member, who simultaneously serves as program coordinator in Lebanon. Professor Joseph D. Coppock, research professor of economics at Earlham College, has served in this dual capacity in 1963–64 and will continue to do so in 1964–65.

This program has been easiest of all to establish, although new features (such as orientation sessions before and after arrival in the Near East) are still being added in the light of experience. The American University of Beirut is sufficiently Americanized to offer only a minimum of student academic readjustment, but all other aspects of the student's experience bring him into association with another culture—Near Eastern students, Islamic and other religions, Arabic language and culture, and fabulously rich history and historical monuments at the crossroads of ancient civilizations. Instruction is in English but Arabic is available. Students take advantage of many courses directly related to the geographic and cultural region. Indeed they are discouraged from enrolling if they are unwilling to break away from the courses which could as well be taken on the home campuses.

While the program is not without minor problems, critical review of it is uniformly favorable both as to academic quality and richness of intercultural experience. This is the judgment of Professor Coppock after several months of observation; of Professor Sherrill Cleland of Kalamazoo College, who visited the program in connection with his service as economic adviser to the Hashemite Kingdom of Jordan; and of the president of the Association, who visited Beirut briefly both in May and October.

*Common Overseas Study Policies.* Overseas opportunities through the Association—not to be confused with opportunities, particularly in Europe, long provided by several member colleges themselves—are governed by several general policies which have emerged in the last year. Generally speaking, programs are to be self-supporting although subsidized in the initial year; costs to students are to be those they would otherwise pay at the home college for an academic year (paid through the college, too, as if enrolled there); opportunities are to be appropriate for students in as many major fields as possible; language requirements are to be flexible and related to multi-level opportunities for language study abroad; selection by the home college will emphasize maturity and readiness to profit from an intercultural opportunity, and a planned program will be provided under the guidance of a faculty coordinator in residence abroad.

*University of Aberdeen.* The Association has not been involved in European programs but it has accepted a clearinghouse function in one case. The University of Aberdeen has reserved six places for students from the Association and has asked the latter to make the nominations. As a result the necessary screening of applicants has been done for the Association by Ohio Wesleyan University for 1963–64 and by Antioch College for 1964–65.

The emphasis which overseas study programs seem to have in this report is a reflection of their stage of development. They will be brought into proper perspective as other aspects of international education are similarly developed. More important than what happens abroad is what happens at home. The foreign study centers are conceived as a reflection, and a point of application, of educational interests on the home campus. They will reach only a fraction of the students who can be reached with intercultural opportunities on the campus, but they can give otherwise unattainable depth to those who go abroad and can supply rich resources and essential feed-back for those who stay home. With the Ford Foundation support and other to be sought, it is reasonable to expect that each college will take both independent and cooperative steps to realize the objectives agreed upon at the Oberlin conference on non-Western studies in 1962. If the international ambitions of the Association are realized, it can later be said, as someone already has, "No college will ever be the same again," and every student will have to some degree an intercultural dimension in his education.

To give point to these objectives and to further the cooperation they will entail, the board of directors in October voted to levy a special assessment on the member colleges to employ a Coordinator of International Programs. (Professor Jackson H. Bailey of Earlham College was named later in 1964.)

## Faculty Development Program

Providing increased professional opportunities for faculty is a cooperative objective which has begun to pay dividends. Sometimes these are explicitly and directly provided for, sometimes they are bound up with another major objective. They fall into these major categories:

opportunities for further study
opportunities for research

opportunities for program participation
opportunities for travel (as related to above)

Four fifths of the half-million-dollar grant from the Ford Foundation will go to faculty fellowships for training and research and related overseas travel, for the promotion of international studies, particularly related to non-Western cultures. Ten to fifteen generous grants will be awarded annually for the next three years on the basis of the applicant's qualifications and the project's relation to his professional goals and the international objectives of his college.

Other fellowships are available through the courtesy of the University of the State of New York—three summer seminars at Columbia and Cornell—and through the American Institute of Indian Studies, of which the Association is a sustaining member.

Finally, program participation of significant professional benefit is available through the overseas study centers. Coordinators are, generally, part-time with opportunity for research or teaching in a foreign country and culture.

## Visiting Scholars and Related Programs

The visiting scholars program has attained only modest success, although broader cultural opportunities are being shared increasingly among the member colleges. The scheduling of distinguished visitors can only add to what each college is already providing on its own and by other cooperative means. Achieving an equitable balance of visits and visitors among all member colleges is a difficult chore, with success possible only as viewed in the perspective of many years.

Nevertheless, cooperative action does gain worthwhile advantages both with speakers and other cultural enrichments. Sir Muhammad Zafrulla Khan, then president of the United Nations General Assembly, gave lectures at three colleges in 1963. Aaron Copland, the composer, is scheduled for similar visits in 1964. Visiting faculty members from foreign countries were brought to the attention of all colleges for such sharing as desired. An excellent exhibit of Japanese prints will tour all colleges in 1964 and 1965, through the courtesy of the Japan Society.

Despite these material gains of 1963, the best gain of all may be that which no one can measure. No precise value can be ascribed to it. It can only be said to exist and to have powers without either certain direction or understood force. Twelve colleges are becoming a family of colleges with kindred relationships. A broader academic community is emerging. Each is aware of eleven others for comparison, for communication, and for added strength. Plenty of areas remain for the exercise of what has been accurately described as a spirit of "fierce independence." But students strive to give the new spirit meaning. Professors recognize a new community of colleagues. Department chairmen meet other department chairmen. Deans share news and academic advantages with other deans. Presidents have a court and forum in the board of directors.

The awareness of being in new company, the making of comparisons, and the sharing of responsibilities are potent stimulants. They help make a genuine community of colleges. If some substantial progress has been made in 1963 toward a greater sense of such community, it has been a good year.

# 15

# THE ST PAUL GROUP

In September 1963 four private colleges in St Paul, Minnesota, began the eleventh year of their cooperative area studies program. It is in several ways a unique program. It is perhaps the oldest integrated area study program on the undergraduate level offered by the faculties of four independent colleges. It is also the oldest program of its type offered cooperatively by Roman Catholic and Protestant colleges: Hamline University, Macalester College, the College of St Catherine and the College of St Thomas.

The program grew out of several earlier interests on the part of the four colleges. All four institutions had been offering occasional courses in non-Western studies. For example, in 1946

College of St Catherine. President: Sister Mary Edward. (Roman Catholic; women; semester system; liberal arts and teacher education to bachelor's degree; 1437 students)

College of St Thomas. President: Monsignor James P. Shannon. (Roman Catholic; men; semester system; liberal arts to master's degree; 1945 students)

Hamline University. President Paul H. Giddens. (Methodist; coeducational; semester system; liberal arts to master's degree; 932 students)

Macalester College. President Harvey M. Rice. (Private; coeducational; semester system; liberal arts to master's degree; 1695 students)

This report is reprinted from an article by Rev. W. E. O'Donnell, academic vice president and dean of the College of St Thomas, published in the *National Catholic Educational Association Bulletin*, LX, 3, February 1964.

the College of St Thomas offered Latin American History, and in the following year, International History of the Far East, (Political) Problems of the Pacific, the United States in International Politics, and Russian language. But these courses, like those in the other colleges, were not interrelated; they stood alone and no attempt was made to integrate them into a core program.

The first attempt at an integrated study of a given geographical or political area was initiated at Macalester College in 1947. At the suggestion of its president, Dr Charles J. Turck, a course on the Area Study of Russia was offered at Macalester College in September 1947. As Dr Yahya Armajani describes it, it was "a single integrated course—given for the entire year to one group of junior and senior students. It carried twelve semester credits and was [taught] by a staff of twelve persons from the departments of history, political science, sociology, Russian language, economics, natural science, literature, geography, philosophy and fine arts. The students could get credits on a major in either history, political science, economics or sociology and fulfilled the divisional minor in the social sciences. The class met for five lectures per week and for one hour of discussion."[1] A similar program, the Area Study of Asia, was offered in 1951 and 1952 in order to take advantage of the presence on the campus of three visiting professors from China, India and Iran.

Although these area studies at Macalester were well received by students and faculty, it became evident by 1952 that there were several factors working against their continuance. The veterans, who as a group were most interested in these studies, were diminishing in number. Moreover, the faculty had been teaching in these area studies over and above their normal teaching duties and without extra remuneration.

Sensing the difficulties of continuing these area studies, and realizing that the other colleges were interested in setting up special courses in non-Western culture, Dr Turck called a special

1.    "Four College Area Studies: A Cooperative Program in the Understanding of Other Cultures," *Association of American Colleges Bulletin*, XLIII, 1, March 1957, pp. 14-22

meeting of the presidents, academic deans and librarians of the other three colleges, and invited the librarian of the Hill Reference Library in St Paul. This group became known as the Central Planning Committee. It drew up a proposal for a three-year area study program involving the four colleges and the Hill Reference Library. The proposal was presented to the Louis W. and Maud Hill Family Foundation of St Paul. The foundation made a generous grant in the spring of 1953.

In presenting their proposal to the Hill Foundation the special committee representing the four colleges and the Hill Reference Library listed the following objectives:

1. To provide students, faculties and administrators of the four colleges with an opportunity to study together, work together and plan together, to the end that levels of scholarship may be raised, interest in serious study may be stimulated, closer bonds of friendship and understanding may be developed and possibilities for financial savings may be explored.

2. To provide opportunity for advanced courses, or new courses, by forming classes comprised of students from all four colleges when enrolment would be too small in a single college to permit the offering of such courses.

3. To offer to students in the four independent Christian liberal arts colleges in St Paul a series of integrated area studies on the upper-class level, given cooperatively by qualified professors in the four colleges, as an unique contribution to American undergraduate education.

4. To contribute to the life of the community by sharing special lectures and programs as widely as possible with the citizens of St Paul within the area selected for special study.

The Louis W. and Maud Hill Center of Area Studies was inaugurated on 22 September 1953. The original grant was for $111,300. A second three-year grant was requested and received in 1956 and a third in 1959. Each successive grant was for a smaller sum, because the colleges assumed an increasing portion of the costs. The grant in 1959 for the third three-year cycle amounted to $31,950.

In these nine years, 1953–62, the classes were held in a specially arranged room in the Hill Reference Library in St Paul.

There were two 2-hour classes each week throughout the academic year. The course was open to juniors and seniors and exceptional sophomores. Eight credits were granted for the two semesters. Although enrolment was supposed to be limited to forty students, approximately ten from each college, there were sometimes more and sometimes less than forty.

The faculty was composed of two members from each college, with one of the eight members as coordinator. The coordinator was relieved of one half of his regular teaching load, and the grant provided for half of his salary. The other professors had no reduction in teaching loads but received a stipend of $25 for each lecture. In the summer preceding a given area study, the faculty members were subsidized generously for study abroad or at some graduate school in the United States. Most professors were not able to travel and study in Russia or the Far East for reasons of distance, expense and limited movement. In 1954, however seven of the eight professors went to the Middle East for study and observation. Each professor was required to prepare a syllabus on his special field. These papers were coordinated at a special workshop preceding the school year and were printed and distributed to the students.

The faculty members were selected to represent the fields of history, economics, political science, sociology, literature, philosophy and religion, natural science and the fine arts. The 116 lecture periods in the first year (Russian Area Study) were divided as follows: history, 20; philosophy, 12; political institutions, 10; literature, 10; social institutions, 8; economics, 10; geography, 8; education, 8; international relations, 6; theater, 4; discussions, 10; tests, 10. The apportionment of lecture periods remained relatively the same throughout the three 3-year cycles on Russia, the Middle East, and the Far East, 1953–62. Most of the original eight faculty members in a given area study remained with the area in subsequent years.

The original grant and the two subsequent grants provided a generous sum of money every year for the purchase of relevant books and periodicals by the Hill Reference Library and the libraries of the four colleges. A separate fund was provided for the drawing up of a union list of periodicals in these five libraries in order to avoid unnecessary duplication in area studies as well as in all other fields. In addition to the literature available in these five libraries, the faculty and students of the area studies had access to the splendid public libraries in the Twin Cities and to the excellent library at the University of Minnesota.

In order to round out the area studies for the students and to give the public an opportunity to benefit from these studies, the coordinator of a given area study arranged a series of public lectures at the Hill Reference Library. These lectures gave way after three years to an annual institute at one or other of the colleges, lasting two or three days and including public lectures, drama, art exhibits and musical presentations.

The impending opening of the first educational television station in the Twin Cities in 1957 was the occasion for a new request made to the Louis W. and Maud Hill Family Foundation. The Central Planning Committee of the four colleges and the Hill Reference Library proposed that the area studies be televised for public consumption the year after their being given in the classroom. The proposal was no sooner made than granted. The grant provided funds for the live telecasting (and, occasionally, pre-taped lectures) of the previous year's area study. The same coordinator and faculty members telecast two one-half hour programs a week for 36 weeks. They reduced their lectures by one half. Viewers were offered an outline and a reading list and could obtain credit for the course by examination. The practice of giving credit was dropped after the first year. The ETV programs, however, were well received by the public and won several awards for their content, interest and production.

During the nine-year period in which these area studies were offered, the central committee of the four colleges and the Hill Reference Library became increasingly aware of the need for study of Latin America and of Africa. In 1962 the committee requested a grant of the Hill Foundation for continuance of the area studies on Russia, the Middle East and the Far East, and the addition of Latin America and Africa. The grant was made.

The new five-year program, 1962–67, is now in its second year. The areas treated are Russia (1962), Africa (1963), Latin America (1964), the Far East (1965), the Middle East (1966). The classes are no longer held at the Hill Reference Library but at one or other of the colleges. The classes have been reduced from four to three hours per week and the semester credits from eight to six. There are four main fields: literature, political science, history and economics. Philosophy, religion, art, geography and education are treated in one or more of the four main fields, either by the professor of that field or by another faculty member more expert in the specific subject. Last year (Russia) there were 60 students in the first semester and 49 in the second. This current year (Africa) there are 33 students. The Russian area study has always drawn the largest class.

Although the original ETV programming of the area studies ended last year with the Far East and no special grant has been received for its continuance, it is possible that the four colleges will try to telecast in shortened version the lectures on Africa and Latin America, using funds from previous grants not fully expended. Africa will probably be telecast in the year 1964–65 and Latin America in 1965–66.

It is much easier to describe a program than to evaluate it. And yet it is more important to know whether a program is worth while in moneys expended, in interest aroused among the students, the faculty and the public and in relationships among cooperating colleges. Has the Area Studies Program been a success or a failure? Perhaps the best way to answer this question is to treat of its weaknesses and strengths in this order.

There are weaknesses and difficulties in every human effort. There is the cost: between $300 and $600 per student per year— an expense beyond the means of any one college or group of colleges without the support of a foundation. There are the differences of opinions and viewpoints among colleges and within colleges. There is the problem of selecting the disciplines to be taught and of the degree of emphasis to be placed on each. There is the problem of the amount of work required of students versus the amount of credit given, as well as the intensity of treatment by the professor versus the extensiveness of his subjects. There is some disadvantage in not having one fixed place for lectures and library. It is a definite disadvantage not to have a knowledge of the language or languages of the area studied. Changes in the faculty of a given area have inevitably occurred. Sometimes it has been difficult to find a professor sufficiently trained in an area to do really efficient work in that area. It has not been possible to have most professors study and travel in certain areas, especially in the Soviet Union and in the Far East.

On the other hand there have been many good results. The program has given special opportunities to more than 350 students and to about thirty faculty members. There has been a growing interest in non-Western studies among the faculties and student bodies of the four colleges: more than twenty students have taken graduate studies in one or other of the areas; several have specialized in graduate studies for work in governmental agencies or private international ventures or in preparation for teaching careers. The program has brought the administrative officers and faculties of the four colleges closer together in mutual respect and understanding of one another. It has also encouraged the four colleges to increase their regular course offerings in non-Western studies, to open these courses to the students of the respective institutions and to list these courses in all four class schedules. It has, moreover, definitely helped the four colleges—and indirectly all private colleges of the state—to present a good image of the private liberal arts college to the general public. In fine, the Area Studies Program has been a unique program, a wonderful experience in inter-college cooperation and a powerful force for the encouragement of non-Western studies on the undergraduate level.

# 16

# THE WINSTON-SALEM GROUP

An Asian studies program was inaugurated in September 1960 by Wake Forest College, Salem College and Winston-Salem State College. Directed by an Asian scholar, Professor B. G. Gokhale from Bombay, it involves cooperation among three quite different institutions. It focuses on South and Southeast Asia, with instruction in Hindi. Participants in the annual faculty seminars prepared seven books and a dozen articles on non-Western topics for publication between 1960 and 1964. The program has developed an institute and seminars for high school teachers throughout Forsyth County.

## Historical Background

The initiative for this program came primarily from former dean William C. Archie and associate professor of political

---

Wake Forest College, Winston-Salem, North Carolina. President Harold W. Tribble. (Baptist; coeducational; semester system; liberal arts and teacher training to master's degree; 2915 students)

Salem College, Winston-Salem, North Carolina. President Dale H. Gramley. (Moravian; women; semester system; liberal arts and teacher training to bachelor's degree; 496 students)

Winston-Salem State College, Winston-Salem, North Carolina. President Kenneth R. Williams. (State; coeducational; semester system; teacher training to bachelor's degree; 1212 students)

science Roy Jumper of Wake Forest College. Former president Atkins of Winston-Salem State College and President Gramley of Salem College pledged the cooperation of their institutions during preliminary discussions in 1958 and 1959. Professor Jumper and Dean Archie took the lead in 1958 by stimulating faculty interest at Wake Forest, doing preliminary planning and making initial contacts with specialists on Asian studies and with foundation representatives.

Professor Jumper, a student of comparative politics with a keen interest in South Asia but no special competence in the area, was convinced along with the dean that it was important to provide better opportunities for undergraduates to learn about Asian and other non-Western societies. They found little competence in such cultures among the faculty, few books in the library and virtually no courses relating to the non-Western world at Wake Forest College in 1958.

One of the first people they approached for advice was Ward Morehouse, educational director for the Asia Society. He arranged for a grant of $1000 to cover the expenses of four visiting consultants who met with administrative and faculty leaders at the three colleges and gave public lectures on Asia during their visits to Winston-Salem in 1958-59. These consultants were Shannon McCune, provost of the University of Massachusetts, James Liu of the department of history at the University of Pittsburgh (now at Stanford), Myron Weiner of the department of political science at the University of Chicago (now at M.I.T.), and Ralph Braibanti of the department of political science at Duke University. David Elliott of the California Institute of Technology also conferred with the representatives of the three colleges in his capacity as consultant to the Ford Foundation.

Faculty members taking part in this early planning agreed that their purpose was "to draw attention to Asia and to introduce material without distorting the existing course offerings leading to the bachelor's degree." They agreed to invite an Asian scholar to direct a program focusing on South Asia, which was to include close institutional and inter-institutional coordination, faculty seminars, seminars for high school teachers, and the building up of library holdings at each college. The Wake Forest College library was to be the main depository, and provision was made for the reciprocal and increased use of library resources on the non-Western world, as well as public lectures and exhibits.

Each of the three participating colleges undertook to make annual contributions from their regular funds to help support the new program. Salem College and Winston-Salem State College were to provide $700 each, with $200 from each college earmarked for the purchase of non-Western library materials in addition to normal library accessions. Wake Forest College agreed to contribute $1000 a year and to care for administrative costs. Five hundred dollars was also to be spent for special library acquisitions.

These plans were well advanced by 1958-59, when the Mary Reynolds Babcock Foundation made a five-year grant of $46,000 to help to start the Tri-College Asian Studies Program. The director's salary and other costs were to be covered by the grant. The East Asian studies program at Harvard University offered to share the major costs of post-doctoral fellowships for professors from the three Winston-Salem colleges who were interested in advancing their knowledge of East Asia. An Indian scholar and diplomat, Professor M. S. Sundaram, accepted appointment as visiting professor of Asian studies in February 1959, but Mr Sundaram's death that summer postponed the program for a year. The Babcock Foundation agreed to have the first year's allocation of $9665 spent on library acquisitions.

The coordinating committee of the three colleges on Asian studies thought that it was important to employ a highly-qualified Asian scholar to develop the new program. This need was underscored by the fact that the colleges wanted to start with expert direction but did not have anyone on their staffs with the disciplinary, area and language skills necessary. They identified a scholar who met these requirements during the interim year 1959-60. This was Dr B. G. Gokhale, an Indian historian who had taught at Siddarth and St Xavier's Colleges in Bombay and at Bowdoin, Oberlin and the University of Washington. He was invited to Wake Forest College as visiting professor of history and director of the projected Asian studies program on a two-year appointment. Professor Gokhale's broad experience as teacher and chairman of a department of history in India and as visiting professor at several American institutions made him unusually well qualified to direct this pioneer, cooperative program.

## Cooperation

Professor Gokhale has worked closely with the Tri-College Coordinating Committee and with faculty committees at each college to stimulate interest in the program. The Tri-College Coordinating Committee consists of the three presidents and academic deans or their representatives and deals mainly with major policy issues. Faculty advisory committees were set up to work with the program at the start. In practice, most of the coordination has been handled by the director working with Ivy Hixson, academic dean and Amy Heidbreder, dean of students at Salem College, and C. J. Parker, professor of history and chairman of the division of the social sciences and Professor D. F. Balsley of the department of English at Winston-Salem State College. Each of these representatives has taken part in the faculty seminar on Asia. This has facilitated the maintenance of good working relationships among the three cooperating institutions. The program has a central office and secretary in a large room next to Dr Gokhale's office in the Reynolds Library and a modest administrative budget. By agreement between the colleges, Wake Forest administers the program funds.

Wake Forest College has served as the center for the Asian studies program, as was expected because it had developed the most course offerings and the strongest library resources on Asia. Its staff has been most active in the program. Professor Gokhale and his colleagues, Professors Banks and Chee from the department of sociology-anthropology, have taught certain courses on Asia at the other two colleges in addition to their normal teaching at Wake Forest College. This has enabled Salem College and Winston-Salem State College to offer, at modest cost to each college, from three to six courses on Asia not otherwise available to their students. Wake Forest College has benefited from the cooperative aspects of the program by sharing its costs, getting a broader base for faculty and student participation in the program and by making the program more attractive to outside support.

## Curriculum

When the program was being planned there were no members of the faculties of the three colleges with special competence in any non-Western area and only a few courses devoted even in part to the non-Western world. Professor Phillip Africa in the history department at Salem taught a course in diplomacy, including the Far East, until he left for Keuka College in 1962. Courses in World Geography at the three colleges and on World Religions at Salem and Wake Forest also gave some attention to the non-Western regions. The same was true to a very limited extent of a course on World Literature and another on the History of Music given at Winston-Salem State College.

The Asian studies program began with Professor Gokhale teaching one course on the history and politics of South Asia at the three participating colleges in the autumn of 1960. Within three years the Asian studies program offered eleven different courses on Asia, with seven focused on South and Southeast Asia, at the three colleges. They were all taught by members of the Wake Forest faculty, three of whom served as visiting professors at one or both of the other colleges. Four of these new courses were in history, four in political science and three in sociology-anthropology. They bore the following titles:

History and Politics of South Asia
History and Civilization of Southeast Asia
Intellectual History of Southeast Asia
Modern India
Government and Politics of South Asia
Government and Politics of Southeast Asia
Introduction to the Political Culture of China and Japan
Asian Political Thought
Oriental Social and Cultural Systems
Ethnography of Southeast Asia
Modern Asia: The Social Impact of the West

Dr Gokhale introduced instruction in elementary and intermediate Hindi. Three students had begun the study of Hindi by the fall of 1963. The class met five hours weekly and each student was expected to spend a minimum of two additional hours a week in language laboratory drill and review. Dr Gokhale also offered two graduate history seminars on India and Southeast Asia for eight graduate students. Two of them have prepared master's theses on South Asia.

By the autumn of 1963 over 590 students from the three colleges had enrolled in courses offered by the Asian studies program. Wake Forest accounted for 432 of these enrolments, Salem for 100 and Winston-Salem State College for 59. This represents respectively about fifteen, twenty and six per cent of the undergraduate liberal arts student body at the three colleges. The Asian courses were open to students at all levels but were mainly upperclass electives.

The Tri-College Asian Studies Program has stimulated the development of other courses devoted to various non-Western areas. Salem College offered a total of ten such courses, including three of the infusion type, by 1963-64. In addition to the four given under the auspices of the Asian studies program, there were two on Russian history and one on Asian art. The infusion-type courses were Great Religious Thinkers, The U. S. in World Affairs, and World Geography. Winston-Salem State College listed nine courses, five of them additional to the courses in Asian studies. They were entitled World Geography, World Literature, The History of Music, Oriental Social and Cultural Systems, and Race and Culture.

By the same year, Wake Forest College had increased its course offerings relating to non-Western areas to 27. Three of these fall into the infusion category. Eleven others represent courses offered by the Asian studies program. The 27 courses were given by five departments and one of them, entitled Approaches to Human Experience, was taught under the interdisciplinary honors program inaugurated in 1961. (Dr Gokhale's two graduate seminars are not included in this total.) The departments of history and political science each gave seven of these courses, languages gave six, sociology-anthropology five and religion one. Ten of the courses dealt with Asia, four with Eastern Europe and the USSR, and two each with Latin America and the Middle East. Two of the language courses were in Hindi and two in Russian. Three students took Hindi and fifteen studied Russian in 1963-64.

## Extending Faculty Competence

The Tri-College Asian Studies Program has helped to develop faculty resources on Asia and other non-Western areas by three chief means: recruitment of staff with non-Western competence, organization of an in-service faculty seminar on Asia, and opportunities for off-campus study and travel.

Wake Forest College recruited Dr Gokhale to direct the program. The college has also employed three younger scholars with non-Western competence. One teaches Latin American politics, another comparative politics of the Middle East and a third Far Eastern sociology. The other two colleges have not added non-Western area specialists to their faculties but instead have used professors from Wake Forest College to teach courses on Asia.

In accordance with initial plans, the main effort has been directed to enlarging the competence of existing faculty members at each institution. Only two members of the staffs of Salem College and Winston-Salem State College have participated regularly in the faculty seminar on Asia. Dr Balsley, a professor of English who teaches World Literature at Winston-Salem State College, spent 1963-64 in Pakistan on a Fulbright fellowship. No other faculty members from the two smaller colleges have done further Asian study at an American university or overseas.

The faculty seminar has met monthly in the library at Wake Forest College. Unlike some other faculty seminars on non-Western areas, this group has not met with visiting specialists. Instead it has depended on the direction of Dr Gokhale and the research interests of participants, who have taken turns preparing a paper which serves as the basis for the evening's discussion. These reports are mimeographed and circulated in advance. Occasionally the group discusses a key issue or document rather than a paper presented by one of the members. Fourteen research papers on Asia, Africa and the USSR had been presented by participants in the faculty seminar by June 1963. The fact that six of these seminar papers had been published or accepted for publication in professional journals in the U.S.A. and abroad suggests the care with which they were prepared.

Twenty-two faculty members took part in the seminars during the first three years. They represented eight disciplines: business administration and law, classics, English, history, political science, psychology, religion and sociology-anthropology. Academic Dean Ivy Hixson, professor of classics, and Amy Heidbreder, dean of students, took part from Salem College. Professors Balsley and Parker came from Winston-Salem State College. The other eighteen represented six departments at Wake Forest. History led the field with seven participants. There were three each from political science and religion, two each from English and sociology-anthropology, and one from business administration and law.

Four other members of the faculty at Wake Forest who did not become regular members of the seminar extended their competence in non-Western areas under the indirect stimulus of the Asian studies program. These were Professor Hamrick in religion (the Middle East); Mr Hitchins, instructor in history, who spent two years in Eastern Europe; Professor Howren, a linguist in the English department, who won a Fulbright award to Burma in 1960-61 but left the college in 1962 to teach in Iowa; and Mrs Lowell Tillett, in Russian language, who visited Russia in the summer of 1962. Thus a total of 21 members of the Wake Forest faculty have extended their competence to non-Western areas in recent years. This represents about ten per cent of the faculty teaching undergraduate liberal arts courses.

Nine of the eighteen Wake Forest members of the seminar have also managed to get first-hand experience in one or more non-Western areas. Three have been in East Asia, three in Southeast Asia, two in South Asia, two in the Middle East, two in Africa, and one in Eastern Europe and Russia. (Some individuals have visited more than one area.)

Wake Forest faculty members have studied and traveled under various auspices. Most have been granted leave and received partial subsidies from the college. They have also won major grants or fellowships, primarily for a year of study and travel, from the American Institute of Indian Studies, and the Babcock, Carnegie, Danforth and Ford Foundations, plus four Fulbright awards and one summer grant under the National Defense Education Act.

Participation in the faculty seminar or further study abroad has not transformed all of these teachers into area and language specialists. But it has given each of them additional knowledge of a non-Western society. Each of these scholars believes that he or she has become a better teacher in the process. The new courses which they offer, along with their publications and professional activities, reflect the effects of this new intellectual thrust.

## Research, Publication and Other Professional Activities

Participants in the faculty seminar have engaged in considerable research and publication encouraged by the program and furthered by field investigation overseas. In addition to the six seminar papers noted above, at least six more articles have been accepted for publication. Seminar members have also published seven volumes on Africa and Asia. They have read papers or chaired sessions at meetings of the American Historical Association, the Association for Asian Studies, the American Anthropological Association, the Southern Sociological Association, and the Southern Political Science Association.

The three colleges acted as hosts to the Second Southeastern Regional Conference of the Association for Asian Studies which met at Wake Forest on 25-27 January 1963.

Many public lectures, two radio talks, a TV program, several cultural programs on the dances and music of Asia, and films about Asia have been presented on the campuses or in the city and neighboring communities by the Asian studies program.

## Seminars and Institute for High School Teachers

The Asian studies program has offered a series of weekly, two-hour evening seminars for high school teachers from Winston-Salem and Forsyth County since 1960. The program also provided an intensive summer institute for teachers for six weeks in the summer of 1963. The seminars have been taught by Dr Gokhale and others and carry credit toward an M.A. from Wake Forest College. South Asia is studied in the first semester and Southeast Asia in the second. Some sixty teachers have taken part in these courses. Six of those who took part in the summer institute in 1963 were taking Dr Gokhale's evening seminar in the autumn of 1963 for credit. Twenty-five teachers registered for the 1963 summer institute and fourteen earned credit. Dr Gokhale taught the two courses, Survey of South Asia, and Survey of Southeast Asia, each of which met five times a week, and a two-hour seminar meeting once a week on The Culture of the Far East. Twelve of the participating teachers received scholarship assistance.

## Library

The Asian studies program has stressed the acquisition of materials on Asia by the libraries of the cooperating colleges. In 1963 general library holdings were 58,000 at Salem, 46,000 at Winston-Salem State College, and 156,000 at Reynolds Library of Wake Forest College. By the summer of 1963 each library had added respectively 700, 100 and 5300 books and periodicals on Asia to its collections. These items were purchased with the $900 in special allocations set aside annually by the three colleges, plus regular library funds of some $2500 per year, supplemented by some $900 from the Wake Forest departmental budgets for history, philosophy, political science, sociology and religion.

These totals include special gifts of 205 volumes from the Asia and Japan Societies and several hundred books on Japan in English and a few in Japanese donated by the Japanese consul in New York. They also include 1202 books and 333 volumes of periodicals purchased with Babcock Foundation funds and 289 works bought with Wake Forest's special appropriation in 1959-60.

Library holdings at Wake Forest were considered "good" for instruction and student research on South and Southeast Asia and "adequate" for other parts of the world except Africa and the Middle East, which were rated as "poor." For faculty research, the staff rated the collections "good" on South and Southeast Asia, "adequate" for Sub-Saharan Africa and East Asia and "poor" for the rest of the non-Western world. The three major needs for non-Western studies were source materials, journals and periodicals, and general works, in that order.

## Conclusion

The Tri-College Asian Studies Program appears to have established itself in Winston-Salem. Wake Forest College has granted Professor Gokhale tenure. The administrative officers of the three colleges are pleased with the program, plan to continue it and to strengthen library resources on Asia. They and the director would like to add a staff member with competence in the Far East, introduce more instruction in Asian languages, and initiate a modest graduate program. They also hope to develop improved summer or year-round courses for high school and college teachers in the proposed Piedmont University Center serving some sixteen four-year colleges in the region. Future plans include increased attention to Asian culture by means of art and handicraft exhibits, concerts, dance recitals, lectures and films. A program to publish monographs, or a journal of South Asian studies, has also been under consideration.

Professor Gokhale has given the program vigorous direction. He has carried an unusually heavy teaching load on the three campuses. He has also managed to continue his research, publishing three books and eight articles between 1960 and 1964. Dr Gokhale has shown what a qualified Asian scholar can contribute to furthering Asian studies in an American college, despite the pitfalls inherent in asking a non-Western scholar to direct a program for U. S. liberal arts undergraduates, and despite the added complications of tripartite intercollegiate cooperation.

This encouraging start need not obscure much that remains to be accomplished. For example, the several new courses on Asia and other non-Western regions do not fulfill standard requirements for the bachelor's degree and thus far reach less than fifteen per cent of the undergraduates at the three colleges. The Asian studies program has not yet developed any lower-level, general education courses which might serve to introduce a large proportion of freshmen or sophomores to an Asian culture. It has not yet elicited broad interest and support from faculty members at Salem College and Winston-Salem State College, nor of teachers in departments such as classics, education, music, philosophy and the sciences at Wake Forest Col'ege. Its impact on the curricula of the three colleges appears to have been more additive than integral.

Yet the young program's accomplishments affirm the usefulness of cooperation and the major contributions which a resident non-Western scholar can make to an undergraduate program. They demonstrate that even relatively modest library resources can, especially when supplemented by a faculty seminar and study abroad, encourage research of consequence on non-Western topics by undergraduate teachers.

# 17

# DARTMOUTH COLLEGE

## Editor's Introduction

The following condensed version of a Dartmouth College proposal for establishing a Comparative Studies Center is included here for two reasons: it shows a particularly wide range of institutional involvements that can first stimulate and then form a part of an effort to incorporate non-Western material into a curriculum; and it affords a glimpse of a rather exceptional approach to that objective.

Since the proposal was written (by Provost John W. Masland in June 1962), the Comparative Studies Center has become a reality on the Dartmouth campus and has gone through its first phase of faculty seminars designed to acquaint participants with techniques of comparison in various disciplines utilizing materials from widely varying cultures. The number of participants and departmental representation were both impressive.

The next phase was the staging of a still more ambitious faculty seminar on Eastern philosophic thought, extending through the winter and spring terms of 1963–64, coupled with other measures to enlarge faculty competence through independent study at home or abroad.

Dartmouth College, Hanover, New Hampshire. President John S. Dickey. (Private; men; quarter system; liberal arts to master's degree, plus certain doctoral programs; 3404 students)

The evident intention is to approach the liberal arts curriculum as a whole, infusing it systematically with non-Western subject matter and attempting to compare and contrast the fullest possible variety of cultural materials in all courses that lend themselves to the approach. The Dartmouth scheme for comparative studies, while promising less depth and intensity in the study of particular non-Western civilizations than does the integrated area program, reflects a compensating concern with the curriculum as a whole and with the maximum exposure of students.

## The Dartmouth Experience Since 1945

### Curricular Developments

In the years since 1945 there has been a steady increase in the attention given by Dartmouth College to international and foreign affairs. In 1945 Dartmouth offered instruction in literature, philosophy, history, economics, sociology and political science common to liberal arts institutions. Beyond this, for some time the College had offered courses in Asian Civilization, Far Eastern History, and Asian Religions, in Russian Literature and History, a course on Spanish-American Literature and one on Spanish-American Civilization. For many years before World War II, instruction in the Chinese language was offered at Dartmouth, and for a short period following 1945 instruction in Japanese was available. Otherwise, relatively little opportunity was provided in the normal course structure for study relating to areas outside of Western Europe and North America.

Immediately following the war, several major efforts were made to relate the curriculum to the changing demands of the times.

The first of these was the establishment of an interdepartmental major program in international relations, administered by a faculty committee representing each of the participating departments. This program was constructed initially of existing courses in history, government and economics, but several new courses were designed specifically to meet the requirements of the major, including a new introductory course in international politics, a course in international organization, a course in European diplomatic history, and a senior seminar. Several additional appointments in international affairs were made to the faculty at this time, including individuals with competence in Far Eastern and Soviet affairs.

The second post-war effort was the Great Issues Course, introduced in 1947 and since that time required of all seniors. Since its inception the Great Issues Course has devoted considerable attention to international and foreign area issues. During the year just concluded, for example, the first term of the course was devoted to issues of war and peace, the second to science and society, and the third to the emerging nations. The lectures in the course are given by speakers brought to the campus for this purpose, including several individuals from overseas. It is expected that the Great Issues Course will follow a roughly similar pattern in the future.

The third effort was the establishment of a department of Russian civilization. Additional appointments to the faculty were made to provide instruction in the Russian language and literature, and in Russian history and politics. Separate major programs are offered in language and literature, and in Russian civilization.

Also in the immediate post-war period, the resources of the department of geography were strengthened. With the addition of new staff, a major program was introduced, and area courses in the Soviet Union, the Far East, and Latin America were offered.

More recently, we have introduced a major program in anthropology and the staff has been relocated in the college museum. One of the anthropologists has been appointed director of the museum and all instruction is taking place in this facility. The collections include considerable non-Western material.

## Faculty Resources

Beyond these special efforts, new appointments to the faculty have enabled us to add a substantial number of foreign area and international affairs courses, particularly during the last three years. For the most part this has been accomplished by replacing individuals who have retired or resigned by others with professional interests beyond those formerly represented in the faculty. Thus faculty with special training or experience in the following fields are now offering instruction at Dartmouth: Oriental art, Latin American history, Latin American politics, Latin American geography, Middle Eastern history, Middle Eastern politics, African geography, Far Eastern politics, Russian literature, Soviet politics, sociology of the Soviet Union, Southeast Asian geography, Southeast Asian politics, polar geography, comparative politics, demography, international law and organization, international economics, and economic development. It should be noted that most of these more recently appointed faculty members participate in the introductory courses in their departments and that their special area interests are reflected in their teaching in these high enrolment courses. They also have made possible the introduction of more numerous and varied advanced seminars directly related to these special interests.

## General Reading Program

In 1958 Dartmouth adopted a new curriculum intended to increase student independence and responsibility in learning. The number of courses carried at one time was reduced from five to three, and to offset the reduced exposure to different areas of study during a term, a program of general reading for the first two years was established. Under this program all freshmen and sophomores are required independently to read challenging books that are not part of their courses. The books, four in number in each of the two years, are selected from a published list, representing works in literature and the humanities, in the social sciences and in the sciences. The list now includes a substantial number of books dealing with non-Western thought and experience.

## American Universities Field Staff

Dartmouth College joined the American Universities Field Staff organization in 1957, bringing to the campus each year specialists representing certain foreign areas in which our own resources have been limited. The most extensive use of AUFS personnel has been made in the departments of government and geography, and in the senior seminar offered for majors in the international relations program. The AUFS members have been frequent lecturers in the Great Issues Course, and they have given public lectures, consulted with students and met informally with members of the faculty on matters of common interest.

The Dartmouth-AUFS relationship has become close as well as effective. Next year, for the second time, an AUFS officer will reside in Hanover during his college tour. Dartmouth, moreover, has appointed K. H. Silvert, one of the senior AUFS members, a professor of government while serving concurrently with AUFS. Professor Silvert is making his permanent home at Dartmouth. During the academic year just concluded he offered a seminar on Latin American politics, and next year he will serve full time for at least two terms, with courses in political modernization and research methods as well as offerings in Latin American affairs.

## Public Affairs Center

In 1961 the trustees established the Public Affairs Center at Dartmouth, as a means of providing leadership for several present and planned activities. The first of these is the Great Issues Course described above. Professor Gene Lyons is serving concurrently as director of the center and of the course. The Public Affairs Laboratory, long a feature of the course, is now part of the center. To the center also has been assigned responsibility for student intern programs, including new experimental overseas internships. In April 1962 the center conducted a student-alumni conference on the theme of individual participation in public affairs. The center also is the focus for various faculty enterprises, including the national security policies research program and an interdisciplinary faculty seminar.

In the spring of 1962, through the cooperation of the Department of State, a Foreign Service officer was assigned to the Public Affairs Center for three weeks. He participated in numerous courses, conducted special seminars and consulted with many students and faculty. We hope to continue this arrangement on a regular basis.

## National Security Studies

Since 1953 a small group at Dartmouth has concerned itself with the study of national security policies and related matters, with the continuing support of the Carnegie Corporation of New York. While the activities of this group have been directed toward research and publication, they have been reflected in courses offered by the members, including the Great Issues Course and a seminar on national security policies. The emphasis of this group, in teaching and research, has varied during the nine-year period. Initially it was upon the educational preparation of military leaders, later upon a study of national security policies by civilian scholars and in civilian institutions, and more recently upon the comparative study of military affairs, the international control of armed forces, and arms limitation and control.

## Northern Studies

As an institution, Dartmouth long has had an interest in northern and polar affairs. Numerous members of the faculty have had experience in the Far North and a few in the Antarctic. Most of these individuals maintain a continuing professional interest in these areas. These include two or three men in geology, two in anthropology, two in engineering and two in geography. The special interests of these men are reflected in the instructional programs in anthropology, geography and geology, an interdisciplinary arctic seminar and an informal series of lectures and special events. The Stefansson arctic collection is located in the Dartmouth library and draws scholars and specialists from beyond Hanover, as well as Dartmouth students and faculty. At the college, the Army ROTC unit conducts an extracurricular mountain and winter warfare program which attracts a substantial number of students. Over the years many Dartmouth students, reflecting these various interests on the campus, have participated in field work and other activities in the Far North. A few have continued as professionals. Hanover also is now the location of the Army Corps of Engineers' Cold Regions Research and Engineering Laboratory. CRREL personnel are enrolled in several Dartmouth courses, and when the new laboratory is completed we hope for many cooperative arrangements between the college and the army facility.

## Canadian Affairs

Apart from northern studies, Dartmouth has had a continuing interest in Canadian affairs. Instruction is limited to a course in Canadian history, but the interest has found expression in numerous other ways. In 1957 we held an Anglo-Canadian-American convocation of several days. In May of this year we sponsored a Canadian-American student conference, involving undergraduate representations of five Canadian and three American institutions. Also this spring term, Professor James Eayres of the University of Toronto served as a visiting professor of government. Next year, Professor Franklin Smallwood will spend six months in Canada, studying regional planning in the Toronto area, and Canadian political affairs in general.

## Hopkins Center

In November 1962 Dartmouth will open its new Hopkins Center for the performing arts. We plan to relate the various activities and programs in art, music and the theater to the larger educational purposes of the institution. Although plans for the first year are not yet complete, we hope to include several activities of a non-Western character. At the present time, for example, tentative arrangements are being made for performances by a group of Indian musicians and dancers, the Bharatiya Kala Kendra, sponsored by the Asia Society.

## Opportunities for Foreign Study and Service

Some years ago the departments of Romance languages and German introduced a foreign study program elected by almost all students majoring in French, Spanish and German, providing for a summer and term of study in a European university. Travel and local arrangements are made by the Experiment in International Living. The Dartmouth Foreign Study Program has since been extended to men majoring in other subjects who meet the language requirements. For the academic year 1962–1963, 68 students have qualified for this program. They will be distributed abroad as follows: France, 33; Spain, 19; Germany, 16, and Peru, 5.

Apart from the Dartmouth Foreign Study Program, numerous other students spend a portion of their undergraduate experience abroad, commonly on one of the established junior-year-abroad programs. We estimate that 203, or 33 per cent of the total membership of 606 of the class of 1962 at graduation in 1962, have had an experience in a foreign country. Of these, 54 will have been abroad for study, 22 as residents, and 84 for travel only.

In 1960 we introduced an overseas intern program, enabling two men to spend six months in the Middle East in work-study situations, one in Turkey and the second in the United Arab Republic. We expect to continue this undertaking on a modest basis, providing similar opportunities in other areas. This year we are inaugurating the Dartmouth Project Asia, sending two men to Hong Kong for two-year teaching assignments. The plan to send two others to Burma was cancelled by the abrupt decision of the Burmese Government to prohibit this kind of relationship, and hopefully these men will be placed elsewhere in Asia. In preparation for the Project Asia some 30 to 40 members of the class of 1962 met together informally for more than a year, informing themselves about the areas to which the four men selected from the group were assigned.

Because of the substantial number of Dartmouth students seeking information and assistance on opportunities for overseas study and service, the assistant dean of the college, Charles Dey, has assumed responsibility for guidance in these matters, working with the Public Affairs Center and members of the faculty. He has not only informed himself about various programs and arrangements but is seeking personal experience that will equip him effectively for this responsibility. The college has granted him leave of absence to serve for one year as a program director with the Peace Corps in the Philippines.

## Foreign Students at Dartmouth

During the post-war period Dartmouth has made an effort to enroll foreign students. In the present academic year 41 foreign students, excluding Canadians, are enrolled in the undergraduate college. Twenty-five of these are receiving financial aid from the college. We have made substantial progress in the selection of students, utilizing the good offices of the International Institute of Education, American Friends of the Middle East, the African-American Institute, etc., as well as alumni groups overseas. We also have made progress in the proper orientation of the new foreign students, including special training in the English language.

## Cutter Hall

In the coming academic year we are undertaking a new experiment in one of the dormitories, Cutter Hall. This will serve as a residential unit for students with a special interest in international affairs. Five of the total of 44 men will be foreign students. We plan to use a small apartment in the unit for visitors to the college, including officers of the American Universities Field Staff, Great Issues speakers and departmental visitors.

## Plans for the Future

This is a creditable record, one of which we are proud. Yet we feel that it is not enough and that our progress should be more systematic, purposeful and speedy. Accordingly the Dartmouth faculty and administration have been devoting increasing attention to these matters. Much of the progress outlined above has been initiated within the normal planning and administrative procedures of the institution. During the past two years, moreover, an organized evaluation of our present resources and program has been undertaken, resulting in the formulation of the plans for a major advance that are outlined below. This effort has been made under the general direction of the faculty Committee on Educational Policy, and has included studies by an *ad hoc* committee on non-Western studies, an *ad hoc* committee on comparative studies, an *ad hoc* committee on Canadian studies, the division of the humanities and the separate departments. Recommendations have been approved for planning purposes, where appropriate, by the executive committee of the faculty and by the trustees of the college. Already some of these recommendations have been implemented.

Our studies and recommendations demonstrate that the Dartmouth experience exhibits the shortcomings that have been identified by the Committee on the University and World Affairs and by others. In the first place, in spite of the marked gains of recent years, the curriculum retains a strong emphasis upon Western civilization, and indeed upon entirely domestic affairs, with too little attention to the infinite variety of man's experience throughout the world. This is particularly true of the introductory courses in the various disciplines with which students satisfy the distribution requirements for the degree, but it is also characteristic of the departmental major requirements. Although we have introduced numerous new foreign area courses, the enrolments in most of these remain relatively low. Thus a large proportion of our students graduate without more than a superficial exposure to international and non-Western affairs. Secondly we still fall short in instructional opportunities in foreign areas and languages and with respect to such problems as economic development, political modernization and comparative cultures.

These major deficiencies of the curriculum at Dartmouth, and indeed in undergraduate liberal arts programs generally, stem from two fundamental conditions, both difficult to overcome. The first is the unprecedented burst of new information and understanding in all fields of human knowledge and the immense problem of fitting this knowledge into an already overcrowded curriculum. If we must introduce additional international and non-Western substance into present courses and add new courses, what shall we cut out? The second condition is equally perplexing. The present domestic and Western orientation of the curriculum reflects the professional training, experience and interests of the majority of the faculty. How can present members of a faculty acquire the competence to provide instruction on unfamiliar areas or subjects? Can these instructional needs be met by means other than new appointments?

Dartmouth now proposes to undertake a large-scale effort to overcome these constraining forces. Projecting our present achievements into the years ahead, we can anticipate substantial progress along the lines already outlined. But as already indicated, we feel that even such progress will fall short of the requirements of our times. We have a sense of greater urgency. Thus we propose to go beyond present measures and to move rapidly and, we hope, effectively to markedly higher levels of accomplishment. We believe that we now have developed both the concept and the strategy that will enable us to achieve our objective. This strategy represents an intellectual response to the problem of integrating new data and knowledge into an overcrowded curriculum, and a practical response to the problem of limited faculty experience and competence. Indeed, we are bold enough to suggest that the approach that we propose offers hope for a major break-through in curriculum development, of significance not only to Dartmouth College but to liberal arts education generally.

Central to this strategy is a sense of institutional purpose and involvement. From our two years of study has emerged a conviction that the basic solution to the dilemma rests not with the introduction of still more subject matter into the curriculum or the appointment to the faculty of individuals with new specialized knowledge, important as both these measures may be, but rather with the development of a new approach to liberal learning, a comprehensive effort involving all relevant elements of the total institution. In part this sense of strategy was suggested by President Dickey in January 1961.

> . . . I find the greatest significance in the "Non-Western Studies" program when I view it as a new dimension in our traditional view of liberal learning rather than as simply an enrichment or extension of our present offerings in international studies. . . . I [am] thinking of

it as an approach to the development of a new strategy for liberal learning in our time. I say "strategy" because I sense that there is potentially a dynamic in this idea and because I believe the idea is more properly conceived of as a new approach to enduring aims rather than a changing of aims. . . . I hold firmly to the view that the aims of liberal learning must always be stated broadly, even sweepingly, simply because in any liberation scope is of the essence. . . .

Accordingly these remarks are aimed not at the formulation of a sense of strategy that will take the place of other valid strategic considerations, e.g., the role of modern science in man's fulfillment, but rather to suggest that "non-Western studies" (to continue using that inadequate phrase) may have a stronger basic role as a new strategic element in modern liberal learning than has been generally realized up to now.

It is a truism to say that the content of liberal studies as we know them in America today is traditionally and dominantly Western in both origin and orientation. It is not equally manifest as yet that this Western dominance represents for us not merely a "nutritional deficiency" of the educated mind but may in fact be a decisive barrier to the ability of our society to relate intellectually and emotionally to the realities of the modern world. . . . We certainly know that there are a few great difficulties and genuinely deep dilemmas that cannot be met or managed in the future unless man is able to see and think about these things from the perspective of *both* the total disparities and the oneness of the world. We are at a juncture in the affairs of men where learning must quickly accommodate to two revolutionary requirements: (1) an unprecedented need for ever greater specialized pentration of all fields of knowledge and (2) an extension of Western man's understanding and "purposes" to embrace the totality of mankind. Being now irretrievably caught up as we surely are with the world's affairs, may it not be that the most fundamental task of liberation facing our society is to free itself from the provincialism of its heritage? Lest a hasty reader misunderstand me, I repeat that the liberation I propose is from provincialism, not from heritage. . . .

Any fundamental change in educational strategy is only likely to win acceptance if it is accompanied by concrete thoughts about how as a practical matter it is to be approached and by some pedagogical theory to give it a rational foundation. . . .

Needless to say I have no panacea for the resolution of this most ancient educational dilemma. I will suggest that greater attention to the possibilities of the comparative approach in dealing with the liberal arts might be a promising, practical way to approach the problem. In all fields of learning we are being forced to accept the fact that the great body of man's knowledge can no longer be taught, at least to one man, and that increasingly the emphasis must be on teaching the approaches to knowledge. . . .

It has been my feeling for some time that the teaching of many undergraduate subjects could be invigorated by greater attention to the comparative approach. It would be a very happy thing, would it not, if we should find in the comparative approach better answers both for improving our pedagogy and for showing the way toward a modern strategy for liberal learning?

Quite independently of President Dickey's thinking, the comparative approach has been advanced by faculty groups as an effective means of meeting the challenge of relating the liberal arts curriculum to world affairs. As separate planning groups moved forward during the two-year interval, the concept of the comparative approach began to take shape as an integrating theme, bringing together various elements in our thinking that initially appeared to be somewhat unrelated and disparate. In fact it emerged also as a reaction to possible over-attention to "non-Western studies." We were reminded frequently that non-Western studies could become parochial in their own way. We recognized that comparisons of political, economic and social institutions, philosophies and the arts between Western and non-Western societies would be meaningful but also that comparisons within Western society itself should not be neglected. Moreover we came to understand that the kind of liberating educational experience should have no bounds in either space or time. Thus, as indicated, the concept of a comparative approach became central to our planning.

What we mean by the comparative approach as we intend to apply it to the undergraduate curriculum is explained in the following statement prepared by Professor Henry Ehrmann:

The constant and intensive interplay between different parts of the world is making it indispensable for all our students, whatever their undergraduate major and their lifetime career, to understand the conditions under which this interplay is taking place. Without such an understanding the liberal arts lose what President Dickey has called their liberating force. Under present conditions of cultural interaction a knowledge of other civilizations and their systematic comparison with the environment which is familiar to the American student becomes necessary to the latter's comprehension even of his own culture. "Without relinquishing the sense of nationality, we have acquired a sense of humanity."

Just as it has long been recognized that all fields of liberal learning are in need of a "historical stretching" (for "he who knows only his own generation remains always a child"), we believe that all disciplines of the humanities and the social sciences (and in the natural sciences at least such applied fields as technology, etc.) need a "geographic stretching" of their scope. This has become the prerequisite of that stretching of the mind which is the goal of undergraduate education. To this end a large infusion of foreign data (and wherever possible of foreign experiences) into the teaching of the various disciplines is necessary.

To a considerable extent this new information will pertain to societies, institutions and cultures which were hitherto regarded as the domain of relatively few specialists. For it is precisely those societies that challenge familiar assumptions based on Western experiences, and it is such a challenge which we wish to provide for our undergraduates. But we consider contrasts and comparisons between the Western and the non-Western World, between developed and underdeveloped, industrial and pre-industrial societies as somewhat too simplistic (or too specialized) for our purposes. To sharpen the understanding of the undergraduate student for the fact that such terms are matters of degree with blurring lines of division instead of sharp breaking points is another goal of our program. The conditions under which change and connected phenomena occur or fail to occur; which structures perform similar or different functions in different societies; which are the models developed in one culture that command assent in another culture and which models are rejected; which factors are favorable to modernization and which are likely to reproduce traditionalism— these are the problems to which the comparative approach addresses itself without necessarily distinguishing between exotic and assumedly more familiar cultures. But there are also many methodologically sound and pragmatic reasons why much of the material to be infused into the curriculum will be sought in the new states and especially those that are building on the foundations of old civilizations.

There is no need here to enter into a discussion of the controversial question, still hotly debated among some historians, whether the comparative approach will ever be able to formulate "general laws" or whether every phenomenon represents a unique combination of features and forces. At the very least comparative analysis can identify and explain uniqueness which is of special importance for the beginning student and his possible penchant for cultural ethnocentricity. But we are also convinced that it can do much more.

We are confident that the comparative approach can lead to a greater unification of the curriculum since it will stress those problems that are common to the humanities and the social sciences and that spring from the "evident interaction that occurs in every society" (developed and developing alike), "between cultural traditions, social organization, and new ideas, new aspirations and new wants." Such a unification can of course be achieved without interfering with the departmental organization common to Dartmouth and other liberal arts colleges.

Finally the introduction of comparative materials into the undergraduate curriculum ought to stress, perhaps far more than this is done by the research scholar cultivating the comparative field in his respective discipline, the role of values in different social and cultural settings. The comparative investigation of the relationship between culture patterns and value orientation, inquiries into the effect of cultural change extending into existing systems of values can become meaningful for undergraduates in almost any of the traditional majors.

## A Comparative Studies Center

To accomplish the purposes set forth in this statement we propose to establish at Dartmouth College a Comparative Studies Center. This center will attack the fundamental task of curricular adjustment and revision, and of faculty development. The experience which it will provide should enable us to employ a comparative approach within existing courses and disciplines without squeezing ever more information and courses into the overcrowded Western-oriented curriculum. We also expect that the center will help members of the Dartmouth and other faculties to acquire a new understanding for areas, institutions and cultures with which they have not been familiar and widen thereby their own horizons as classroom teachers.

While the center will be a separate entity, serving for a period as long as ten years, it will be *of* the faculty and will work *within* the framework of regular faculty processes. At the same time, as a distinct entity, it will provide the leadership and the resources required to bring about fundamental changes. We are convinced that an endeavor of this scope and magnitude must represent a commitment of the total institution, involving all relevant parts. Yet we believe that a separate organizational device is appropriate as a means of providing the "cutting edge" by which insitutional goals will be accomplished. Likewise, the separate center will provide the means of making an impact not only at Dartmouth but broadly in American higher education. We feel that although a period of up to a decade will be required for the center to complete its objectives, it should be phased out, at least in the form we have suggested, when its reasons for being have been accomplished.

In broad outline, the Comparative Studies Center will operate as follows. It will be headed by a director, a teacher-scholar of the Dartmouth faculty who will provide leadership for the enterprise and at the same time relate its activities to the larger purposes and programs of the entire institution. He will be assisted by a small steering group representing faculty and administration. At any one time there will be assigned to the center up to ten or twelve members of the faculty from the humanities and social sciences, and hopefully now and then a scientist, on a full- or part-time basis, for periods of a year or two. Some of these individuals are presently on the Dartmouth faculty. Others will be appointed, both in the normal process of faculty replacements and appointments, and on either a temporary or on an open-ended basis. Some of the latter will participate in classroom teaching by taking over on a part-time basis the teaching assignments of present members of the faculty who will be assigned to the center. Others will develop new areas of instruction presently not represented in the Dartmouth curriculum.

Individuals assigned to the center whenever possible will continue with some teaching, unless overseas study and travel preclude it. Indeed a continuing link with the classroom will be essential for an enterprise devoted to the alteration and improvement of the curriculum, at Dartmouth and elsewhere. Hence the feedback from the center to the instructional process should not be interrupted.

The principal feature of the center will be a joint faculty seminar and a series of sub-seminars, that will bring all members of the enterprise together in a common experience, to share their separate findings, their insights and their perspectives. Basically this central part of the center's program will be to determine the degree of validity of the comparative approach as a means of providing a more effective liberal education.

In contemplating the faculty seminar and its related sub-seminars, we are consciously endeavoring to avoid what might readily become just another curriculum study. Rather we are hoping to work outward from fundamental substantive problems and issues of study, bringing about curricular changes by indirect rather than direct means, that is, in response to the intellectual interests and experiences of an increasing number of faculty members instead of by some "grand design" imposed from without. We contemplate that several sub-seminars will be operating concurrently, focused on topics arising from the mutual interests and aspirations of individuals assigned to the center at that time.

The kinds of topics we have in mind, and all suggested by faculty members from the various departments, are indicated by the following partial list:

Modernization and change

Basic concepts and values such as authority and freedom

Studies in comparative philosophy and religion

The place of the drama and other forms of literature in different cultures, and the role of nature, the hero and the family in different national literatures

The place of science in different cultures

The outlook on and the organization of education

The influence of the military, of other interest groups.

The larger seminar, in which all center participants will take part, will serve as a forum in which the experiences of the sub-seminars as well as those of individual members will be discussed. But the seminar also will be concerned, as we gain experience with the institutional aspects of our undertaking, particularly with the application of comparative analysis to the separate disciplines and to the liberal arts curriculum as a whole.

We assume that the seminar will become the initiating force in bringing into being *ad hoc* groups that will undertake to revise existing courses in the light of center experience, and devise new experimental courses that might ultimately replace existing courses, such as the introductory courses that are elected by a large number of students to satisfy the distribution requirements for the degree.

We do not plan to introduce new survey or interdisciplinary courses; rather we expect to work within the established disciplines. Our deliberations suggest to us that the comparative approach can be applied and developed in this manner. We shall seek not to crowd more data into these courses but rather to develop selective techniques and a new approach to the presentation of knowledge. Ultimately we seek to determine whether, through such an approach, the social sciences and the humanities can make gains comparable to those in mathematics and the sciences, in which large blocks of knowledge can, in effect, be leaped over as the student moves forward to higher levels of analysis and understanding.

Here we face a critical issue. We must ask ourselves, how can the teacher-scholar be a master of several fields without the loss of integrity in his chosen field? That there is danger of superficiality we do not deny. Obviously we must acquire more knowledge of more areas and more fields if we are to be capable of valid comparative analysis. But it is our belief that by pooling knowledge through the center and its seminar and sub-seminars we can avoid superficiality and preserve the integrity of the individual scholar. What we hope to achieve for him is a wider perspective within which he can develop his special competence.

As one of our members has expressed it, as we know more we can provide better generalizations. As we provide better generalizations we can simplify more, and as we simplify more we can teach more things, even when faced with a greater volume of information. Moreover in this manner we hope to resolve the dilemma of breadth versus depth faced by the *ad hoc* faculty committee on non-Western studies.

Thus, the center will have a primary concern for the large introductory courses. Since we are convinced that almost any problem in the humanities and the social sciences should be analyzed on a comparative and multi-national basis, the question of which subjects are most deserving of comparative study becomes of secondary importance. It amounts to asking which part of the entire curriculum should have priority for our scrutiny. On this question answers are bound to differ; the establishment of a strategy of priorities will be among the first tasks of the proposed faculty seminar.

Some of the introductory courses will be more open to change than others. The introductory courses in geography and anthropology, for example, already draw upon materials of a non-Western nature and employ comparative techniques in their presentation. Our preliminary studies suggest that there are substantial opportunities for the new approach in such introductory courses as Government 5 (Political Ideas), Government 6 (American and Foreign Governments), Sociology 1 (Introduction to Sociology), and Philosophy 1 (Problems of Philosophy). The division of humanities has proposed that a student be permitted to elect Religion 2 (Living Asian Religions) as well as Religion 1 (The Judeo-Christian Tradition) to satisfy the humanities distribution requirement for the degree. The division has suggested also that ultimately the two courses be redesigned to provide a comparative approach throughout the two-course sequence. Likewise, the separate introductory courses in art might be similarly redesigned. Several of the younger historians have proposed a new sequence in world civilizations to replace the present introductory courses in European and American history. The economists too have expressed interest in experimenting with comparative techniques in the introductory courses.

These introductory courses usually are the responsibility of the departments as a whole rather than of a single instructor. We plan to bring into the center individuals who are directly involved in the planning and instruction of these courses, with the expectation that upon their return to their regular teaching duties they will provide leadership within the departments in bringing about experimentation and innovation with these courses.

Ideally these changes will take place by an evolutionary process within these established courses. In many cases we believe this can be accomplished. In others built-in rigidities may make this more difficult. Thus we believe we should contemplate the development in some situations of experimental introductory courses, offered in parallel with the established courses and open to a limited number of students, as pilot operations.

The center also will be concerned with intermediate and advanced courses. Here its influence will be more immediate and direct, since instructors usually have a more personal responsibility for such courses, and will be able to relate their center experiences intimately to their classroom instruction.

The seminar and sub-seminars described above have been planned for the faculty. We anticipate, however, that the latter in many cases may evolve into courses for undergraduates. Initially, a few advanced students might participate in a sub-seminar. Subsequently, one or two of the faculty participants might offer the topic as an advanced seminar. Ultimately, and hopefully, the subject matter will find its way into some of the regular courses open to students more generally. This may well prove to be the most effective process by which curricular changes will be initiated.

We expect that each member of the center will continue with his own individual research or other form of creative activity. This will not only provide an opportunity to advance his scholarship and professional development but also will enable him better to contribute to the seminar projects. We assume, for example, that the choice of topics for sub-seminars will be made, in part at least, on the basis of the research or related interests of the participants.

Our experience suggests that we shall also be able to develop numerous and fruitful opportunities for student collaboration in faculty research.

Likewise the center will provide opportunity for overseas observation, study and research by its members where such activity is appropriate. This will be an essential experience for individuals who will be concerning themselves with new foreign areas for the first time. In the case of individuals who are area specialists, there must be continuing opportunity to return to the field overseas.

So far, we have described participation by members of the Dartmouth faculty in this enterprise. We also plan to secure the services of visiting scholars. We plan to appoint to the center, for periods of up to one year, individuals of outstanding competence in their fields, with more specialized knowledge and experience than most of us here have acquired. We would expect them to contribute as specialists to the seminar and sub-seminars and also to provide advice and guidance in achieving the larger objectives of the center. We would expect the scholarly contributions of these visitors to pervade the entire undertaking.

Likewise we wish to appoint visiting scholars from overseas. Such individuals, on one- or two-year appointment, would engage in some teaching but also would participate in center activities, including the seminars.

We have emphasized in this presentation our expectations that the Dartmouth experience in the Comparative Studies Center will have an impact upon the liberal arts curriculum generally. In part this effect can be accomplished to the degree that new curricular developments will serve as models or proto-types for other institutions to follow. We are hopeful, however, of establishing a more direct and effective relationship between the Dartmouth experience and other institutions. Accordingly, we propose that provision be made for up to ten or twelve one-year fellowships in the Comparative Studies Center, to be held by representatives of other liberal arts institutions. These individuals will have the same opportunities and responsibilities as members of the Dartmouth faculty assigned to the center. In some cases it may be appropriate for them to engage in part-time teaching while in residence. They will participate in the faculty seminar and sub-seminars and will return to their own institutions not only enriched by the experience but prepared to exercise leadership in curricular innovation.

We propose also that, as we at Dartmouth gain experience in the center, we conduct, particularly during the summer months, a number of other shorter and more specialized programs to serve other institutions. These will include short conferences for the exchange of information and analysis of common experiences and problems, and longer institutes that will be more in the nature of training opportunities for other teachers. Several of the institutes might be planned for secondary school teachers. We also propose to take advantage of the summer term that we are inaugurating in 1963, using this period as an opportunity to introduce new, experimental courses.

Beyond these measures, we anticipate that the center will prepare course outlines and syllabi, bibliographies and other descriptive materials that will be of value to other institutions. While we do not at this time expect to engage in a larger publications program, it is possible that we may wish to move modestly in this direction.

In order not only to utilize the advice of experienced individuals elsewhere but also to relate the Dartmouth Comparative Studies Center to other institutions, we propose the establishment of an advisory group of five or six individuals. During the first phase this group will provide guidance to the center's activities, and the individual members will serve as consultants in their fields of special interest.

The comparative studies project outlined above is a large and ambitious undertaking. It is one that falls squarely within the institutional purposes and commitments of Dartmouth College. We are confident moreover that it is within the capabilities of this college.

The focus of the project is upon undergraduate liberal learning. Dartmouth is committed to providing for its students a liberal arts program of preeminent quality. But the goals of the comparative studies project are to be accomplished by bringing the larger world of scholarship to bear upon the processes of teaching and learning. This Dartmouth is now achieving in other fields. In a sense Dartmouth stands between the college and the university. While retaining and strengthening its primary concern for undergraduate education, it has developed certain of the characteristics of the university. It possesses an outstanding library. In its associated schools of medicine, engineering and business administration it has had long experience with professional education at the graduate level. Its faculty in the arts and sciences is composed of individuals of substantial scholarly achievement. Recently Dartmouth established doctoral programs in mathematics and molecular biology. While we do not anticipate a large-scale advance into graduate education, we are prepared to consider programs in those areas in which, because of the proper combination of factors, we may be able to make a worthwhile contribution.

Thus Dartmouth College will provide an environment appropriate for the conduct of the scholarly pursuits of the center project but within the context of deep concern for undergraduate liberal learning. The goals of the project already are those of the institution.

# 18

# UNIVERSITY OF THE PACIFIC

The University of the Pacific's approach to non-Western studies for undergraduates is novel in two respects. The first is its pioneer enterprise at Elbert Covell College, where the U.S. liberal arts curriculum is being taught in Spanish, as are courses on the history, economy, literature and social development of Latin America. The second is Raymond College's approach, with non-Western studies required of all students but studied primarily through reading and independent research projects. The two different approaches to learning embodied in Raymond and Elbert Covell Colleges are results of the university's decision to plan its further expansion primarily on the basis of small residential "cluster" colleges of some 250 students. Each will have its own students and, at least partly, its own resident faculty but will share library, laboratories, other general services and some courses with the College of the Pacific, which is the main undergraduate liberal arts core of the institution, and with other schools of the university.

## Historical Background

The University of the Pacific, a Methodist church-related institution founded in 1851, was the first chartered college in

University of the Pacific, Stockton, California. President Robert E. Burns. (Methodist; coeducational; semester system; liberal arts to doctor's degree; 2561 students)

California. It is relatively small, with some 1800 undergraduates in the College of the Pacific, 124 in the new Raymond College, 60 in Elbert Covell College, and the remainder, about 350, enrolled in the professional and graduate schools. The emphasis has always been on liberal arts undergraduate education for men and women, with ninety per cent of the students in residence.

Over the years President Robert Burns became convinced that the pressure for substantially increased enrolments in all public and private institutions in California would not only be hard to resist but would also challenge the residential, liberal arts character of the College of the Pacific. It was clear that simply to grow bigger and bigger, along with the state university campuses, the new state college system and the proliferating junior colleges, was not the answer for a private institution of this sort. Therefore, he and some of his key associates decided that the university should grow in such a way as to preserve the best values of the small residential liberal arts college. They planned to achieve this by the gradual addition of semi-autonomous residential cluster colleges alongside the existing College of the Pacific.

President Burns and some key faculty members visited Oxford and Cambridge three times between 1959 and 1963 and invited the secretary general of the faculty at Cambridge to spend some time at the University of the Pacific in 1962. They also visited Latin America in 1960 and 1961.

In assessing the situation President Burns recognized that he "probably couldn't change the College of the Pacific's curriculum by a direct reorganization." He wanted to "avoid the heartbreak and revolution that usually occur around conservative colleges when major changes are introduced." Consequently, he and a few key members of the administration and faculty worked out the plans for Raymond College without reference to the faculty in general. The president said that he wished to develop a "brand new approach with no departmental organization or major requirements." He and Samuel L. Meyer, professor of botany and academic vice president, did most of the initial planning for Raymond College. The key ideas on controlled growth and curricular revision developed during these years, were adopted by the board of regents, and announced publicly in 1961. They have been implemented thus far primarily through the creation of Raymond and Elbert Covell Colleges.

The ideas embodied in Elbert Covell College were first mooted at a faculty retreat in February 1959. The general plan of the college was worked out by President Burns and Vice President Meyer in discussion with Ambassador Robert Woodward at the United States Embassy in Montevideo in 1960. Substantial strides have since been made in putting the plan into effect. The nucleus of a bilingual staff (some drawn from the faculty of the College of the Pacific) has been appointed, and in September 1963 forty Latin American students, from fifteen countries, and twenty U.S. students registered for the four-year B.A. program.

The development of the two colleges was expedited by the fact that the university had land available for them. It has since acquired more land fairly close to its present campus for further expansion as faculty and funds become available for the addition of more cluster colleges. Plans for the first new residential college proved so attractive to two interested men that they deeded valuable property to the university to endow Raymond College. The imaginative plans for a new Spanish-speaking college have elicited the support of several people who have established testamentary trusts with substantial assets which will form the endowment for Elbert Covell College.

For the time being, the major attention of the university is being focused on the development of these two new colleges. Plans are also going forward, however, for the development of a third cluster college, St Michael's, related to the Episcopal Church. There are prospects that a fourth, sponsored by the Presbyterian Church, will also be established during the next few years.

### Raymond College

Raymond, the first of the cluster colleges, housed in its own quadrangle and having its own faculty and student body, began instruction in the fall of 1962. It provides an intensive, essentially traditional liberal arts curriculum based on a sequence of courses in the natural sciences, social sciences and humanities leading to a B.A. degree in three years.

Students at Raymond take three terms per year. The Raymond term is longer than the traditional quarter and shorter than the traditional semester, but each term (approximately thirteen weeks) has the weight of a semester in terms of "contact hours" with the professors, owing to a sixty-minute class hour and five meetings per week. Students take only three courses per term. The methodology of the college features seminars, tutorials, independent study and writing. The Raymond curriculum allows for few electives, but there is considerable flexibility within the general course divisions of the curriculum.

The college is entirely residential and emphasizes the advantages of keeping students within "the climate of learning." A provost and four other faculty members reside in the quadrangle. There are seminar classrooms and faculty studies in each residence hall. The quadrangle also contains a common room with paperback library and a multipurpose central dining room called Great Hall. Weekly "High Table" talks, discussions and artistic performances by distinguished guests are presented in Great Hall and are open to the entire college and guests from other parts of the university and the community. These features, plus a student-faculty ratio of about 10-1, are all designed to strengthen close student-faculty association and to provide a continuous learning experience.

## A Reading Approach to Non-Western Cultures

During the first and second years each student devotes two terms (10 units) to a seminar in Readings in World Civilization and two terms to a seminar called Readings in World Literature. A fifth term may be given over to independent study in one of these areas. The course called Readings in World Civilization is described as follows:

The course in Readings in World Civilization builds upon a background of political, social, economic and intellectual history of Europe and selected concepts in the social sciences developed in the antecedent course Introduction to the Modern World. It is designed, first of all, to give the student a comprehensive grounding in a number of original classics, from Plato to the present, which represent contributions to theories of the state and society. Essentially, the so-called Lockean and non-Lockean schools of thought and their precursors are examined and an effort is made to assess the historical significance of the various writers and their works. More specifically, writings by Plato, Aristotle, Cicero, St. Augustine, St. Thomas, Machiavelli, Hobbes, Locke, Rousseau, J. S. Mill, Marx, Engels, Lenin, Stalin, Lippmann, Mannheim, and some other selections, like the New Program of the Communist Party of the USSR, are included in the reading assignments.

All students read these works, discuss them in class, and also write reports on selected works. The second part of the course in Readings in World Civilization is designed primarily to familiarize students with histories and current problems of cultures largely outside the Western tradition. Each student makes an intensive study of the history and an analysis of the contemporary social, economic, and political problems of one non-Western country. His findings are shared with all through seminar presentations and discussions. A final term paper of thirty-five to fifty pages provides the synthesis of the individual's research. In addition the research of each student is shared with several others who study and critically evaluate this final term paper in seminar. The author defends his work. Thus each individual has an opportunity to study the work of several other students and each has the opportunity of having his own work critically evaluated by several classmates.

The seminar is further enriched by each student being responsible for a general theme (e.g., nationalism, political transformation, social change) in addition to the country he is studying. These topics are selected so each student can contribute conceptually to the seminar discussions on the countries. Among the topics chosen for consideration are: theory of evolution, nationalism, concept of progress, mechanisms of political transformation, population, motivation, agrarian reform, social or cultural change, imperialism, theory of power, theory of economic development, communism as an ideological force, liberal democracy as a political instrument.

In order to introduce the students to certain basic economic and cultural considerations of the underdeveloped world, one of the faculty members, Professor Walter Wagner, delivers a series of lectures to all sections at the beginning of the term.

Countries selected for study by students vary but the following is a representative list: India, Cuba, Thailand, Pakistan, Korea, Egypt, China, Paraguay, Afghanistan, Japan, Russia, Yugoslavia, Israel, Burma, Turkey, Brazil, Venezuela, Vietnam and Zanzibar.

Vera Micheles Dean's *The Nature of the Non-Western World,* and Eugene Staley's *The Future of Underdeveloped Countries* are assigned as reading for general orientation to the non-Western world. The major emphasis for learning is placed on student research and self-education. The seminar, meeting four to five times weekly, is used primarily for exploration of ideas, interpretations, challenge, critical evaluation and dissemination of information.

Provost Warren Bryan Martin and Professors Walter Wagner, Eugene Wise and George Blum, who teach the course, intend to give even greater attention to non-Western cultures in this course as well as in a freshman team-teaching course entitled Introduction to the Modern World, by inviting authorities on special themes from other parts of the University of the Pacific, or from other universities, under the terms of a grant proposal which is now being evaluated and arranged.

The college does not now itself offer more advanced courses in non-Western fields as electives or as a part of the core program. But Raymond students may arrange to take courses relating to the Arab World, Latin America, India, Southeast Asia, the Far East, and the USSR offered at the College of the Pacific or at Elbert Covell College, provided they can find time to do so in addition to their normal required courses at Raymond.

In the course entitled Introduction to the Modern World, Raymond students are introduced to anthropological, cross-cultural analysis and an "international" perspective. The teachers involved in this course are intent on developing an introduction to the modern *world.* Raymond students at the senior level do "Study in the Area of Specialization" as well as independent study, and some of these students are doing their work in areas that will contribute to international understanding—Islamic culture, international relations and various areas in anthropology. Students in independent study at Raymond often meet in informal seminars under student leadership to share their material and experiences.

## Elbert Covell College

The university's second new approach to non-Western studies focuses on Latin America through the program at Elbert Covell College. Elbert Covell College, which welcomed its first sixty students in September 1963, has its own quadrangle adjacent to Raymond, which it resembles in many physical respects. Elbert Covell differs from Raymond in that its faculty and curriculum are not autonomous but are partly shared with the College of the Pacific. It offers a four-year B.A. program in the liberal arts patterned on that of the College of the Pacific but requires all students to take at least half of their courses in the Spanish language. Elbert Covell students major in the traditional disciplines but the college stresses three areas of particular importance to Latin America. These are the sciences and mathematics; economics and business administration; and teaching and administration in elementary and secondary schools. Since virtually all courses are to be taught in Spanish, with the exception of English, which is included in the curriculum as a foreign or second language, Latin American students will be able to study in the United States "free of the language barrier which is all too often an insurmountable obstacle to satisfactory academic progress. On the other hand, North American students who seek functional proficiency in Spanish may take content courses in their field of major interest in this Spanish-speaking college, as their ever-increasing facility in the use of the language permits."

Dr Arthur J. Cullen, director of Elbert Covell College, and Vice President Meyer have characterized the objectives of Elbert Covell College as: (1) to train men and women as inter-American specialists; (2) to give Latin American students the highest quality of educational and technical knowledge in their own language; (3) to give North American students superior training in inter-American studies; (4) to encourage Latin-American students, if they so choose, to take part of their general program in the English-speaking divisions of the university, when proficiency in English permits; (5) to give students from both the Americas the opportunity to study and live together, to represent their respective cultures to each other, and to accept the responsibility of understanding each other; and (6) to make available within the framework of a truly inter-American concept the traditionally sound North American program of education in the liberal arts.[1] The founders of Elbert Covell College insist that:

The Spanish-speaking college of the University of the Pacific is not interested in changing Latin Americans into North Americans, nor the

---

1.  *Liberal Education*, XLIX, 1, May 1963, p. 221

opposite. It is dedicated to the creation of a new American: the inter-American specialist, the American who is prepared to contribute to the common progress—social, economic, political—of *all* the Americas here or there, wherever these Americas are concerned about solving the problems of today with the tools provided through modern educational preparation.[2]

They go on to define "the inter-American specialist" as follows:

He must be, first of all, a specialist in one of the critical needs of the Americas. He completes a major of sufficient breadth and depth to allow him to pursue graduate work toward an advanced degree in his subject matter area or in a professional field related to it. The inter-American specialist is bilingual. He understands, speaks, reads and writes both the English and Spanish languages sufficiently well to communicate professionally and socially. The inter-American specialist has been well-grounded in "area" courses; he knows the history, the forms of government, the literature, the art, the music, the traditions, the economic problems, the way-of-life of his own people as well as those of the other America. The traditional Latin American studies program becomes only a part of his training, equal in importance to —but of questionable value unless accompanied by—language skills and professional ability.[3]

## Program

During the academic year 1963-64 students at Elbert Covell College could take a wide selection of courses offered in Spanish, including United States history, history and civilization of Latin America, geography of the Americas, general economics, algebra, trigonometry, analytical geometry, calculus, biology, chemistry, learning and the learner, foundations of American education, fundamentals of speech, and basic Spanish composition. Elbert Covell College is thus breaking new ground in Spanish-language teaching of the regular liberal arts program.

Dr Cullen said in January 1964 that his three greatest problems were: (1) how to get and retain able faculty members who can and will teach courses in their discipline in both Spanish and English; (2) how to attract well-qualified non-English-

---

2. Op. cit. p. 222
3. Ibid.

speaking Latin American students; and (3) how to identify adequate texts for the various subjects in the U. S. liberal arts curriculum which are being taught in the Spanish language.

## Faculty for Elbert Covell College

Elbert Covell College was fortunate in being able to draw upon one full-time and seven part-time faculty members from the College of the Pacific who were able to teach their respective disciplines in Spanish. Nine new full-time faculty members were appointed in 1963 to teach history, Spanish, mathematics and English as a foreign language. Six of these seventeen teachers are South Americans. Five graduate assistants, two of them in Spanish and one each in English as a foreign language, home economics and chemistry, complete the present roster of instructional staff. There also are head residents for men and women and two bilingual secretaries.

## Students at Elbert Covell College

Ideally, Dr Cullen hopes to attract about two thirds of the maximum of 250 students at Elbert Covell from Latin America, and one third from North America. He estimates that half of the Latin Americans, or a third of the total, will require scholarship help but hopes that the other half can attend at their own expense. In order to recruit students for the first year, Dr Elliot Taylor, dean of admissions, made a four-week trip through ten Latin American cities in the spring of 1963. By the summer of 1963, 115 applicants from fifteen Latin American countries had sought admission. Of these, 59 were considered academically qualified. Twenty-seven of these applicants did not indicate the field of study they wished to pursue. The others selected a wide range of subjects, with strong emphasis on engineering, teaching, economics, business administration and science. Nine of the first group of forty Latin American students admitted in September 1963 were from Honduras and came under U. S. AID auspices.

Dr Cullen calculated that the college needed some $40,000 in scholarships for 1963-64, and that the scholarship funds necessary for subsequent years will rise by multiples of $40,000 until they stabilize at $160,000 a year for some 80 Latin American students annually by the time the college reaches its optimum size of 250 students in the academic year 1967-68. Thus far the college has no guaranteed funds for scholarships and has been raising them as necessary. Dr Cullen believes that loans are healthier than outright scholarships and that a revolving loan fund for this purpose would prove more economical and would help to develop self-respect among recipients. Gifts of scholarship-fund books have already been made to Elbert Covell College by Rotary clubs and other groups in Latin America. The Mexican government donated the Adolfo López-Mateos collection of some 3,000 volumes in 1963.

In 1963-64 and for the following three years, a number of regular students at the College of the Pacific will reside at Elbert Covell College to occupy the excess dormitory space until the college's full complement of Latin American and North American students is reached. For the time being, this means that a majority of the students residing in Elbert Covell College are English-speaking North Americans and that each of the forty Latin American students can and does share a room with a North American student who does not speak Spanish. This provides an unusual opportunity for the Latin American student to develop a competence in English and for the North American student to practice Spanish.

Elbert Covell reports that its first Latin American students got off to a good start during their first semester and performed better than the North American students. Their teachers believe this was partly because the Latin Americans were able to take virtually all their courses in Spanish and so felt at ease from the beginning without a new language to master along with other adjustments.

Elbert Covell College may make a unique contribution to inter-American studies if it can foster the development of adequate Spanish textbooks in various subjects common to the U. S. liberal arts undergraduate curriculum. The faculty of the college is already engaged in intensive preparation to develop further courses and texts in Spanish for the second or sophomore year. The staff's ability to develop appropriate courses and texts during the next few years will be crucial to the achievement of the college's goals.

## Other Non-Western Courses

In addition to the offerings relating to the non-Western world at Raymond and Elbert Covell Colleges, the College of the Pacific has itself developed a number of non-Western courses. The offerings relating to North Africa and the Middle East, primarily taught by Professor Rom Landau, are of particular interest, as he has had long experience in the Arab world, especially Morocco, and has written extensively about this area. These courses have been offered over the past decade but they remain essentially upperclass electives and do not draw large numbers of students. They represent to some extent the residue of the American Academy for Asian Studies established for some years in San Francisco, which was affiliated in the 1950's with the College of the Pacific. When the affiliation was dissolved in the mid-1950's, the college decided to retain Professor Landau to teach courses on North Africa and the Islamic Middle East. He continues to reside in San Francisco and normally spends only one day a week on the campus in Stockton. This may be one reason why the study of North Africa and the Middle East has not permeated notably into underclass general education courses.

## Faculty at the College of the Pacific

Besides the substantial number of faculty members with Latin American competence mentioned in discussion of Elbert Covell College, five faculty members in the College of the Pacific have had substantial experience relating to the non-Western world, although little systematic effort outside of the department of history and political science has been made to secure staff members with particular competence in international affairs or the non-Western world. Nevertheless, eight members of the faculty have resided or taught abroad. One of them is an Iranian who is an assistant professor of education. Four others have had experience in Japan and one of these learned some Japanese during a three-year visit. The others have had experience in Asia and the USSR, Pakistan and Syria. With the exception of one man teaching political science, including some work on the USSR, none of these professors is now teaching courses in which he uses this non-Western experience to any significant extent.

## Library

The university library now has 120,000 volumes and is spending some $32,000 annually for books and $11,000 for periodicals. It receives annually 1,150 periodicals, and the librarians estimate that four per cent of the new book accessions and three per cent of the periodicals relate to the non-Western world. For purposes of instruction, library holdings are rated as "good" for East Asia and Latin America, and "adequate" for Africa (general), North Africa, Asia (general), South Asia, and the Middle East. No evaluation is made of the holdings relating to areas not included in the curriculum, such as Southeast Asia and Slavic and East European studies. Otherwise, the library is rated as "poor" for all major world areas in terms of student research and faculty research. The first three priority needs are: (1) to build up original and current materials on Latin America; (2) to develop a back file of periodicals and non-current books on Latin America; and (3) to build up original materials and current accessions in relation to Africa. The library plans to build a new wing in 1964-65 to provide space for the Adolfo López-Mateos Latin American collection and other materials relating to Latin America.

## Foreign Students and Study Abroad

In 1963-64, 67 undergraduate students from non-Western areas were enrolled, 40 of them in Elbert Covell College. Twenty-five held scholarships from the college and another eighteen held scholarships from other sources. Only from five to seven scholarships had been granted each year between 1958 and 1962. This big increase in scholarships granted to students from the non-Western world indicates growing institutional commitment to developing a more international student body. Most of the increase represents scholarships for Latin American students at Elbert Covell College.

The office of the dean of the College of the Pacific issues a periodic newsletter called "Academics Augmented," reporting on both summer and year-round, on- and off-campus, educational service and travel opportunities for students. For many years members of the faculty have organized tours sponsored by the university. Recently these have averaged two a year with half the tours going to Europe. Such tours, combined with preparatory study and subsequent reports, can enrich course offerings on non-Western areas and give students direct experience in other cultures. Few undergraduates have benefited from the opportunities offered by the tours, although some graduate students have participated.

### Conclusion

The University of the Pacific's two main approaches to non-Western studies are still in the early experimental stage. They appear to have elicited general support from the faculty but they represent a method of introducing curricular change which largely by-passes the existing liberal arts college. Three issues affecting further development may need more consideration.

The first concerns faculty competence. Will the university develop plans to enable faculty members to extend their competence in non-Western areas systematically, or will it depend mainly on recruiting new teachers with the special skills required? If the university continues its present emphasis on recruitment it may wish to formulate more specific and explicit criteria for the identification of non-Western competence. Experience elsewhere suggests that it may be necessary to develop opportunities for present faculty members to learn more about the non-Western world. Even the teachers at Raymond College now responsible for the reading courses relating to non-Western cultures recognize their need for more experience in the non-Western world and for special study about it in order to teach more effectively.

Dean Jacoby of the College of the Pacific is hopeful of strengthening the curriculum by adding upperclass offerings on the non-Western world. He would like to encourage more attention to it in lower division general education courses, starting with the introduction of non-Western data and perspectives into introductory courses in history and political science. The dean would also like to build upon existing interest and faculty competence in Japan and the Far East as the first non-Western area focus in the college and as a complement to the Latin American concentration in Elbert Covell College. But Dean Jacoby believes that as a result of the efforts at developing residential colleges on new patterns there is little likelihood that any special programs in the area of non-Western studies will be undertaken by the College of the Pacific in the next few years.

In its focus on Latin America, Elbert Covell College appears to have adopted a curricular pattern little changed from that of the College of the Pacific rather than the Raymond model. There may be opportunities in the future for the university to assess whether a foreign-study college such as Elbert Covell might dispense with the usual curriculum and departmental structure and might benefit by patterning its program on Raymond College. In either case, the residential environment and the emphasis of these new colleges on reinforcing the formal learning process offer a milieu conducive to continuous learning.

In the long run, perhaps, one of the most important questions will be whether Elbert Covell can remain a truly liberal arts college if it maintains its strong pre-professional concentration on developing "the inter-American specialist." Elbert Covell asserts that it offers "professional preparation based on the needs of the twentieth century in all the Americas and on the talents and interest of young men and women who must satisfy those needs." The college may have difficulty in reconciling this vocational aim with its hope that in the study of the sciences and mathematics, economics and business administration, or teaching and administration in elementary and secondary schools "in his own language . . . (the Latin or North American student) can acquire the basic liberal arts prerequisites for later technical and professional training. . . ."

It remains to be seen how the College of the Pacific and its new sister colleges will develop their programs in relation to non-Western studies and to each other. President Burns hopes that Raymond and Elbert Covell Colleges, with their different curricula and emphases, may stimulate further innovations in the College of the Pacific and possibly serve as models for other liberal arts institutions.

# 19

# UNDERGRADUATE FOREIGN AREA STUDIES: THE CASE OF THE MIDDLE EAST

The partisans of undergraduate non-Western studies contend that such courses, which have been spreading across the country like wildfire, have been the most salutary development on the American campus since colonial times, because they are deparochializing American higher education. The foes of what is claimed to be no more than a fad charge that the colleges in the past decade have made a mess of non-Western studies, and that now non-Western studies are making a mess of the colleges. Somewhere between these extremes lies the truth, which it was the purpose of a recent ACLS conference[1] to help uncover.

The original purpose of the conference was to examine undergraduate instruction on the Middle East in selected liberal arts colleges to see what, if any, special problems these colleges faced

This is a shortened version of a report written by J. C. Hurewitz, professor of government at Columbia University and director of the conference which he describes, and published in *ACLS Newsletter*, XV, 4, April 1964.

1. At the Gould House, Dobbs Ferry, 6–7 March 1964

when they introduced such courses into the curriculum. The ACLS decision to sponsor the conference grew out of a nationwide survey that reflected the situation in the spring of 1961.[2] The survey demonstrated that most undergraduate schools, especially the liberal arts colleges, with Middle East offerings had still not begun to overcome the difficulties arising from inadequate library resources, the virtual nonexistence of textbooks, and intrafaculty rivalries and tensions. The administrators of such colleges, moreover, continued to be baffled by the high cost of incorporating into the curriculum courses on non-Western areas, or what might perhaps be more simply and appropriately designated "foreign areas," in view of the recent rediscovery, by social scientists, of Latin America as a zone that appears to share much in common with the underdeveloped areas of Asia and Africa.

The number of undergraduate schools offering one or more courses on the Middle East has multiplied since 1950 from fewer than a half dozen to well over 200. Present indications suggest that the rate of growth is likely to quicken in the decade ahead. The seven graduate Middle East training centers have not yet reached their full stride, and an eighth may come into being soon. The universities with centers are already capable of turning out each year some two dozen Ph.D.'s with Middle East specialization. The NDFL and the ACLS/SSRC Foreign Area Fellowship programs assure in the foreseeable future an uninterrupted flow of able students into the centers. The quality of training that they receive steadily rises so that today's center graduates display a wider range of skills and greater area expertise than those who have already come through the mill.

With the prospect of progressively better teachers, it might be assumed, offerings on the Middle East in undergraduate schools can hardly fail to improve. Indeed, since the overwhelming majority of the present instructors on the Middle East are nonspecialists, or at best semispecialists, we should seem at first blush to have cause for cheer. Yet such a conclusion would hardly

---

2. J. C. Hurewitz, *Undergraduate Instruction on the Middle East in American Colleges and Universities*, American Association for Middle East Studies, New York, May 1962

be sustained by the facts. The only valid assumption that we might make is that colleges and universities seeking to introduce courses on the Middle East need no longer be satisfied with substandard instructors. Middle East specialists, as perhaps specialists on other foreign areas, are likely to go begging, if they should insist on academic employment that would give adequate scope to their expensively acquired area skills.

A Middle East specialist, it should be noted, is one who has been expressly trained for teaching and research, with reading fluency in one or more of the area's languages and a demonstrated capacity to conduct original research on that area. Once a scholar has spent as many as six to eight years learning an uncommon language (or two or more unrelated uncommon languages), steeping himself in Middle East history and culture, and mastering an academic discipline, he can hardly be blamed for wishing to devote himself in substantial measure to teaching and research in his chosen field. This, of course, should not mean work wholly on the area, not even for the historian. As a practitioner of an established discipline, he should be encouraged to keep abreast of developments in that discipline by regular non-area teaching responsibilities and perhaps even occasional research on non-area problems. Only the training centers and a handful of the larger institutions, private and state, offering graduate as well as undergraduate courses are equipped to make maximal use of the Middle East specialists' area expertise.

This cluster of institutions apart, the general situation is far from reassuring. Under the prevailing undergraduate dispensation, the area expert must give almost all his time to teaching and most of his teaching time to non-area courses. In the circumstances his area instruction in a liberal arts college does not, on the average, exceed a third of his total teaching assignment, and often it may be no more than a sixth. In a university that offers graduate/undergraduate instruction on the area, the specialist may be somewhat better off, for the likelihood is greater that he will be permitted to devote as much as half time to the Middle East, and on rare occasions perhaps even more. Yet denied him altogether at most schools is the opportunity to do research on the Middle East in the regular academic year.

The conclusion would thus seem inescapable that these schools as presently constituted cannot sustain the "luxury" of instructors with a two-thirds area specialization, divided between teaching and research. But even when the area specialist attempts such research on his own time, almost invariably the area resources of his institutional library are hopelessly insufficient. With little area teaching and no area research time or facilities, the Middle East specialist begins to lose his hard-won skills. Little wonder that those specialists who have gone to teach in good colleges and universities that lack supporting Middle East libraries and are remote from such collections frequently look for employment in one of the metropolitan universities. They are, in short, instructors who are overtrained for the uses to which their talents are being put.

The underemployment of such specialists reflects a general condition of unresolved difficulties that have obstructed the sound development of undergraduate teaching on the Middle East. What has hindered Middle East studies, I suspect, has probably also hindered foreign area studies in general, although manifestly the specific problems must differ in degree—and at times also in kind—from one area to the next. Spanish and Portuguese do not present the same complexity to the American student as does Arabic (or Chinese); nor is the literature on Latin America as hard to locate and catalogue and maintain as that on the Middle East (or the Far East). Clearly, too, the length of time in which graduate area training centers have been in operation and their number will determine the flow of area specialists into the academic market.

The very adoption of courses on non-Western areas (the Middle East included) is designed, from a strictly curricular viewpoint, to redress the balance in a liberal arts tradition that has been preoccupied with Western civilization. The mere addition of courses, however, does not assure automatic integration into the curriculum. The obstacles to integration are manifold, particularly if high academic standards are to be achieved. Such decisions must be taken as: the number and variety of courses on the Middle East that should or might be offered, whether these should or might include offerings on the region's languages (and, if so, which ones), whether the Middle East courses should be offered only as part of a larger program on foreign areas, and, if the last, how to maintain an equilibrium between foreign areas and the traditional offerings as among the foreign area courses themselves. Almost all liberal arts institutions discover, at the start of instruction on the Middle East, that their area library resources are sparse, even for teaching, to say nothing of faculty research. With appropriate guidance a basic collection in Western languages—what is basic will clearly vary with the number and diversity of courses offered—may be assembled. But decisions must also be taken on the advisability of including works in Middle East languages.

This is merely a sampling of problems that beset the liberal arts schools that either have taken—or are merely contemplating taking—the plunge into Middle East studies, or into a more comprehensive foreign area coverage. These schools have faced a serious dilemma: they can no longer avoid foreign area studies, but neither can they afford them. Nor are they likely to overcome the impediments by individual action. The larger foundations have shown what can be done by collaborative endeavor. The experiments, however, have been no more than marginal and suggestive.

## Organization of the Conference

So as to encourage full and frank discussion, we decided to organize a small, closed conference of seven colleges with courses on the Middle East as part of an undergraduate liberal arts curriculum. In view of the great diversity in undergraduate education, institutional homogeneity was important for the study of common problems. Yet it was no less essential, for maximal benefit, to select a group of schools that was as broadly representative as possible.

The conference was therefore built around a homogeneous core. The New England trio (*Amherst, Dartmouth* and *Williams*) and *Antioch* seemed to respond in roughly the same way to the challenge of foreign area studies. Still each had reached a different stage in its development of the studies. Amherst joined Smith,

Mount Holyoke and the University of Massachusetts in 1960 to initiate the Four-College or Connecticut Valley cooperative program of non-Western studies, which became known in 1963 as the Asian-African Studies Program, directed by a coordinating committee of the consortium. The program, which provides for the free movement of faculty and students among the four colleges, embraced the Far East, South and Southeast Asia, the Middle East, and sub-Saharan Africa. Williams College in 1962 started an Area Studies Program on Latin America, Russia, the Middle East and Africa, and South and Southeast Asia. Dartmouth in 1963 launched a Comparative Studies Center, which aimed to coordinate all instruction and research on foreign areas (Russia, the Far East, Latin America, the Middle East, and Southeast Asia). Antioch cooperated with Earlham in 1959 to start a common program in non-Western studies. Among other activities, the partners have conducted a joint seminar to enlarge faculty familiarity with non-Western cultures. So far with the cooperation of visiting scholars the seminar has considered in annual succession: China, India, Japan, Islam and the Middle East, and Africa.

The four colleges confer the M.A. as the highest degree; two others are B.A. schools—*Kenyon* and *Portland State*, each offering courses on the Middle East but on no other foreign area. These two colleges served as excellent controls for the conference, since Kenyon with only 600 students could not consider any lavish program, while Portland State, with 7,000 students and still rapidly expanding, nevertheless continued to limit its foreign area coverage in depth to the Middle East, on which an integrated interdisciplinary studies center offers language and area training. Finally, *George Washington* furnished yet another control by providing an opportunity to compare and contrast the experiences of the self-contained colleges with an undergraduate program that formed part of a university and that admitted to the same foreign area courses graduate and undergraduate students.

Diversity was achieved in yet another way. Three of the colleges (Dartmouth, Portland State and Williams) could be labelled foreign area studies thrusters; the remaining four, stragglers. It is of course understood that no normative significance attaches to these labels.

The basic modification of the traditional liberal arts curriculum resulting from the introduction of foreign area studies was bound to be disruptive. We therefore felt that we could best evaluate the problems by having institutions represented by an administrative officer (preferably the president or the dean) and an instructor. Such representation would make it possible to look closely at the instructional difficulties without losing the institutional perspective. Each school was requested to prepare a brief paper describing its experience with the introduction and development of Middle East studies, focusing on the problems encountered and the solutions evolved.[3]

The institutional statements were prepared in accordance with explicit instructions, so as to furnish as relatively uniform data as the divergent experiences of the participating schools allowed. The case histories were circulated among all participants in advance and, by drawing attention to many common themes, provided the conference agenda.

## The Case Histories

The case histories revealed a remarkable degree of uniformity in the development of foreign area studies in the participating schools. This does not mean that the same pattern would hold true for all undergraduate institutions in the United States. But it does suggest that this may be a pattern worth looking for.

In all the schools that submitted case histories, the postwar foreign area studies traced back to the presence on the faculty of instructors with an established interest in a particular foreign area, acquired through field and/or academic experience (but not under the auspices of a training center). In six of the seven schools Middle East studies also began in the same informal way; in only one case was an area specialist—that is, a graduate of one of the training centers—expressly employed for introducing courses on the Middle East; and when the first Middle East

---

3. Cf. Item 5 of this Appendix.

specialist left the college at the end of two years, he was replaced by another.

If the experience at the selected schools is typical, and there is little reason to believe otherwise, the decision to experiment with foreign area studies is usually taken at the departmental level. In most colleges the departments enjoy the freedom, within reason, of determining what new courses they will introduce, provided always that these offerings satisfy the academic standards of the institution and entail no additional cost. What is doubtless atypical, the six Middle East instructors in the schools that did not resort to special recruitment either came to the college equipped with a research knowledge of at least one Middle East language or began the study of that language with the blessings—in the form of released teaching time and often material assistance as well—of their departments and administrations.

The first or experimental stage in the development of an undergraduate foreign area program would thus appear to be wholly informal. The institutional budget is largely unaffected, and the department's trial may even get under way without serious challenge.

In two M.A. colleges (Dartmouth and Williams) popularity led to the multiplication of foreign area courses. The second or proliferating stage is generally an untidy one, for certain departments (chiefly geography, history and political science) begin enthusiastically to accumulate areas, even accepting occasional long-range obligations by hiring area specialists to replace instructors who have retired or departed. These are still intradepartmental actions taken without reference to other departments and without benefit of general institutional guidance. At this stage the quarrels between the classicists and the modernists, the humanists and the social scientists break out into the open, and the defenders of the traditional curricular bias in favor of Western civilization sharpen their claws. At this stage, too, the curriculum itself is thrown into imbalance, because the new courses have not been thoroughly assimilated.

It is precisely the imbalance and the untidiness that bring the intrafaculty tensions to the surface. The faculty as a whole are drawn into the dispute, and it becomes necessary to take a comprehensive decision to rationalize the foreign area program and convert it into one that is compatible with the over-all curriculum. In the light of the changing institutional image, the college defines afresh its objectives for instruction and research. It is at this third stage that the bedeviling questions must be answered. How far and how fast shall the college go in the adoption of foreign areas? Shall it include languages for every area or, if only for selected ones, which ones and why? How will the program be financed? The answers, which the faculty at large must frame together with the administration, lay down a strategy for future development. The college accepts durable commitments and establishes priorities. It takes stock in the relevant departments of instructors about to retire, so that their replacements might serve the new dispensation at little or no added cost. Where new subjects may demand new manpower and with it library expansion, retraining of existing faculty, and encouragement of faculty research, the college may also have to appeal for outside help.

Dartmouth, which most nearly exemplifies this experience, received a substantial grant from the Ford Foundation late in 1962 to create its Comparative Studies Center as the focus of foreign area activity on the campus.[4] The center idea, it should be noted, emerged from more than a year of faculty discussion and debate. Williams, by contrast, financed entirely with its own funds the expanded and rationalized foreign area program—approved after two years of debate following a faculty decision in 1960 to "attempt some meaningful curricular reform"—without language offerings for the Middle East and Africa and for South and Southeast Asia. The college has sought NDEA grants for teaching these languages, thus far without success. Instructively, even a college as richly endowed as Williams cannot realize its foreign area aspirations without external assistance.

Thus Dartmouth and Williams fell, for the purposes of the present discussion, into the thruster class. Antioch and Amherst, on the other hand, were foreign area stragglers and also joiners—again to choose a term for descriptive and not normative reasons.

---

4.    Cf. Item 17 of this Appendix.

Both entered with neighboring schools into shared programs, supported by the Ford Foundation. In the Antioch-Earlham partnership, it was Earlham that had taken the initiative; in the Connecticut Valley group, it was Smith and Mt Holyoke. Amherst and Antioch tended to display characteristics of the second and third stages at once. Foreign area instruction expanded swiftly as each institution opened its courses to the students of all participating schools. Yet even after joining the consortiums neither Amherst nor Antioch seemed to display the same enthusiasm for foreign area courses or the same mastery over them as their partners. Still all the partners valued the benefits that derived from their common endeavors. The pooling of instructors and library holdings enabled them to stretch their investments, to offer a greater variety of languages and other courses, and to attract area specialists for permanent employment.

Kenyon adopted its minimal coverage of the Middle East simply because there happened to be on its faculty a semi-specialist with long field experience in the area and a knowledge of two of its languages. Kenyon has nevertheless remained at the first stage for nearly a decade. Still, it has been under pressure to diversify its foreign area treatment after affiliating with the Great Lakes Colleges Association (created in 1962 with a Ford grant) and is planning to respond as the college itself expands in the decade ahead.[5]

In establishing a Middle East Studies Center, Portland State jumped from the first to the third stage in a single foreign area but otherwise showed little interest in such studies. Available federal aid under the NDEA, the lack of fixed precedents in a college that had received its charter less than five years earlier, and the presence of an instructor with strong area interest combined to make it possible to develop a comprehensive program on the Middle East that resembled a graduate training center in structure and course distribution (the major area languages included). The twelve members of the center's teaching staff were drawn from seven departments, whose executive officers proved

---

5.  Cf. Item 14 of this Appendix.

willing to hire staff with Middle East competence while the center shared in payment of salaries.

George Washington, on its part, remains essentially at the second stage. Its undergraduate liberal arts faculty in 1953 approved, as part of a master plan for broadening the curriculum, expanded coverage of Russia, the Far East, and the Middle East. Its graduate faculties however avoided the establishment of training centers, primarily because they felt that this would duplicate unnecessarily what other universities were already doing in the Washington area. The subdued handling of foreign areas at George Washington's graduate level also held in check the undergraduate offerings.

All participating schools, in conspicuous unanimity, favored area instructors who are well equipped in their disciplines and for whom area knowledge is an added skill, and opposed their engaging in full-time area activity, even if divided between teaching and research. These schools preferred to retrain existing staff in expertise in the area of their choice to the hiring of area experts because of fear that these experts would not stay. On the other hand, the few specialists employed in these colleges felt isolated.

On the value of language instruction, the case histories showed that the attitudes ranged from the feeling that "the advantages of a non-Western study . . . can still accrue even when somebody does not have the language" to the belief that language is indispensable. The record reveals, however, that all institutions teaching multiple areas—on an individual or shared basis—have added new languages to the curriculum, often the uncommon Asian variety.

All the colleges, even those with outside support, expressed bafflement over the problem of amassing library collections on foreign areas to serve students and faculty adequately. In this connection, an abundance could prove as embarrassing as a paucity. Thus, the Middle East Studies Center at Portland State began receiving a flood of Arabic books, under Public Law 480, only to discover that it had no cataloguer linguistically qualified to process them.

## The Present State of Foreign Area Studies in the Liberal Arts College

Given the interests of those attending this conference, no participant could have been expected to question the value of foreign area studies. All participants, however, seemed to agree that such studies, whether focused only on one area or on several, enabled the students to see their own culture in a new perspective, to learn about other cultures for their own sake, and to appreciate intercultural relationships. Furthermore, the students might capture something that lay at the heart of a liberal education: a broadening and a deepening of understanding through the observation of relationships within a whole civilization, as the classicists and the medievalists still do, since their documents are so scarce that all the evidence must be examined. Foreign area studies tend to lessen the rigidity of the departmental structure and of the curriculum as a whole and thus provide a means of pulling the disciplines together again. By compelling the students to step out of their own culture, moreover, such studies make the students less parochial in their daily lives and in their later professions. A decade ago any discussion of foreign area studies would have focused on American security; at the conference only one spokesman mentioned in passing that "the national need must not be overlooked." All stood to gain from foreign area studies, it was agreed: the liberal arts curriculum, the several engaged disciplines, and the faculty of the pertinent departments, whether or not they serve as area instructors.

Similarly, the discussion on instructional procedures did not stir basic controversy. Almost all the conference participants endorsed the allocation of foreign area courses among the established disciplines. Only one institution seemed to favor setting up a separate department, so that the area specialist might teach his courses without ties or obligations to any particular discipline. This would suggest the near absence at the participating colleges of those points of tension, so common at the graduate schools, between the departmental approach of the traditional orientalists and the disciplinary one of the area specialists. The advocates of the disciplinary approach, while opposed to an area major for undergraduates, were nevertheless offering disciplinary majors that included area courses.

Furthermore, no one questioned the commitment of the participating schools to foreign area studies. One college officer stated his belief that commitment had to be understood in relation to the different parts of the college: the faculty, the department and the administration (the trustees included). Commitment, he felt, implied a willingness to make structural changes in the college, to set aside vested interests, and to rethink staffing procedures. While leadership was indispensable for such comprehensive action, fewer new resources than often assumed were in fact required, once a college became engaged.

The start with one course on one area at the experimental stage immediately leads into the numbers game, for the foreign area promotional group in the faculty want to make the non-Western component in the curriculum effective but have no clear notion of what it takes to do so. How does a college check such built-in pressures for the proliferation of foreign area instruction? One president observed that resisting proliferation was the normal business of the president and the dean. Every college, he continued, has its guidelines for taking such decisions. His own criteria included limited funds, limited personnel and limited time. Another declared that his college, in working out its reasonably coherent foreign area studies program, discovered local area talents, so that all that needed doing was to shift resources rather than enlarge the staff.

In view of the poverty of monographic literature and teaching aids for some foreign areas and the absence of trained instructors, it was suggested that two standards of instruction might be unavoidable at the experimental stage: one for the traditional disciplines and another for area studies. All denied the intimation of dual standards, insisting that the quality of area study was at least as high as that of the others, if not higher. A more important question arose, it was argued, when it appeared essential to abandon a traditional course to make way for one on a foreign area.

The conferees were asked about the minimal conditions that would make the best use of an area specialist's expertise. The response reaffirmed the principle enunciated in the case histories: the area specialist ought not to teach area courses exclusively, since the colleges could not afford such specialization. Besides, the very question conveyed the idea that area experts somehow form a breed apart. Actually they do not differ in kind from other members of the faculty, since each claimed his own specialization. The danger must be avoided of repeating the mistake of allowing too narrow a specialization. Care must be taken to ensure against provincializing the area experts. More germane than whether an area specialist should teach a general course, therefore, is whether a generalist without area training should be invited to teach an area course.

This led directly to a consideration of the fate of the area specialist in a college. Even the training centers, it was pointed out, discouraged absolute specialization. The college procured in an area expert an instructor with two strings to his bow: an area expertise and mastery of a discipline. But in employing such an instructor just emerging from a training center, the college often did not allow him to develop any secure area competence. He was immediately overwhelmed with preparations for general courses within the discipline that had nothing to do with his area; the latter possessed for the department no more than supplemental value. In the long run this kind of distribution, it was contended, might make little difference. But in the crucial first years, when the area expert was still a novice and only feeling his way, he had to sink his area roots. For this, research was the best guarantor. Yet his college often denied him research facilities and research time.

To this argument strong objection was voiced. One college officer suggested that, if the specialist could not adjust to the type of teaching required, he was in all likelihood not properly trained. In his view the problems for the area specialist were no more acute than for the scientist, although it was conceded that young scientists did enjoy in sponsored research advantages over area specialists. The issue here, however, was to ensure that the social scientists and the humanists also received comparable help. Here the large universities and the foundations ought to recognize their responsibilities by continuing to help the people they had trained.

Conferees and observers alike took exception to the view that there was for some areas an effective oversupply of experts. To support their contrary view they pointed to the inability of the colleges to find such trained teachers. This appeared to confirm, they held, that graduates were not streaming but only trickling from the training centers. There seemed to be an unawareness at the conference of the general reluctance among newly trained area specialists to accept academic employment in colleges which were remote from the large universities and which combined inadequate library resources with teaching commitments that for all practical purposes crowded area instruction out. Even area experts who find their first posts in metropolitan districts occasionally complain that they have no opportunity for research, because they have been so thoroughly inundated with non-area obligations.

The colleges might wish in the future to consider modifying their practices. When they employ a budding area specialist, particularly if his expertise dictates the use of one or more uncommon languages, they might relieve him of all non-area obligations in the initial two or three years. He might then devote himself to converting a dissertation into a book, writing articles for scholarly journals and structuring at least two area courses. Thereafter he would assume progressive responsibility for non-area teaching in his discipline. If such a procedure were followed (with external aid for most colleges), the hiring institution would at the end of the period have what it thought it was obtaining, but is not now: an instructor with a dual competence in a discipline and in an area. This is the kind of activity that the NDEA or some equivalent federal program might ultimately encompass, supplemented in the larger states by state financing.

The discussion of the role of language in undergraduate foreign area studies confirmed the existence of two schools of thought. One argued that without language non-Western instruction was meaningless. The other contended that the students benefited substantially from foreign area study even without the languages. The mere mention of instruction in Asian languages elicited the view from this group that such study represented a form of pre-professional training. In any case, they continued, the demand for such difficult languages as Arabic, Chinese and Japanese would be insufficient on most campuses to sustain the courses.

Dr Charles A. Ferguson, the director of the Center for Applied Linguistics, brought the language discussion into focus. He explained that the reasons for teaching foreign languages were essentially four in number: broadening the horizon, providing a tool in linguistic study, communication and the pursuit of a career. At least four general courses met some or all of these differing needs: the ordinary course which demands four to five class hours and perhaps an equal number in the laboratory; the intensive course which requires at least double or possibly triple the time of ordinary courses; the special-purpose course which serves those concentrating on the structure of language; and self-teaching methods (that are now being devised) which will use tapes and carefully worked out materials that should make it possible to acquire a language where no regular teaching facilities are available. The last method, when finally developed, would open important new possibilities on the college campus. The varying difficulties among the languages and the different kinds of competence within a language would determine the varieties of the teaching materials. Thus, for example, different levels of preparation were needed for speaking Arabic, for reading an Arabic newspaper, and for reading a classical Arabic text.

It was the consensus of the discussion that for almost all undergraduate students the learning of Asian languages is not important. It is, however, almost imperative for those who plan to become experts on an Asian area. Foreign area studies in such cases constitute a species of preprofessional training; and the more difficult the language, the earlier the area candidate ought to start its study. The evolving method of training should furnish a satisfactory means of including such languages in the liberal arts curriculum.

In the case histories and at the conference the question was reviewed of where the liberal arts curriculum ends and professionalism begins. It could be argued, for example, that a foreign area program might be labelled quasi-professional if it were sufficiently intensive so that it gave the student a detailed knowledge of the area in the major disciplines, trained him in one or more area languages, and enabled him upon completion of his studies to procure employment that would utilize his skills. A college graduate with such training, in other words, could use it to qualify for a specialized job, since the instruction manifestly aimed at producing a trained person. Arrayed against this argument was another: such training did not essentially differ from that of a French or German major in any college. He too had a marketable education. No one would think of terming as quasi-professional the training of a student of French or German language and literature. According to the consensus, no matter how comprehensive or even quasi-professional the student's instruction in foreign areas, this was not incompatible with a liberal arts education, provided the student was required to take courses in the general disciplines along with those on the areas. Still, one college president advised that we ought to think of liberal arts as designed to enlarge experience. To this non-Western studies certainly contributed. But the effort required for the serious study of uncommon languages represented a loss, if the undergraduate had to devote three fourths of his time to it.

The experience of all the participants underlined the need for external financial assistance to help the colleges cope with the open-ended problems created by the growth of foreign area studies. At the same time it was recognized that the future developments depended on more than dollars and cents. It also depended on the sense with which the dollars were expended. Although money still remains a matter of concern even for the wealthiest schools, this does not seem to arise because of their having undertaken excessive obligations. Manifestly, more has to be done by all engaged—the foundations, the government, the national scholarly associations, and the college and university associations—to shift the emphasis in foreign area studies from simply promoting interest to raising, as well, instructional standards.

# DIRECTORY OF RESOURCES

A. Select Bibliography

B. Major Conferences on Non-Western Studies

C. NDEA Language and Area Centers

D. Organizations and Agencies

# DIRECTORY OF RESOURCES

## A. Select Bibliography

Axelrod, Joseph and Bigelow, Donald N.: *Resources for Language and Area Studies* (Washington: American Council on Education, 1962)

Bennett, Wendell: *Area Studies in American Universities* (New York: Social Science Research Council, 1951)

Bidwell, Percy W.: *Undergraduate Education in Foreign Affairs* (New York: King's Crown Press, 1962)

Bigelow, Donald N. and Legters, Lyman H.: *NDEA Language and Area Centers; A Report on the First Five Years* (Washington: U. S. Office of Education, 1964). Bibliography

Bigelow, Donald N. and Legters, Lyman H. (eds.): "The Non-Western World in Higher Education," *Annals of the American Academy of Political and Social Science,* November 1964 (forthcoming)

Bureau of Intelligence and Research: *Language and Area Study Programs in American Universities* (Washington: Department of State, 1964)

*The College and World Affairs* (New York: Education and World Affairs, 1964). Bibliography

Fenton, William Nelson: *Area Studies in American Universities* (Washington: American Council on Education, 1947)

Gibb, Sir Hamilton A. R.: *Area Studies Reconsidered* (London: University of London, 1963)

Hall, Robert B.: *Area Studies; with Special Reference to their Implications for Research in the Social Sciences* (New York: Social Science Research Council, 1947)

Mintz, Sidney W.: *A Sample Survey of Area Programs at American Universities* (New Haven: Human Relations Area Files, n.d.)

Morehouse, Ward: *The International Dimensions of Education in New York State* (Albany: The University of the State of New York, 1963)

Parker, William R.: *The National Interest and Foreign Languages* (Washington: Department of State, 3rd ed. 1961)

Swift, Richard N.: *World Affairs and the College Curriculum* (Washington: American Council on Education, 1959) Bibliography

*The University and World Affairs* (New York: The Ford Foundation, 1960)

## B. Major Conferences on Non-Western Studies

1947, Wagley, Charles: *Area Research and Training: A Conference Report on the Study of World Areas*, November 28–30, 1947. (New York: Social Science Research Council, 1948)

1954, Frenz, Horst and Anderson, G. L. (eds.): *Indiana University Conference on Oriental-Western Literary Relations*, June 28–July 2, 1954. (Chapel Hill: University of North Carolina Press, 1955)

1957, Singer, Milton (ed.): *Introducing India in Liberal Education*, May 17–18, 1957. (Chicago: University of Chicago, 1957)

1957, Boardman, Eugene (ed.): *Asian Studies in Liberal Education*, December 28–30, 1957, and April 2–4, 1958. (Washington: Association of American Colleges, 1959)

1958, Cline, Howard F. (comp.): *Latin American Studies in the United States*, November 6–8, 1958. (Washington: Library of Congress, 1959)

1958, Creel, H. G. (ed.): *Chinese Civilization in Liberal Education*, November 28–29, 1958. (Chicago: University of Chicago, 1959)

1958, Byrnes, Robert F. (ed.): *The Non-Western Areas in Undergraduate Education in Indiana*, September 18–20, 1958. (Bloomington: Indiana University Publications, 1959)

1959, de Bary, William Theodore (ed.): *Approaches to the Oriental Classics*, 1958. (New York: Columbia University Press, 1959)

1959, Teng, S. Y. (ed.): *Asian Studies and State Universities*, November 11–13, 1959. (Bloomington: Indiana University, 1960)

1960, Brown, W. Norman (ed.): *Resources for South Asian Language Studies in the United States*, January 15–16, 1960. (Philadelphia: University of Pennsylvania Press, 1960)

1960, Bordie, John G. (ed.): *National Conference on the Teaching of African Language and Area Studies,* March 11–12, 1960. (Washington: Georgetown University, 1960)

1960, *Sino-American Conference on Intellectual Cooperation,* July 10–15, 1960. (Seattle: University of Washington, 1960)

1961, Lambert, Richard D. (ed.): *Resources for South Asian Area Studies in the United States,* February 23–25, 1961. (Philadelphia: University of Pennsylvania Press, 1962)

1961, Morehouse, Ward (ed.): *Asian Studies in Liberal Arts Colleges,* March 1961. (Washington: Association of American Colleges, 1961)

1961, de Bary, Wm. Theodore and Embree, Ainslee T. (eds.): *Approaches to Asian Civilizations,* September 13–14, 1961. (New York: Columbia University Press, 1964)

## C. NDEA Language and Area Centers

The University of Arizona, Tucson
Professor Earl H. Pritchard,
  Director, Language and Area
  Center in Oriental Studies

*University of California, Berkeley
Professor G. D. Berreman, Director,
  South Asia Language and Area
  Center

University of California, Berkeley
Professor Lawrence L. Thomas,
  Director, East European Language
  and Area Center

*University of California, Los Angeles
Professor James S. Coleman, Director,
  African Language and Area Center

University of California, Los Angeles
Professor Henry J. Bruman,
  Director, Latin American Language
  and Area Center

*University of California, Los Angeles
Professor Gustave E. von Grunebaum,
  Director, Near Eastern Language
  and Area Center

The University of Chicago
Professor Edwin McClellan, Director,
  Far Eastern Language and Area
  Center

*The University of Chicago
Professor Edward C. Dimock and
Professor J. A. B. van Buitenen,
  Co-Directors, South Asia Language
  and Area Center

*University of Colorado, Boulder
Professor Robert P. Browder,
  Acting Director, Center for Slavic
  and East European Studies

Columbia University, New York
Professor L. Gray Cowan, Director,
  African Language and Area Center

*Columbia University, New York
Professor Charles Wagley, Director,
  Language and Area Center for
  Latin American Studies

*Columbia University, New York
Professor Alexander Dallin, Director,
  Soviet and East European Lan-
  guage and Area Center

*Columbia University, New York
Professor Wm. Theodore de Bary,
  Director, East Asian Language and
  Area Center

Columbia University, New York
Professor John Lotz, Director,
  Uralic Language and Area Center

Cornell University, Ithaca, New York
Professor G. B. Kelley, Director,
  South Asia Language and Area
  Center

*Cornell University, Ithaca, New York
Professor George McT. Kahin,
  Director, Southeast Asia Language
  and Area Center

Cornell University, Ithaca, New York
Professor Harold Shadick, Director,
  East Asia Language and Area
  Center

*Duke University, Durham, N. C.
Professor Ralph Braibanti, Director,
  Center for Southern Asian Studies

*Duquesne University,
  Pittsburgh, Pennsylvania
Professor Geza Grosschmid, Director,
  African Language and Area Center

*University of Florida, Gainesville
Professor Lyle McAlister, Director,
  Latin American Language and Area
  Program

---

* Has been host to summer intensive language program.

*Fordham University, New York
Reverend Walter C. Jaskievicz, S.J.,
Director, Russian Language and
Area Center

*Harvard University, Cambridge, Mass.
Professor Donald H. Shively, Director,
Language and Area Center for East
Asian Studies

*Harvard University, Cambridge, Mass.
Professor D. W. Lockard, Associate
Director, Center for Middle Eastern
Studies

Harvard University, Cambridge, Mass.
Professor Horace G. Lunt, Director,
Slavic Language and Area Center

*University of Hawaii, Honolulu
Professor Ronald S. Anderson,
Director, Language and Area
Center in Chinese, Japanese, Korean

*University of Hawaii, Honolulu
Professor Ronald S. Anderson,
Director, Language and Area
Center in Indonesian, Javanese,
Thai

Howard University,
Washington, D. C.
Professor Mark Hanna Watkins,
Director, African Language and
Area Center

University of Illinois, Urbana
Professor Ralph T. Fisher, Jr,
Director, Center for Russian
Language and Area Studies

*Indiana University, Bloomington
Professor William B. Edgerton,
Director, Slavic Language and
Area Center

*Indiana University, Bloomington
Professor Denis Sinor, Director,
Uralic and Altaic Language and
Area Center

State University of Iowa, Iowa City
Professor Y. P. Mei, Director,
Center for Far Eastern Studies

The Johns Hopkins University,
School of Advanced International
Studies, Washington, D. C.
Professor Majid Khadduri, Director,
Middle East Language and Area
Center

*University of Kansas, Lawrence
Professor Thomas R. Smith,
Acting Director, Center for East
Asian Studies

*The University of Michigan,
Ann Arbor
Professor Joseph K. Yamagina,
Director, Far Eastern Language
and Area Center

The University of Michigan,
Ann Arbor
Professor William D. Schorger,
Acting Director, Center for Near
and Middle Eastern Studies

*The University of Michigan,
Ann Arbor
Professor John Mersereau, Jr,
Director, Slavic Language and
Area Center

*Michigan State University,
East Lansing
Professor Charles C. Hughes,
Director, African Studies Center

*New York University, New York
Professor John Edwin Fagg,
Director, Portuguese Language and
Area Center

*University of Pennsylvania,
Philadelphia
Professor W. Norman Brown,
Director, South Asia Language and
Area Center

---

* Has been host to summer intensive language program.

University of Pennsylvania,
Philadelphia
Professor Alfred Senn, Director,
Slavic Language and Area Center

University of Pittsburgh,
Pittsburgh, Pennsylvania
Professor Frank W. Wadsworth,
Acting Director, East Asian
Language and Area Center

Portland State College,
Portland, Oregon
Professor Frederick J. Cox,
Director, Middle East Studies
Center

*Princeton University,
Princeton, New Jersey
Professor T. Cuyler Young,
Director, Language and Area
Center for Near Eastern Studies

*University of Southern California,
Los Angeles
Professor Theodore H. E. Chen,
Director, Asian-Slavic Studies
Center

*Stanford University,
Stanford, California
Professor P. D. Hanan, Director,
Chinese-Japanese Language and
Area Center

The University of Texas, Austin
Professor Edgard G. Polomá,
Director, South Asia Language and
Area Center

The University of Texas, Austin
Professor Walter Lehn, Director,
Middle East Language and Area
Center

*The University of Texas, Austin
Professor John P. Harrison,
Director, Language and Area
Center for Latin American Studies

*Tulane University,
New Orleans, Louisiana
Professor Bernard Gicovate,
Director, Language and Area
Center for Latin American Studies

*University of Utah, Salt Lake City
Professor Aziz S. Atiya, Director,
Middle East Language and Area
Center

Vanderbilt University,
Nashville, Tennessee
Professor Josef Rysan, Director,
Russian Language and Area Center

University of Washington, Seattle
Professor George E. Taylor, Director,
Far Eastern and Russian Language
and Area Center

*The University of Wisconsin,
Madison
Professor Richard H. Robinson,
Director, South Asian Language
and Area Center

*The University of Wisconsin,
Madison
Professors Norman P. Sacks and
Alberto Machado de Rosa,
Co-Directors, Language and Area
Center for Latin American Studies

*Yale University,
New Haven, Connecticut
Professor Karl J. Pelzer, Director,
Southeast Asia Studies Center

---

* Has been host to summer intensive language program.

# D. Organizations and Agencies

## (i) Sources of General Information and Advice

American Association of Colleges for
Teacher Education
1201 16th Street, N. W.
Washington, D. C.  20036

American Council on Education
1785 Massachusetts Avenue, N. W.
Washington, D. C.  20036

Association of American Colleges
1818 R Street, N. W.
Washington, D. C.  20009

Bureau of Intelligence and Research
External Research Division
Department of State
Washington, D. C.  20520

Council of Protestant Colleges and
Universities
1818 R Street, N. W.
Washington, D. C.  20009

Education and World Affairs, Inc.
522 Fifth Avenue
New York, New York  10036

Language and Area Centers Section
Division of College and University
Assistance
U. S. Office of Education
Department of Health, Education, and
Welfare
Washington, D. C.  20202

## (ii) Sources of Information and Advice on Cultural Areas

African Studies Association
Columbia University
409 West 117th Street
New York, New York  10027

American Association for the Advancement of Slavic Studies
112 Davenport House
620 East Daniel Street
Champaign, Illinois  61822

American Association for Middle East
Studies
11 West 42nd Street
New York, New York  10036

The Asia Society
112 East 64th Street
New York, New York  10021

Association for Asian Studies
P. O. Box 606
Ann Arbor, Michigan  48106

Hispanic Foundation
Reference Department
Library of Congress
Washington, D. C.  20540

## (iii) Sources of Specialized Information and Advice

American Universities Field Staff, Inc.
366 Madison Avenue
New York, New York  10017
(reports and visiting specialists on
current affairs)

Center for Applied Linguistics
1755 Massachusetts Avenue, N. W.
Washington, D. C.  20036
(language teaching)

Committee on International Exchange
of Persons
Conference Board of Associated Research Councils
2101 Constitution Avenue, N. W.
Washington, D. C.  20418
(availability of foreign scholars)

Consultant in Foreign Area Studies
University of the State of New York
State Education Department
Albany, New York 12201
(services available to colleges in New
York State)

Consultative Service on U. S. Undergraduate Study Abroad
Institute of International Education
809 United Nations Plaza
New York, New York 10017
(overseas study programs)

Modern Language Association of
America
6 Washington Square North
New York, New York 10003
(language teaching)

National Association for Foreign Student Affairs
Field Service Program
601 Rockwell Avenue
Cleveland, Ohio 44114
(foreign student problems)